STOMP and SWERVE

American Music Gets Hot

1843–1924

DAVID WONDRICH

CHICAGO
REVIEW
PRESS

An A Cappella Book

Library of Congress Cataloging-in-Publication Data

Wondrich, David.
Stomp and swerve : American music gets hot,
1843–1924 / by David Wondrich.— 1st ed.
    p. cm.
Includes bibliographical references (p. 243), discography, and index.
ISBN 1-55652-496-X
1. Popular music—United States—History and criticism. 2. African Americans—Music—History and criticism. 3. Jazz—History and criticism. I. Title.

ML3477.W69 2003
781.64'0973—dc21

                                        2003004480

Cover photo: Mamie Smith and Her Jazz Hounds,
courtesy of the Frank Driggs collection

Cover and interior design: Laura Lindgren

Published by A Cappella Books,
An imprint of Chicago Review Press, Incorporated
814 North Franklin Street
Chicago, Illinois 60610
ISBN 1-55652-496-X
Printed in the United States of America
5 4 3 2 1

For Karen

Contents

Preface

The eighty-odd years between 1843, when a new, indigenous style of music-making first came to the attention of the American general public, and the early 1920s, when its full spectrum—black and white, urban and rural, sophisticated as silk lingerie and crude as cotton overalls—finally made it on record for all to hear, are the caveman period of American music. An age of firelit darkness, sundered by the screech of badly tuned fiddles. For the eighty years since, on the other hand, the story is a familiar one. The key players, in this age of Britney Spears, might not all be the household names they once were, but they suffer no lack of recognition; all their records are in print and there's no shortage of books about 'em. Louis Armstrong, Bessie Smith, Robert Johnson, Jimmie Rogers, Bob Wills, Duke Ellington, Count Basie, Billie Holiday, Benny Goodman, Charlie Parker, Hank Williams, Elvis Presley, Little Richard, Jerry Lee Lewis, so on and so forth. Benchmark names. Names that you can't ignore in any serious discussion of American music.

Against those monumental names, those early decades have only three to offer: Scott Joplin, Stephen Foster, and John Philip Sousa (although Sousa's often not taken as seriously as he deserves). There are plenty of others who should be there, but aren't. This book is an essay, not a formal, comprehensive history; an attempt to bring the missing names into the conversation; to treat the music made by fiddling minstrels and brass bands, ragtime piano "professors" and concert banjoists, singers of "Coon songs" (we'll get to that in a minute), ragtime dance orchestras, vocal quartets, novelty drummers, and Broadway cakewalkers with the same honesty, sympathy, and passion we're accustomed to find in writing about the music that followed them.

♪

The roots of this book reach back to the fall of 1977, when I was in eleventh grade, living with my folks in Port Washington, out on Long Island. One afternoon, a friend and I took the Long Island Railroad into Manhattan to buy posters or some such thing. On the way home, we stopped at the Sam Goody's record store in Penn Station, and I bought *Never Mind the Bollocks, Here's the Sex Pistols*. Usually, I listened to the Allman Brothers, the Grateful Dead, that sort of thing, but an impulse came over me and I obeyed it. Later, when I played the record, I thought it was...*intense*. More intense than *anything*. *Ever*. (I was sixteen.)

A few days later, on my way home from school I stopped in at the Neergard Pharmacy on Main Street, one of those mom-and-pop affairs that had a small record department—top-twenty new releases and a rack or two of $2.99 cutouts. Leafing through the cutouts, I came across a Columbia LP called *King of the Delta Blues Singers, Vol. II* by Robert Johnson. I'd never heard of Robert Johnson, but it looked like a goof—old and weird and good for springing on my friends, tormenting them with. Besides, for $2.99 plus tax, I could be a sport. I didn't get around to playing it for a couple of days.

When I did, I learned a lesson. It's an old one; as Anthony Cooper, Earl of Shaftesbury, formulated it in 1710, those who are ignorant of history and the evolution of taste "are apt at every turn to make the present age their standard, and imagine nothing so barbarous or savage but what is contrary to the manners of their own time." Of course, in this case it was me imagining "nothing so barbarous or savage" as the music that was a product of the manners of my own time, but the principle's the same. I had been making the present my standard, and I was wrong. The recordings on that LP were forty years old when I first listened to them, and yet they were just as intense, just as punky, wild, weird, and modern, as anything Johnny Rotten and his mates were churning out.

PREFACE

I know that by comparing Johnny Rotten to Robert Johnson I risk completely alienating any blues fanatics who may be reading this; I can only beg your patience. In fact, here I should probably assure those among you who find rock 'n' roll distasteful that this is not a book about rock 'n' roll, or, for that matter, soul music, funk, or rap. This is a book about the music of the past; old music. But it *is* a book that treats that music as if it were made not by the solemn, still faces in old black-and-white photographs, but by young (mostly) men and women, people with the same hormones, the same nerves, the same needs and desires and capacities for fulfilling them that drove Elvis Presley and Jerry Lee Lewis, Aretha Franklin and James Brown, Jimi Hendrix and, yes, even Ozzy Osbourne. This means that while discussing ragtime and early jazz, minstrel shows and brass bands and all the other foundational manifestations of hot music in America, I shall be drawing the occasional analogy from the vernacular music of the present (or at least the recent past). Since these days the odds are pretty good that even the most hardened bluegrass fiend, blues scholar, jazzbo, or ragtimer grew up listening to the same crap as the rest of us, I think it will do most no harm. Anyway, the line of influence from antebellum minstrel Daniel Decatur Emmett to Kid Rock, from Bert Williams, the first black man to appear in a Broadway show, to Outkast, is unbroken, though rarely acknowledged.

There are two reasons why this tradition has so often been ignored. One is technical: the kind of energetic, informal music we're dealing with here has always been difficult to get down on paper. Transcriptions miss the vigor and charm of the performers, without which this music is nothing, while written descriptions—how can you really write about music? It's like writing about the taste of malt whiskey. To really do justice to it, you need to preserve the performance itself. You need records. Unfortunately, for the first four decades of our period, there were none. Then came December 7, 1877—a day that shall live in harmony—when a certain John Kruesi, one of Thomas

[ix]

Edison's mechanics, put the finishing touches on the master's design for a device to pluck vibrations out of the air and imprison them in the narrow track a needle leaves on a rotating cylinder of tinfoil. By the early 1890s, this simple technology was mature enough to support an industry. By 1910, thousands upon thousands of different records had been made of all kinds. Many were of classical music, opera, parlor songs, that sort of thing. Others, though, were in the direct ancestral line of Robert Johnson and the Sex Pistols. Not that you'd know that from the amount of attention they receive from historians of popular music. True, they're kind of hard to listen to—scratchy and often dimly recorded. That's no excuse, though, for the serious listener; those records were cut on the same equipment that Caruso's were, and folks write about him plenty.

This brings us to our second, bigger, reason. During the eight decades covered by this book, as during the eight since, the dominant issue in American music was the tense, dynamic relationship between its African elements and its European ones. Which is a polite way of saying that white men and women were imitating (often very poorly, and not always with the best intentions) what they heard black men and women playing and singing. Much of this imitation involves language and stereotypes that make people very, very uncomfortable—misty-eyed evocations of plantation days, crude and violent tales of the supposed realities of ghetto life, like that. A lot of it is just plain racist trash, music made with the intent to insult. As the wise and worldly Lord Chesterfield instructed his son, "Mimicry...is the lowest and most illiberal of all buffoonery.... The person mimicked is insulted; and...an insult is never forgiven." Whether it should be forgiven is not mine to say.

Whether it should nonetheless be examined, though, is a different question. Distressing as this stuff can be, it's all we've got. Even after the introduction of recording, the industry was run on a strictly Jim Crow basis until the very last years of our period. You could count the black artists who recorded in the 1890s and 1900s on the fingers of both hands, even if you were down a couple of fingers. Scott Joplin never made a record, while many a white mediocrity made hundreds. (The 1910s saw some small loosening of this hateful attitude, and the success of Mamie Smith's "Crazy Blues" in 1920 washed it away entirely. Not that the music of rural white America fared any better—they didn't let anybody but a city slicker into a recording studio for purposes other than custodial until 1922, some thirty years after the industry was established.) Critics tend to dismiss unheard the scads and scads of blackface records that survive from the period—many of them written by black songwriters. Imagine if the same conditions had prevailed in the 1950s; if instead of Little Richard doing "Tutti Frutti," all we had was white cover versions. Pat Boone cut it. But so did Elvis. Which is why I'm going to talk about this stuff. The language is offensive; words such as "nigger," "coon," "darky" abound. I do not use them in my private life (and I hope I would not have used them back then), but neither will I shy from them when necessary. They're not my words. To let them scare us off from understanding our history, from experiencing it in all its awfulness and beauty, is to grant them far too much power.

Barbara Walters: When you're onstage...see, it's hard for me to say. I was going to say, you talk about "niggers." I can't...you can say it. I can't say it.

Richard Pryor: You just said it.

Walters: Yeah, but I feel so...

Pryor: You said it very good.

Walters: ...uncomfortable.

Pryor: Well, good. You said it pretty good.

Walters: O.K.

Pryor: That's not the first time you said it.

—*The Barbara Walters Special*, 1979

Acknowledgments

With a book as full of opinions, assertions, theories, judgments, omissions, and questionable inclusions as this one, it's as important to absolve the people who've helped make it as to thank them. And so: it's not their fault. They tried to talk me out of it. They told me not to leave her out; to forget about him. With that said, I'd like to heartily thank the following people, without whom this book would not exist:

Yuval Taylor, my long-suffering editor, whose idea this book was. There were times when he regretted it, I'm sure.

My brother Nick, who brought Elvis into our house.

My friends Kenneth Goldsmith, Cary Berger, David Goldsmith, Nick Noyes, Marcus Boon, and Alex Halberstadt (listed in the order that I met them), with whom I have spent roughly one-eighth of my life engaged in intense, often circular discussions about music.

Will Friedwald, who solicitously deluged me with CDs full of music otherwise unavailable and did not think my tastes were strange (and a special shout-out to Al "OM5" Simmons).

Mike Kieffer, Dave Sager, Brad Kay, and John Zeiderman, who generously taped their rare 78s for me and endured my questions re same.

Richard Martin and Megan Hennessy, of Archeophone Records, and Mr. Chris Ware, who unquestioningly and at a moment's notice supplied rare material for illustrations.

Chuck Eddy of the *Village Voice* and Fletcher Roberts of the *New York Times,* excellent editors who taught me that music writing is as exacting a discipline as any other.

Vince Giordano, Frank Gresham, and Craig Ventresco, three phenomenal musicians who, by playing old music with drive and swerve and without irony, helped me to hear what was really on those 78s.

CDs were generously provided by Don Kent of Yazoo Records, Dave Freeman of County Records, Alastair Robertson of Hep Records, Colin Bray of Jazz Oracle Records, Bruce Bastin and Kevin Worrell of Interstate Music, Mark Best of www.besmark.com, Glenn Sage of www.tinfoil.com, and the kind person from Timeless Records whose signature I can't decipher.

Finally, there's Sherwin. Sometimes I think that everybody who's ever gotten a lift as they've blown the dust off a thrift-shop 78 to discover an E-copy of Fred Hall's Hometowners on Cameo, everybody who's ever picked out the chords to "Santa Claus Blues" or blown the melody line to "Clementine from New Orleans," knows Sherwin Dunner. For a curmudgeon, he's got an awful lot of friends, and without him (and them) this book would have been a much, much thinner affair—and not just because of all the records he's taped for me, books he's lent, rants he's listened to, misconceptions corrected (or attempted to), illustrations supplied, and on and on. Plus, he makes a mean mai-tai.

Note: fragments of Part II, for the most part greatly altered, have appeared in the *New York Times*, the *Village Voice*, *LCD*, and *The Cartoon Music Book*, edited by Daniel Goldmark and Yuval Taylor (A Cappella, 2002).

INTRODUCTION

Love and Strife

When you hear
Dem a bells go ding ling ling,
All join 'round
And sweetly you must sing,
And when the verse am through,
In the chorus all join in,
There'll be a hot time
In the old town tonight.

—JOE HAYDEN,
"A Hot Time in the Old Town"

Drive and Swerve

This book is about hot music. We all know what that means, or at least what it sounds like when we hear it. We grew up knowing. The Rolling Stones are hot, at least through *Exile on Main St*. The Beatles are usually not, and often anything but ("When I'm Sixty-Four"). James Brown is very hot, James Taylor is not at all. Jimi Hendrix is hot, Pink Floyd is cool for a while, and then just uncool. Nirvana is hot, despite its cool name. Merle Haggard and George Jones are hot, Alabama and the entire cast of the CMA are not.

[1]

Louis Armstrong is hot, always; Benny Goodman usually is, Glenn Miller rarely if ever. Bessie Smith is hot, Billie Holiday tries very hard not to be, not always successfully. Some kinds of music are hot in general: fifties rock 'n' roll is almost always hot, fifties jazz is clearly not, which is why they call it cool jazz (hot is usually cool, but cool isn't necessarily uncool, it's just not hot—Miles Davis is, of course, both cool and cool). Hip-hop is hot, ambient is most defiantly not. Techno is sometimes hot, but usually not. Punk is hot, new wave... etcetera. Pretty obvious—unless you're dealing with music over a century old, with no pumping bass or booting solos to tip you the nod.

If we're going to put our enterprise on a sound scientific footing, we'll need a theory. This isn't easy, since hot music at first appears to be one of those phenomena beyond definition, subject to Armstrong's Paradox ("If you gotta ask you'll never know"). You know and I know it's got something to do with sex, but saying that doesn't help much. The standard *New Grove Dictionary of Jazz* tells us that "in jazz parlance, the term is used to suggest the qualities of excitement, passion, and intensity," which doesn't help us much either, and that "hot solos were generally performed at considerable speed and were characterized by a frenetic quality, an urgent sense of rhythm, agitated syncopation, eager anticipations of the beat, and an earthy or 'dirty' tone."

This gives us a little more to work with, although it's only part of the story. Louis Armstrong's "Alligator Crawl" from 1927 (Ok. 8482; wherever possible, I shall identify any recording mentioned in these pages by its original catalog number: reissues come and go, but the original release remains constant) is a slow grind without frenzy or agitation, and it's so hot that it seems to melt the grilles on your speakers. And what if our ears tell us that "Possum in the Hayloft" by a cracker fiddle band from Georgia, "Nichts Bei Mir" by a Yiddish clarinet combo from Hester Street, and "Peephole Drag" by a black cornet blower from the South Side of Chicago are equally hot, although they seem to have nothing in common? Any theory that would cover all three musicologically—that would explain what they're all doing in terms of rhythm, timbre, harmony, melodic development, etc.—would have to be impossibly complex. Luckily, for you and me both, I'm not a musicologist. And there are other ways of approaching this question. We don't need musicological exactness here (we just want to listen to the stuff, not vivisect it), we need what the thought gang likes to call a heuristic: a simplified way of making sense out of a complex situation, of enabling the mind to grasp it sensually, rather than rationally. A model, in other words.

The model I propose for hot music has just two parts, both fairly commonplace: let's call them "drive" and "swerve." Without either of these, a record can't be hot; with just one, it may be hot; with both, in various combinations, it will be scorching.

Since drive is fairly obvious, we'll start there. We can define drive as the quality that gives a piece of music momentum, that pulls you in and makes your body want to move with the music (and I mean *move*, not swing and sway); drive is what gets your toe tapping, your foot pounding, your fingers drumming, your head nodding. It's purely physical, purely unconscious. Drive isn't the same thing as speed— "The Flight of the Bumblebee" is fast indeed, but it doesn't drive you (even when some mook turns it into the Green Hornet theme), while Bessie Smith's seminal 1925 version of "St. Louis Blues" (Col. 14064-D) isn't particularly fast, but it drags your body along with every beat. Drive demands repetition: rhythmic and/or melodic figures have to be played over and over, and off against each other; this usually lets out the Paganiniesque violin breakdown as well as much of free jazz. Now, this repetition can't help but instantly remind those among us whose hormones are at spring tide of the act of generation, a fact that has never failed to cause paroxysms of hand-wringing and tut-tutting in the custodial classes; but more on this later.

Usually, drive involves some kind of syncopation, whereby the accent is shifted off the strong beats of the measure without losing them altogether. So if you have a piece of music where the first and third beat of each four-beat bar are supposed to be accented, you might hold those notes just a little too long or hit them just a little too late, stretching them into the spaces where two and four are supposed to fall; this makes it seem like the beat is being pulled forward headlong. Or you can lay another pattern on top of the 1-3, accenting those other beats (this is how ragtime works). Or you can do both (think boogie-woogie). No matter how you do it, and myriad are the ways, syncopation is the key to every kind of hot music from the nineteenth-century minstrel walkaround to Jay-Z and beyond.

There are different kinds of drive. The brilliant (if stiff) musicologist and jazz historian Gunther Schuller draws a distinction between "horizontal" and "vertical" momentum. Vertically oriented rhythms feature accents where the whole band comes in at once: they stomp rather than swing. Drive is difficult to annotate: before there were records, we can't really tell how it was handled. But in the 1890s, at least—judging from the earliest surviving records—the brass bands and ragtime orchestras would take their 2/4 rhythm and goose it up so that everyone would come down on the one like a steam hammer, lay off a little on the two, and then whomp on the one again. The rhythm sections tended to feature tubas and banjos, both of which add a percussive pop to the beat.

You swing, on the other hand, horizontally—the various members of the band place their accents at different places in the measure. The band may stand on the one, but they won't whomp it. Swing is in an even 4/4 time, a smoother measure but still powerful—a rushing steam locomotive to the two-beat's washing machine rocking in place. Since the turn of the century, New Orleans musicians tended to give their rags and marches a 4/4 feel. They also relied on string bass and guitar in the rhythm section, instruments with less punch than tuba and banjo, but more sustain—you could hold a beat longer, drag it out through the measure. Ultimately, their way prevailed.

That doesn't mean it's "better." Unfortunately, Schuller and his fellow jazz critics tend to use this distinction between vertical and horizontal movement to put down anything that doesn't swing, or at least to imply that swinging is the higher musical development: as far as they're concerned, all kinds of rhythm music (ragtime, marching band, stomp) inherently want to swing, if only they can—as if all those thousands of stompers were just waiting around pogoing up and down until someone could figure out how to get off the dime. Any who underlaid their 2/4 stomps with a 4/4 beat were of course ahead of their time, a couple rungs higher up the evolutionary ladder. This is bilge, although the basic distinction is nevertheless a useful one.

But enough about drive. What about this "swerve"? Let's go back a bit. In the course of sorting out the physical composition of the universe, the Roman poet Lucretius talks about the origins of the phenomenal world—that is, the world of things that we can see and touch, taste and smell and hear. In the beginning, he says, the universe was nothing but a steady rain of minute and indivisible atoms falling—driving—through an infinite void. Their trajectories were strictly parallel: no one atom could possibly cross paths with another, interfere with it in any way. Then,

> ... *incerto tempore ferme*
> *incertisque locis spatio depellere paulum,*
> *tantum quod momen mutatum dicere possis* (II, 218-20)

> At some uncertain place in space and time
> They deviated from their given course
> By just enough so you could say it changed.

The swerve is what makes life possible—without it, all is static, permanent, sterile. One little bend, completely without premeditation or plan, just because—call it God, love, free will, anarchy, whatever your name for the unknowable. Then POW! The universe as we know it: the willful atom swerves into its straight neighbor's path, the neighbor gets bent and crashes into a few others; soon you've got a cosmic pool table. Then the atoms begin sticking together in

[5]

clumps and the next thing you know you've got Carteret, New Jersey (so the process isn't perfect; what is?).

But what in the name of all that is holy does any of this have to do with music? In an article wistfully titled "James Taylor Marked for Death," the enfant terrible of rock criticism Lester Bangs lays it out: "It always begins with that glorious 'mistake,' the crazy unexpected note kicking out sideways to let us loose again no matter what you call it. It reappears periodically every few years, the next new absurd and outrageous squeak that no one could calculate till ten years after it molders buried under wretched excess in the slow-down twilight, but the Craze will come again in new clothes!"

So every time music starts to follow its natural tendency to sink and begins to fall like those atoms, zip! something swerves. Or rather, somebody. When Billie Holiday starts slurring her notes, bending away from the melody and then rushing ahead to catch it up, she's working the swerve. The swerve is ragtime-obsessed trombonist Arthur Pryor smearing and blatting his way through "Trombone Sneeze," back in 1902 (Vic. 1223). It's the keening, free-falling elevator wail of Johnny Dodds's clarinet at the beginning of his 1926 "Perdido Street Blues" (Col. 698-D). It's Lester Young, ten years later, walking his tenor dreamily away from the chords he's supposed to be riffing on. It's Rock 'n' Roll Trio guitarist Paul Burlinson figuring out, one day in 1956, that the weird fuzzy sound his Telecaster is making is due to a loose tube in his amp, and not fixing it.

Whenever there's a proper, legit, "dicty" way of phrasing the tune in question and a musician plays something arbitrary, irrational, spontaneous, unexplainable, that's the swerve. Here's where we'll find those "eager anticipations of the beat," that "earthy or 'dirty' tone" that the *Grove Dictionary* calls hot. But they're only part of the story: melody, harmony, tone, timbre, rhythm can all be swerved. Bends, slurs, growls, rasps, howls, moans, slides, stretches, takeoffs, inversions, fits, starts, even stomps and syncopations—all ways of swerving. Country music scholar Robert Cantwell has a beautiful paragraph in his *Bluegrass Breakdown* on what the European ear hears when Africa is in the house:

> ...tones grow hair, go blind, or explode; notes bend, break, weaken, collapse or leave home; melodies compulsively juggle handfuls of notes or fling them wildly away; rhythms spill over in syncopations...horns growl, hiss, cough and squeak; banjos snarl, snap and bite; fiddles cry and wail; singing voices shout, holler, call, moan and weep, fill with gravel, smoke or weeds, cower in the nasal cavities or in one corner of the mouth and sink luxuriously into some lower region of the anatomy, and sometimes even slip into mere speech or something worse, like nonsense syllables.

That's the swerve.

Some kinds of music institutionalize the swerve, build it into the basic structure—into the rhythm, the harmony, the melody. Thus the springy spaces between notes in a Scott Joplin rag; the poignant harmonies of a Duke Ellington tone poem; the searching melodic surge of a Beethoven symphony. Some seek to exclude it entirely—manifesto by Maurice Ravel: "the work of art appears only in mature conception where no detail has been left to chance." The impulse to want to turn Carteret back into atomic rain is understandable, a natural reaction to the chaos of the physical world, but.... Some kinds of music vigilantly keep it out of one door only to let it in through another (the straight melodies and wild voices of hillbilly music). Many try to carve it in stone, at which point it ceases to be a swerve. In 1958, fuzztone guitar was frightening; in 2003, it's cute: they're using it in kiddy cartoons and car commercials.

Applying rigid logic to this system, we realize immediately that drive and swerve in their purest forms have to be antithetical, like yin and yang or gin and tonic. If a musician's following the wisp of his fey Muse, note leading note hither and yon into the rarefied aether of pure invention, he can't at the same time fix the rigid patterns and earthy repetitions that cement a groove.

The same goes for groups: when you get everybody doing the same thing at the same time over and over again—oom-PAH oom-PAH oom-PAH—you get maximum drive, but it's powerful dull. When everybody does her own thing, each avoiding any kind of overlap with the character in the next chair, you get a circus of swerve, but it sure ain't gonna be a toe-tapper. Drive demands repetition, swerve surprise. It's big band versus free jazz, Glenn Miller versus Archie Shepp. Neither one of these is hot; heat demands compromise—paradoxically, the hottest music is the most thoroughly compromised.

Now, a little reflection will lead to the conclusion that drive and swerve are relative: if it's only a swerve until everybody gets thoroughly used to it, then it's only drive until something louder or punchier comes along and folks get with the new groove. But you can go home again: after a while, old swerves and worn-out drives fall out of the popular consciousness. Then some big-eared types, bored with the modern wave, will start digging for something new to dig. The old bones get polished up and joined together in new and fanciful ways, and the old swerve bends a new drive, the old drive pushes a new bend.

This model isn't perfect; no model is. At least it gives us a way to approach the barely comprehensible chaos that is the real world with a little more confidence. Yet lest we be slaves to a theory that is in itself imperfect, let us you and me remind ourselves that not all music can be plotted with two vectors, that there are hundreds and thousands of ineffably hot performances that will somehow fall off the axes of our little graph. Some of these we'll deal with; others remain hovering on the edges of our consciousness, tantalizing us with faint echoes of harmonies unfathomable and rhythms beyond quantification.

In weakness we create distinctions, then
Believe our puny boundaries are things
Which we perceive, and not which we have made.

William Wordsworth said that, back before his brain turned to muesli. On to American music. Hot music.

Afro-Celtic Fusion

A country's music isn't the same thing as the music that exists in that country; it's not the sum total of every note that is played and sung within its territorial limits. Just because, say, Buenos Aires has an opera house where you can hear Verdi, that doesn't mean that *Rigoletto* is Argentine music (I would, however, be the first to agree that it says something about the people of Argentina that they're staging Italian opera). No, a country's music is born of its earth and partakes of the character of its inhabitants—although precisely how can be far from obvious. Like a dialect, it's a vessel into which people pour their most unguarded emotions, a first means of expression that, at its most basic level, isn't studied so much as absorbed from the earliest age (which of course means studied very intently, as only small children can). When I say that this book is about American music, therefore, I don't mean that it's in any way a survey of musical activity in America. It's about one, enduring, musical dialect.

America has had more than one such dialect in its history, of course. Before the Europeans came, there was music. That was truly American music, but it's not what this book is about. Nor is it about the Spanish music of the Southwest, the French music of the Mississippi Valley, or even the ballads brought here by the English and nurtured in the hollows and hills of Appalachia. Neither is it about the various species and genera of music that followed the waves of immigration of the mid-nineteenth century, at least not directly—American music was already a done deal by then. And it's certainly not about the composed, pan-European art music that you had to go to school to study, and still do.

This book is about the music that two subject peoples, brought here by the English and often—if not generally—antagonistic to each other, created between themselves, and, with one of the supreme ironies in cultural history, thrust burning into the American heart where it remains to this day; the music from which jazz and R&B, honky-tonk, country, and bluegrass, have all descended, not to mention soul, rap, and all the various subspecies of rock 'n' roll.

I won't get into the sordid history of African slavery in the Americas, much; for that, see Hugh Thomas's magisterial *The Slave Trade.* By the mid-1700s, suffice it to say, Africans were present in large numbers in just about every corner of the Americas, and in many cases had been there for two hundred years or more—the first African slaves had arrived in the New World in 1510. They were in English North America by 1619. Now, everybody knows what happened when these Africans, their children, and their descendants, encountered European music; how they began to blend their extraordinarily complex concepts of rhythm with European developments in harmony. The evidence is strewn all about the Americas. In Argentina, it's the tango, in Uruguay, the candombe. Brazil has all kinds of African-inflected music, none more famous than the samba (although the maxixe used to be quite popular in the States, back before the Great War). Colombia has its loopy, driving cumbia. The Caribbean is stuffed to the gills with Afro-beats, from the Trinidadian calypso to the Martiniquaise beguine, the Haitian konpa, the Jamaican mento, the Puerto Rican bomba and, of course, all the multitude of Cuban genres—the rumba, guaguancó, mambo, danzón, and all the others that extraordinarily musical island has produced. Even Mexico's mariachi has African roots. And, of course, the United States has gospel, ragtime, jazz, the blues—and, as I shall make clear below, so-called "hillbilly music." And those are just the traditional types.

Yet if you had to take one of those "which of these objects doesn't belong" tests about the music of the African diaspora in the Americas, the answer would be obvious. Something happened to African music in Anglo-Saxon North America that didn't happen to it anywhere else. If you were to collect representative samples of all those other musics, and even of the indigenous musics of West Africa— preferably samples from the beginning of the twentieth century, before cross-pollination via phonograph record had time to occur—you'd find they share a loping, lilting sense of rhythm that's very different from the harder-edged, more urgent beat that underlies their North American analogues. Both are hot; both have plenty of drive and that African swerve built into the bones of the music. But at their most animated—when everybody's going flat out—theirs trot, ours run. Whenever North American musicians approach the edge of chaos, they've got a distinct tendency to want to lean over it as far as they can go.

This difference has to do with the particular origins of the men and women transported to the British colonies of North America, with the peculiar conditions of servitude they met with here, with the people whom they served and the people they served with. Of the roughly 11,000,000 African slaves who survived the horrors of the Middle Passage (following Thomas's statistics), only 500,000 came directly to our shores. A number more were taken here indirectly from the Caribbean, but the total is still small in comparison to the 4,000,000 that went to Brazil alone, the 2,500,000 sucked up by the Spanish Empire, the 2,000,000 by the British West Indies. Here in North America, to a far greater degree than elewhere in the Americas, the Africans were scattered, often even deliberately dispersed, among the European population. According to the first census of the United States, in 1790, of the 3,898,874 new Americans, 694,207 were slaves. Even if you assume that every single one of the 59,196 free persons left over after you deduct all the white folks was of African descent and add them to the total, that's still just over 20 percent of the population. Nowhere in the colonies was the concentration above South Carolina's 43 percent. Compare that to the situation prevailing in Brazil, according to figures from 1798: 1,986,000 Africans (about 25 percent free) out of 3.25 million people; some parts of Brazil were over 70 percent African.

What this means, of course, is that the Africans in North America were forced into much closer contact with the Europeans. There were exceptions, where you'd find the massive plantations characteristic of the Caribbean and Brazil; places like the rice-growing areas of the Carolinas. But they were far from universal. In many areas, particularly on the southern frontier, a slaveowning family would rarely have more than five slaves, and often just one or two. Imagine the difficulty of preserving your native language, culture, music under those circumstances, impossibly far from home, stuck among a hard, often cruel people in a vast, dangerous, and above all alien land. And yet African music persisted in North America, if in a form less "pure" than one finds in other lands of the diaspora.

Almost from their first arrival in North America, the Africans would have encountered representatives of another group of exiles, often as unwilling as they were; a people the English regarded as just as barbarous, savage, uncivilized (and, I should point out, musical) as the Africans. I refer, of course, to the Celts. When Oliver Cromwell, regicide and Lord Protector (i.e., dictator) of England, landed his armies in Dublin in 1649, it was with no kind intentions toward the Irish people. The campaign that followed was savage and ended with much of eastern Ireland cleared of its population and distributed to Englishmen, who in turn leased much of it out to their Lowland Scottish Presbyterian allies. Some fifty thousand Irish slaves were sent to work the plantations of Virginia and Barbados, to live side by side with England's other slaves. In the early eighteenth century, it was the allies' turn—their dour brand of Protestantism was no longer in favor with the English, and the cheap leases started dry-ing up. Between 1718 and 1746, a third of the so-called Scots-Irish left Ulster for America, many as indentured servants (who often lived with and served alongside slaves). In 1745, Bonnie Prince Charlie led the assembled clans of the Scottish Highlands against England to claim the throne that was rightfully his; after his defeat the next spring at Culloden, the English moved to pacify the Highlands ("solitudinem faciunt, pacem appellant"; "they make a desert; they call it peace"—Tacitus). The Highlanders decamped to America, in droves. The 1790 census lists a hair under two hundred thousand Americans who claimed themselves as Scottish or Irish.

The Celts and the West Africans were both particularly musical peoples, peoples who liked to sing and, especially, to dance. The English thought so, anyway. In 1623, Richard Jobson, an English sea captain, published an account of what he saw in Senegambia, at the very western tip of the Dark Continent. He was a keen observer:

> I would acquaint you of their most principall instrument, which is called a Ballards [the balafon, or gourd-resonated xylophone], made to stand a foot above the ground, hollow under, and hath uppon the top some seventeene woodden keyes standing like the Organ, upon which hee that playes sitting upon the ground, just against the middle of the instrument, strikes with a sticke in either hand, about a foote long, at the end whereof is made fast a round ball, covered with some soft stuffe, to avoyd the clattering noyse the bare stickes would make...the sound that proceeds from this instrument is worth the observing, for we can heare it a good English mile, the making of this instrument being one of the most ingenious things amongst them: for to every one of these keyes there belongs a small Iron the bignesse of a quill, and is a foote long, the breadth of the instrument, upon which hangs two gourdes under the hollow, like bottles, who receives the sound, and returnes it againe with that extraordinary loudnesse.

There are not many of these, as we can perceive, because they are not common, but when they doe come to any place, the resort unto them is to be admired; for both day and night, more especially all the night the people continue dauncing, untill he that playes be quite tyred out; the most desirous of dancing are the women, who dance without men, and but one alone, with crooked knees and bended bodies they foot it nimbly, while the standers by seeme to grace the dancer, by clapping their hands together after the manner of keeping time; and when the men dance they doe it with their swords naked in their hands, with which they use some action, and both men and women when they have ended their first dance give somewhat unto the player.

The Celts, too, had their popular musicians and indefatigable dancers. In 1845, Charles St. John, an English gentleman hunter, was stalking a stag in the Scottish Highlands, attended by his local ghillie, Donald. Night fell, and it was raining. Then they heard a fiddle, wild in the darkness. "'It's all right enough,'" St. John recalled Donald saying, "'it's that drunken deevil, Sandy Ross; ye'll never haud a fiddle frae him, nor him frae a whisky still.'"

They followed the music to a "whisky bothie"—an illicit still house—where they witnessed an extraordinary scene:

On a barrel in the middle of the apartment—half hut, half cavern—stood aloft, fiddling with all his might, the identical Sandy Ross, while round him danced three unkempt savages; and another figure was stooping, employed over a fire in the corner, where the whisky pot was in full operation.... We got rest, food and fire—all we required—and something more; for long after I had betaken me to the dry heather in the corner, I had disturbed visions of strange orgies in the bothie, and of my sober Donald exhibiting curious antics on

the top of a tub...when daylight awoke me, the smugglers
and Donald were all quiet and asleep, far past my efforts to
arouse them.... From the state in which my trusty companion was, with his head in a heap of ashes, I saw it would
serve no purpose to wake him, even if I were able to do so.

Small wonder the fiddle was nicknamed "the devil's box."

As far as I know, unlike the devil's box, the ballards didn't turn
up in American music until the vaudeville era, when the xylophone became a popular novelty instrument (although it was much
used in Central and South America). For a population as dispersed
as the Africans in North America, one that had to travel to congre-
gate (if at all), it would be cumbersome. Worse, anything whose
sound could carry "a good English mile" would be, let's say, prob-
lematic for the overseers. That went for the big drums that the
Africans used for communication, and it would've gone for this
as well. In 1764, James Grainger, a cohort of Samuel "Dictionary"
Johnson's who had spent some time on the island of St. Kitts, published a poem on the art of cultivating sugarcane, titled *Sugar Cane,
a Poem* (the eighteenth century isn't known for the imagination of
its poets). Much of it is occupied by the care and feeding of slaves.
Though Grainger imagined himself humane and benevolent in this
regard, he nonetheless warns the would-be planter:

But let not thou the drum their mirth inspire;
Nor vinous spirits: else, to madness fir'd,
...
Fell acts of blood, and vengeance they pursue (IV, 602–5).

Exactly.

What the slaves needed was something more portable and less
threatening to their uneasy captors—like another instrument Jobson
saw:

...that [instrument] which is most common in use, is made of a great gourd, and a necke thereunto fastned, resembling, in some sort, our Bandora [a species of lute]; but they have no manner of fret, and the strings they are either such as the place yeeldes or their invention can attaine to make, being very unapt to yeeld a sweete and musicall sound, notwithstanding with pinnes they winde and bring to agree in tunable notes, having not above six strings upon their greatest instrument.

This wouldn't cause nearly such a problem with the powers that be. Grainger again:

Permit thy slaves to lead the choral dance,
To the wild banshaw's melancholy sound (IV, 583–4).

He adds a note to this: "*Banshaw*. This is a sort of rude guitar, invented by the Negroes. It produces a wild pleasing melancholy sound."

Somewhere along the way, the music the Celts brought with them began to get tangled up with the music the Africans had brought with them. (While some of the Scots and Irish pushed themselves up on the backs of their African fellow-chattel, shunned them and hated them, others did not; Maryland was passing antimiscegenation laws as early as 1661.) Whether this tangling happened first in Virginia, during the days of Cromwell; on the western frontier of Pennsylvania or North Carolina, where the Scots-Irish betook themselves; or elsewhere, we don't know. I like to think it took place exactly as in William Sydney Mount's 1845 painting *Dance of the Haymakers*: in an open barn, two men, clearly Irish, dance a jig to a third's fiddle, while a young black boy beats time on the barn door with a pair of sticks.

In any case, there are certain affinities between the two musics that would've expedited the process. In the western bulge of Africa, where the bulk of the slaves transported to North America came

from, Arab Africa and black Africa met, mixed, and brought forth
a music that (as Robert Palmer points out in his classic *Deep Blues*)
was string-oriented, with long, twisty melodies and plenty of rhythm—
not entirely unlike Celtic music, in fact.

There were also some key differences, polarities that have shaped
all American music since. Consider how two performances captured
during the early days of ethnic recording, one Irish, one African,
handle something as basic as the beat. In October 1921, the fiddler
Michael Coleman—a slender, intense thirty-year-old native of County
Sligo, where the Celtic traditions of Irish music were particularly
strong—went into Columbia Records' New York studio and recorded
"The Monaghan," a jig dating back to at least the 1840s (Col. E7470).
As a dimly recorded piano clomps away briskly in the background,
Coleman's fiddle starts off slowly, carving out a set of rather monotonous, relentlessly regular minor-key figures. With each repetition,
however, he grows more insistent, darting slightly ahead of the beat
and then falling back right on top of it; riding it, pushing it, tacking
it down to the ground. His playing, skirting as it does the very edge
of chaos, threatening to break free and skitter away, is nonetheless
absolutely fluid, confident and, ultimately, controlled. "The Monaghan" is no anomaly; on record after record, Coleman—the most
celebrated Irish fiddler of his generation, if not all time—demonstrates the same fierceness, the same implicit violence.

There's no one record as typical of West African music as a Coleman disc is of Irish music. This is especially so for the twenties, when
the cross-pollination and homogenization that invariably occurs when
outside music is introduced had not yet had much of a chance to
occur. West Africa is a complicated and very, very diverse part of
the world. That said, "Yaw Donkor" by the Kumasi Trio (not to be
confused with the Nairobi Trio) at least covers many of the most
common elements (Zon. 1008). Recorded in London in 1928 for
Zonophone Records' new West African series—an attempt by its par-
ent company to squeeze a few more shillings out of the colonies—

the record features the virtuoso Ghanian guitarist Jacob Sam playing with a percussionist and another guitarist; all three sing (in Fanti, one of the many languages of the region). Like Coleman, Sam surges ahead of the beat—or where we feel the beat should be—with a series of complex, tumbling runs. But this propulsion is where the resemblance ends. There's this clicking, you see (the record label calls it "castanets," but it could be anything) that's lagging behind the guitar, pulling the beat back. And then the vocals. Call and response, the call ahead of the beat and response behind it. And that's it—there's no normative part to the music, no on-the-beat accompaniment like Coleman had to play against. In fact, there really is no beat as Michael Coleman would've understood it; it's implied, not stated; something to dance around. There's a backspun sort of drive, sure, but more swerve than we know how to handle. The result, to our ears, sounds lazy, ragged, almost chaotic. In fact, it's anything but, as lending a careful ear to the deliberate, precise percussion demonstrates.

By the mid-eighteenth century these very different forms of music had begun to send tendrils out to each other, making American music as we know it a done deal. The runaway-slave notices found in the colonial newspapers of the time are rife with items like the one from the *South Carolina Gazette* in 1741, seeking a "middle-sized Negro Fellow named Sam" who "can play upon the violin," or the 1743 one from the *Boston Evening Post* seeking a certain Cambridge, who "plays well upon a flute, and not so well on a violin." If any detailed description of the music these men were making has survived, I have not seen it. But we can be pretty damn sure the person advertising for "any white person that can play on the violin, or a Negro" in the September 17, 1737, *South Carolina Gazette* wasn't looking for someone to play the likes of "Yaw Donkor."

In his seminal *Country: The Twisted Roots of Rock 'n' Roll*, Nick Tosches quotes from the diary of Nicholas Cresswell, an Englishman who attended a Virginia barbecue in July of 1774: "A great number of young people met together with a Fiddle and Banjo [which he elsewhere described as "a Gourd…with only four strings"] played by two Negroes, with Plenty of Toddy, which both Men and Women seem to be very fond of. I believe they have danced and drunk till there are few sober people amongst them." Whatever they were playing in the slave quarters, it's a pretty safe bet that when they were working for the young white folks, this anonymous little string band was playing, among other things, a selection of the (hot) Celtic-derived jigs, reels, and hornpipes that were all the rage. I sure would like to hear what that banjo player was up to.

These two men, and thousands of other men and women just as anonymous, black and white, free and enslaved, built American music. Collectively, away from the eye of history, they welded African and Celtic elements (with, to be sure, a goodly portion of English hymns and ballads) together into a musical language resilient enough to pass the test that all national musics must pass if they are to survive. It encountered, and continues to encounter, other musical traditions, digested what was digestible in them, spat out the rest, and moved on with its central characteristics unchanged.

♪

I have divided the story of this new music into three unequal parts; as we move closer to the present, the amount of available evidence increases, and there is more to say. Part I deals with the minstrel era, when our raw fusion was first recognized as something new, and something characteristically American. Part II deals with the ragtime era, when the music absorbed the influences of European formal music. The last part covers the birth of jazz, when this fusion was reexposed to African music in the form of the blues. A coda mentions hillbilly music, or the rebirth of minstrelsy; and the text is followed by a bibliographical note and a discographical one.

Daniel Decatur Emmett, when he wasn't working.

PART I

Minstrelsy, or Get Out De Way

[Ministrallorum] sunt duo genera. Quidam enim frequentant
publicas potationes et lasciuas congregationes, et cantant ibi
diuersas cantilenas ut moueant homines ad lasciuiam, et tales
sunt damnabiles. Sunt autem alii qui cantant gesta principum
et uita sanctorum et non faciunt innumerabiles turpitudines.

There are two kinds of minstrels: some frequent public drink-
ing-places and indecent gatherings, where they sing all sorts of
popular songs in order to move people to indecency; such minstrels are damnable. There are others, however, who sing about
the deeds of princes and the lives of the saints and don't do
those countless filthy things.
　　　　　　　　　　　—THOMAS DE CABHAM (OB. 1313)

America's First Music Craze

In late January 1843, Daniel Decatur Emmett hosted an impromptu
jam session in his room in Mrs. Brooke's boarding house at 37
Catherine Street, in New York's impressively unsavory Fourth Ward.
(The tenement that's been camping out on the site for the last century
or so now holds a Chinese beauty parlor and no plaque.) Emmett

[21]

fiddled and Billy Whitlock picked on a banjo that Emmett had lying around, while Dick Pelham and Frank Brower kept time on tambourine and bones (nothing more than a pair of cattle ribs that you rattled together like musical spoons). The young men—Emmett, the oldest, was twenty-eight—played "Old Dan Tucker" (words by Emmett, tune by... somebody else), and it was good. Better yet, it was *hot*. Within hours, they had a gig at Bartlett's Billiard-Room in the Branch Hotel, a couple of blocks away at 36 Bowery (no plaque). Or maybe they secured the gig first and jammed later; memories, as always in revolutions, differ. In any case, they were overnight stars. They began calling themselves the Virginia Minstrels, evidently playing off a quartet of yodeling Tyrolese Minstrels that were touring at the time; we'll get to the Virginia part in a moment.

The Virginia Minstrels were the first truly American band, playing American music—or at least the first to be publicly recognized as such. When Billy Whitlock added his percussive banjo to Dan Emmett's fiddle, he was doing something new and dangerous, at least for white folks. Before the Virginia Minstrels, white performers kept the (white) fiddle and its music segregated from the black banjo and its music. One doesn't hear of white banjo players much at all before the Virginian Joel Walker Sweeney, who began touring with the instrument in 1836; he was Whitlock's teacher (he's also credited with changing the body of the instrument from a gourd to a proper European drum shell). If the Virginia Minstrels were merely presenting something to the larger ofay public that had been going on quietly for ages back in the hood, the fact remains that this particular lineup, and especially the conjunction of the banjo and the fiddle, doesn't seem to have been attempted before on the stage, at least in New York (and then, as now, if it ain't in New York, it's out of town). Billy Whitlock himself had played one night with a fiddler in Philly, a couple of years before Mrs. Brooke's, but he remembered it only as a "novel idea," a freak.

What did they sound like? The songs are basically "Turkey in the Straw" (Emmett's name for it; before him, it was "Zip Coon") and the like—lightly syncopated variants of English/Scots/Irish fiddle tunes; repetitive melodies with rough, usually satirical lyrics often chanted in unison. But, as a witness to their antics observed, "it could be very difficult to describe [their performance] in libretto, and musical score would not do it justice." Pelham, for instance, "seemed animated by a savage energy," and, in an age where real musicians were supposed to sit still, his frenzied tambourine-bashing "nearly wrung him off his seat." Whitlock frailed away at his gut-stringed banjo with "complete abandon," Emmett furiously hacked a fiddle held backwoods-style at his chest, and Brower kept popping up from his chair to stomp around the stage in his boots while rapidly rattling a pair of rib bones in each hand, putting the whole arm into it. How can you notate that? *Fortissimo* doesn't quite cut it; *allo Negro* might be more appropriate.

For—as you may have surmised—Emmett, Brower, Pelham, and Whitlock were all well-established professional "darkies," or "Ethiopian delineators," which were the contemporary terms of art (it should go without saying that the bulk of white America at the time, North and South, slaver and abolitionist, was casually, thoroughly, and institutionally racist in speech and deed). They were white men who spent the greater part of the working day in loud, tattered clothes, with nappy wigs on their heads and large quantities of burnt cork besmirching their pasty Anglo-Irish complexions. Thus decked out, they would present themselves before their equals—mostly deracinated rustics newly come to the metropolis and recent immigrants from the various islands and mains of northern Europe, with a stiffening of the established petite bourgeoisie and even the occasional slumming swell— and pretend (albeit not very hard) that they were real African slaves on one of the great Southern plantations (hence the "Virginia"). And thus they would dance and sing, pick the banjo and rock the bow, give mangled speeches and tell corny jokes. Always tell jokes. Before the Virginia Minstrels, they did it in ones and twos, as part of someone else's act or variety show. After, they *were* the show. If there were other, earlier, white musicians who turned imitating black ones into a musical genre, rather than a one-off novelty, their names have fallen into the cracks of history.

The music of the minstrel show, as codified by Emmett and his boys, was the first recognized, fully documented eruption of American music. Although many have tried and oft, none has yet found a way beyond the mere assertion of tain't so to escape the plain fact that all that is American in American music, and all that is good, traces its bloodlines through the minstrel show—an institution through which white America stole, plundered, colonized; raped, prostituted, and pimped; contaminated and diluted; misinterpreted and misunderstood; ridiculed, patronized, bucked, scorned and—in some strange way—passionately loved the music and the culture of black America.

In the past few years, minstrelsy has become something of a hot topic among academics. A lot of convoluted sentences have been spun out to the effect that this peculiar institution illuminates the patterns of race, class, and wampum that shaped and continue to shape the culture of our great and oppressive nation; that it is a manifestation of the alienation working-class white males felt in a society where the rich and powerful looked to European norms of acculturation to reinforce the status that their penises, pennies, and power gave them; that the blackface minstrels had to fashion themselves into the only people to whom they could feel superior in order to both reinforce their precarious place in white society through ridicule of an excluded Other (whose cultural practices in many ways inconveniently recall their own), and appropriate some of the freedom and—more importantly—sexual power of an Other who is both feminized through his powerlessness and hyper-masculinized through his very alterity.

Waaall, sure. Only a fool would fail to perceive, and only a knave deny, the obvious patterns of power flowing through the enterprise of minstrelsy, the commingled contempt and envy. That's not the whole story, though. When white men—and always men—got themselves up like Coons (let's rehab that odious little word as a technical term for the bulge-eyed, red-lipped virtual—as in, strictly pretend; ersatz; stereotypical; without meaningful correlation to objective reality—African of the minstrel stage; for all the dandified Zip Coons and countrified Jim Crows, whatever their tint from collar to cuff) and sang their mangled little songs, sure, they were alienating black from white, making blackness appear foreign when in fact blacks were as American as anyone and a damn sight more so than the recent Irish immigrants who made up so large a part of the minstrels' audience. At the same time—a contradictory idea, but minstrelsy was nothing if not contradictory—by the very act of smearing blackness on and sloughing it off again, they were making the idea of "blackness" more white, and "whiteness" more black. If you can put on another race and take it off again just like that, then skin color and behavior might not necessarily be linked with bonds of iron.

Ultimately, minstrelsy was an institution with an ideology, and that ideology was not a benign one. But it was also a human institution; an American institution; worst of all, a showbiz institution. As an American human with showbiz experience, I feel entitled to a little skepticism about just what the average minstrel's degree of interest was in the ideological aspects of his trade. For many, I'm sure it was just a good wheeze, a throwaway joke told by people who didn't know, think, or care nearly so much about whom they told it on as about the laughs they were getting. It was entertainment. It was rock 'n' roll. And, if minstrelsy was anything like any of the crazes that followed it—like ragtime, like jazz, like swing, like rock and soul and hip-hop—some of those blacked-up ofays must have felt a sincere and unfeigned admiration for the black musicians they were imitating. Some of them must have internalized the music, understood it, played it with sympathy, skill, and creativity. Minstrelsy must have had its Joe Lambs and Jack Teagardens, its Elvises and its Eminems.

Some people who saw these acts were fooled (the rubes!). For their benefit, early minstrels often included before-and-after engravings on their song folios, just so you would *know*. Many others thought that they knew more about black people because they had seen blackface; that they had witnessed something "authentic" (when anybody in American culture tries to pawn that word off on you, best break out your bifocals and get the shotgun down from over the mantle). After all, early minstrels like Thomas Rice (whose hit ditty was "Jim Crow," of Jim Crow fame), Dan Emmett, and George Christy claimed to base their shtick on diligent and acute observation of real live black people, and some of them were sincerely anthropological about it. Even the Virginia Minstrels, who were far from scientific about their delineation, billed their act as the "sports and pastimes of the Virginia Colored Race, through medium of Songs, Refrains and Ditties as sung by Southern Slaves."

Unfortunately, we cannot judge the accuracy of their claim. In the 1850s, at least one foreign observer who had seen both imitators and imitated, the Frenchman Oscar Commettant (a musician himself), thought that the minstrels of his day painted a vivid and accurate portrait of their subjects. But then again, there are folks who consider Eric Clapton a bluesman. Doubtless, some minstrels were more sensitive to their subjects than others; heard the music more accurately and were able to reproduce it with more suppleness. The thing is, the Virginia Minstrels kicked off a craze, and you know how those work in America. As in the jazz craze of the 1920s, the rock 'n' roll craze of the 1950s, or the gangsta rap craze of the 1990s, public demand was such that everyone and his uncle thought they'd give the thing a try. When you expand the pool of would-be entertainers beyond the seasoned professionals, you tend to get higher highs and lower lows. In the 1920s, when the craze for hillbilly music caught Daniel Decatur Emmett's least-evolved musical descendants on disc, you find minstrel performances as sublimely baroque and weird as Emmett Miller's, and as embarrassingly stiff and shitty as Herschel Brown's "Talking Nigger Blues" (Ok. 402001).

One thing did result, though, from the first rush of the minstrel craze: documentation. Within months of the Virginia Minstrels hitting it big, the music business of the day—with that industry's perennial promptness to jump on a loose dollar—churned out a torrent of "Ethiopian Songbooks," "Celebrated Ethiopian Melodies," "Banjo Instructors," and, of course, "Songs of the Virginia Minstrels." The average prospective minstrel being a nice, economically challenged Irish boy from the North (a disproportionate number of the early minstrels came from the new Hibernian underclass that was flooding into the country), and travel to the actual slave states being difficult and very expensive, these would've been invaluable.

The same reservations apply to the published music as to its performance, but nonetheless this stuff provides, if in attenuated form, our first inkling of what all those anonymous fiddlers and banjo strummers had been up to. The harmonies are simple, even crude—two or three chords, nothing fancy. The tunes, the melodies, are generally drawn from Scottish and Irish fiddle tunes. As musicologist Hans Nathan illustrates, the Scottish "Jenny's Babee" becomes "My Long Tail Blue" (the black dandy character of the minstrel stage was preternaturally fond of his swallowtail blue coat); the Irish "I Wish the Shepherd's Pet Were Mine" becomes "Jim Crow," the English "Bow Wow Wow" becomes "Gumbo Chaff." Not exactly, though—the melodies tend to be chopped up into short, two-bar phrases, with more stops and starts than in their European sources, and more repetition. At first, this might seem anything but hot.

Consider Emmett's version of "Old Dan Tucker," which he published in 1843. The melody—with a range of about five notes, it's not much of one—is in straight eighth notes, one per syllable, with strategically placed quarter and sixteenth notes, mostly in the chorus:

> I come to town de
> ud-der night, I
> hear de noise an
> saw de fight, De
> watch-man was a
> runnin roun, cry-in
> Old Dan Tuck-er's
> come to town, so—
> *chorus:*
> get out-de waay!
> [fill: four eighth notes]
> get out-de waay!
> [fill: four eighth notes]
> get out-de waay!
> Old Dan Tuck-er
> your to [*sic*] late to
> come to sup-per.

If the verse is plain, the chorus injects a sudden, offbeat rush to the proceedings, providing release after the monotonous stomp of the verse. That's not the whole story, though. There are accents that the lead-sheets of the day don't indicate. Add the eighth-note stomp of the banjoist's foot. Add the castanet rattle of the bones (an instrument that goes back to *A Midsummer Night's Dream*, at the very least. "*Titania*: What, wilt thou hear some music, my sweet love? *Bottom*: I have a reasonable good ear in music. Let's have the tongs and the bones." Badum-sha.) Add the bass thump of the tambourine, the puh-ching of the clawhammer banjo (that is, one played by plucking with the thumb while strumming down with the fingernails), and you've got something. As Nathan explains,

> ...the principle of pitting highly irregular accentuations in the melody...against a precise metrical accompaniment, which

characterizes all American dance music up to the present, is anticipated by early banjo tunes and undoubtedly derives from them.

He then goes on to list eight riffs and patterns that would be familiar to anyone who's ever played air guitar or patted hambone to "Jungle Boogie."

Unfortunately, the Virginia Minstrels were fifty years too early for the recording horn; by the time it arrived, Emmett was seventy-five. Some folks have tried recently to re-create the music of Dan Emmett and his buddies, using the instruments they must have used, the documents they left behind, and our own modern sense of what their influences, goals, and aesthetics must have been; too bad this dodge never really works. Not that their attempts aren't interesting.

In 1989, banjoist Joe Ayers recorded a cassette titled *Old Dan Tucker: Melodies of Dan Emmett & the Virginia Minstrels, 1843–1860* (it's still not available on CD, as far as I know—which indicates the amount of call there is for this kind of thing). It's a sincere, skilled, historically informed attempt to reproduce the music of a century and a half ago. It's helpful—you get an idea of what the instruments sounded like, learn a couple of the songs. The mellowness of the gut-string banjo is surprising, as is the muscularity of the tambourine-thumps. The songs—the ear instantly types them as hillbilly music—have a peculiar, stiff-legged stomp to them that sets the body to unconscious rocking. But no matter how well executed, Ayers's is an impossible project. It just doesn't have, can't have, that first-time-around, hell-we-don't-know-we're-just-makin'-this-shit-up-as-we-go-along *spark*. There's a distinct lack of "savage energy," and the abandon on display is very far from complete. For better or worse, the early Coons were stars, and it takes a star to play a star. The kind of folks with the patience and eccentricity for careful reconstruction of obsolete forms of music just ain't star timber. Stars don't like to work that hard.

On the other hand, much of the Minstrels' repertoire made it into the foundations of country music—massive, roughhewn stones, black with antiquity and more than half-buried in the muck from which American culture grows, stones upon which the whole huge edifice teeters with increasing precariousness every year. As the music got watered down on stage, professionalized and orchestrated, in its more rumbustious form it went to ground in the South, where it was kept alive in obscurity (at least as far as the national entertainment industry was concerned) by three generations of backwoods fiddlers and banjo-pickers until the recording industry finally turned its attention to the peckerwood market in the early 1920s. It's only natural to turn to these discs to hear the shades of Emmett, Brower, Pelham & Whitlock.

The magic of living tradition is powerful juju, to be sure, but no matter how "primitive" a record like Fiddlin' John Carson's 1924 "Old Dan Tucker" (Ok. 73039) may sound, it can't sound like the Virginia Minstrels' own version of eighty years earlier. It's sort of like turning to Shakespeare's *Comedy of Errors* to commune with Plautus's *Menaechmi*, its Roman source. Too much pop has happened—too much hokum and humbug has eaten its way into the "authentic" wood of the music, been absorbed, been rubbed with a patina of age. Still, running through all the first-wave hillbillies is a current of urgency that can't be accidental.

♪

If not the Virginia Minstrels, it would've been someone else. Sooner or later, somebody was going to bring this stuff to the surface. The Virginia Minstrels happened to be the surfers who first crested the surging wave. Since the early part of the nineteenth century (at least), white America had been running a mild case of jungle fever, musically speaking. The music that blacks, subjugated or emancipated, were making was just too interesting, too apt for expressing that intangible spark which made Americans unrecoverably not European (no matter how much the opera-hat-and-lorgnette set might yearn to the contrary) to be left unmolested.

Even a high-hat like Antonin Dvořák saw this. When they dragged him to America in 1893 (exactly fifty years after the Branch Hotel gig) to head the National Conservatory of Music and teach us how to be high-class, musically speaking, he maintained to the *New York Herald* that he didn't come all the way to New York to conduct the same old Beethoven and Wagner. He was here to help us find our own national music. And where was he looking? "In the Negro melodies of America I discover all that is needed for a great and noble school of music." Needless to say, we didn't need the help of any longhaired foreigners to figure that out; we'd been onto that tip for decades. Of course, the 'Merican way of assimilating black music into white culture involved all the crassness, commercialism, insensitivity, hypocrisy, sublimation, and brash vigor that distinguish us among nations. The European way was the conservatory; the American, the minstrel show.

As numerous folks have pointed out, this is America's only indigenous form of theater. It's ugly as muleshit, but it's ours. More than that, in the 1800s it was our chief cultural export, our best foot forward on the world stage. (That, and our cocktails—but that's another book.) It was something nobody else had, and we were good at it. The Europeans ate it up—"*Henry James? Herman Melville? Feh! Emerson, Thoreau, Whitman? Gib uns den Jim Crow da und den Zip Coon! Wir möchten gern Herrn. Bones und Tambo länger gehören.*" They was laughin' at us out there, but at least they wanted *something* of ours beyond our cotton, our timber, and our gold (and our juleps, corpse-revivers, fizzes, cobblers, and crustas).

Here in America, though, it was more than just a fun curiosity. Before the minstrels, if you couldn't feature Beethoven and such—European art music—your pop options were few: basically, Anglicized, pseudo-Irish airs like Thomas Moore's "Believe Me, If All

Those Enduring Young Charms" (the tune that Yosemite Sam uses to try to blow up Bugs Bunny on that rigged piano) and tear-jerkers like Henry Russell's "Woodman, Spare That Tree"—sentimental parlor pap. European music, anyway. Even the hot dance music, all those traditional fiddle tunes, had been born in a time and place ever receding from the realities of life in a new world, in a new country.

The minstrels provided a tough, brawling, aggressively modern alternative to all that. An American alternative. They were Mitch Ryder to Russell and his ilk's Wayne Newton; Mark Twain to Henry James. Sure the minstrels were white and way racist, yet they opened a window for black culture to come streaming through and light up the darkest recesses of America's musical heart. From our perch a yard and a half down the road, the Virginia Minstrels are as much symbols, good and bad, for everything that followed in American music as real, live individuals. Even if their run as rock 'n' roll was short—they lasted as a group barely six months, although the individuals all went on to be fixtures of the minstrel trade—it made waves whose ripples we're still feeling. The most important thing about the Virginia Minstrels and the early roughnecks who followed them is that they were making sure that, in the American mind, drive and swerve would take on a color; that hot music would be generally perceived as being in some way synonymous with black music, whatever its actual provenance.

This is not without its ironies. Sitting around in his New York rooming house in what is now the very fahionable district of Soho on "one rainy Sunday" in early 1859, as he later recalled it, Dan Emmett wrote, or wrote down—note the distinction—a rousing little "Plantation Song and Dance." That's how Bryant's Minstrels billed it when they performed it for the first time on April 4 of that year. Within two years, "Dixie's Land," as he called it, had become the national anthem of the Confederacy. That's no coincidence, nor is it a coincidence that the sullen and whupped postwar South made minstrel music—originally northern stage music—into its own folk music. Dixie became the Minstrel Nation and its music, composed of equal parts Coon, corn, and Celtica, became the vernacular music of the American cracker. The banjo, once a signifier for "black," came to signify, as it still does, "too white."

♪

Like many a supergroup since, the Virginia Minstrels self-destructed, and quickly. In a pattern followed by their spiritual and musical descendants the Original Dixieland Jazz Band (and—in reverse— the Sex Pistols), Emmett and the boys rode their overnight stardom straight onto the first thing smoking for England. The band formed in late January and arrived in Liverpool on May 21. On July 14, in London, they broke up. Egos had run high on the boat, when they weren't working; and on land, when they were, the money wasn't what it should have been. But the damage had been done. They had knocked 'em dead in London, with predictable results. Soon you had Brits doing it, Frogs doing it, even Irishmen in bogs doing it. And, as usually happens in these matters, before long the Europeans started telling *us* how to play the Coon—and we listened. Minstrelsy got refined—at least, as refined as any crude, derogatory product of the people's collective lizard-brain can get. By the 1860s, the Virginia Minstrels' brand of mayhem was strictly for rubes. As the stereo-type took on a life of its own increasingly unattached to any kind of African American reality—not that the tether was ever a short one— the citizens enacting it leached out the funk and left the insult.

The process of refinement began early, but then again, Elvis didn't wait so very long either before bringing in the Jordanaires. In fact, there's always been a current of sap and corn as broad as it is deep running beneath American music. Hearts start out cheatin' and end up achy breaky. Almost as soon as the minstrel show came on the scene, Emmett's great rivals the Christy Minstrels added four-part harmony singing to the mix, which couldn't help but smooth out the music's ragged frontier whoop. (The Beatles to the Virginia Minstrels' Rolling Stones, the Christy troupe was led by E. P. "Ned" Christy and his sidekick George Harrington, who soon changed his name to Christy and blew past his mentor.)

Pittsburgh's own Stephen Foster, however, added something much worse—*sympathy*. In 1845, the young songwriter answered Emmett's tough and rowdy "Old Dan Tucker," who's "come to town— get out de way!" with poor old "Uncle Ned," who's "gone whar de good Niggas go," leaving "Massa" and "Old Missus" behind to weep. Not hot. If you're snuffling back tears, you're not thinking of that *carnal act*. Foster, musical genius that he was and whatnot, hit it big by tempering the Jackson-era frontier crudity of "Ethiopian delineation," as it was known, with the aching pseudo-Irish sentimentality of the definitely not hot parlor song. His songs, spread by the hugely popular Christy Minstrels, were everywhere. This was the new music's first test. Could it be more than a rowdy dance thing, a novelty? Could it move hearts as well as butts? It could. Stephen Foster was the animating spirit behind the sentimental, plantation-reverie strain of minstrelsy, a strain that gained new poignance to many when the Civil War added a dimension to it which the nineteenth-century public prized above all other: nostalgia.

Not that it did Foster much personal good—when Dan Emmett was passing his sunset years in proud and penurious semi-obscurity, Foster was already long dead, eaten hollow by cheap booze. For those who like to pick out patterns in the random whorls of time, it should be noted that his last address was the hardscrabble North American Hotel at 30 Bowery, where some dissenting scholiasts say the Virginia Minstrels had their first gig, twenty-one years earlier almost to the day. Emmett was made of tougher stuff; he lasted until 1904, the year—as Nick Tosches points out—that Al Jolson first started blacking up. He last went before the public in 1895–96, when he fiddled "Dixie" with Al G. Field's Minstrels—the troupe with which Emmett Miller, the last great minstrel, would later appear.

Meanwhile, after Emancipation, black musicians began to figure that if Mr. Charlie accepts Coons as entertainment, he might possibly just as well have black ones as white—"Let's take it to the stage," as Funkadelic used to say. The long-running all-black Georgia Minstrels were the first. They were a smash. In fact, the Georgia Minstrels were so popular that their name became generic for any black minstrel show; white minstrels called themselves "Nigger minstrels." Over the next eighty-odd years many others were to follow, including such seminal troupes as Callender's (featuring, among other luminaries, the great Billy Kersands—the fellow with the billiard balls in his mouth on the cover of *Exile on Main St.*), Mahara's (where W. C. Handy got his start), Silas Green's from New Orleans (vets include Ma Rainey and, in 1949, the teenage Ornette Coleman!) and the Mississippi-based F. S. Wolcott's Rabbit Foot Minstrels (Ma Rainey again; the great songster Jim Jackson, who put in twenty-five years with the outfit; blues artiste Skip James; the young Louis Jordan; and veteran Stax star Rufus Thomas).

Of course, even black performers sometimes had to burn the cork and smear it on if they wanted to be taken seriously as Coons: the natural variation in skin tone found in the African American population proved puzzling to the white consumer. Besides, Coons—being essentially the product of a virtual reality—should all be the same uniform black, no? People are people, and stereotypes are stereotypes, and never the twain &c. As with so many other indignities, they got used to this too, grudgingly turning it to their advantage. In a later age, when Pigmeat Markham had to stop blacking up he felt it killed his humor.

The black minstrels' shtick ultimately differed little from that of the whites; they were just better at it. So much better, as a matter of fact, that they pretty much cornered the market on plantationica, on the happy-darky-singin'-and-grinnin' element. In other words, as long as they didn't rock the boat, they had a semi-comfortable niche in the biz whereby they could feed their families. Semi-comfortable, because the unabated savagery of white racism guaranteed that any group of traveling blacks would lead a life of dodging insults, objects, and threats of lynching. On the other hand, some made real money—Billy Kersands was pulling in eighty dollars a week in 1882, about the same as a top white Coon. Sure they were demeaning the race—the black intelligentsia was anything but fond of minstrelsy white or black—but if it was going to be caricatured anyway, at least they were getting some of the gravy. And a whole passel of brilliantly talented performers got to step out and make their mark on the world. Anyway, Georgia minstrelsy was enormously popular with "average" black folks, people who worked hard for every penny and weren't about to throw them away on lame shows. But white folks went to see them too, and in the process learned to accept and even sometimes admire blacks as entertainers.

Since Nigger minstrels could never be as authentic as Georgia ones, authenticity ceased to be an issue in mainstream (i.e., ofay) minstrelsy. "Accurate" Ethiopian delineation, and nothing more, was left to the black minstrels—"if y'all wanna horn in on my Coon act, fine, but that's all y'all *evah* gonna be"—while white minstrelsy went off in ways of its own, emancipated, as it were, from the burden of truth.

Beginning in the 1850s, groups such as Christy's, who made a point of featuring Foster's new-model senti-minstrel songs, progressively watered down the Ethiopian part of their delineation and pumped up the corn and the novelty; Irish, Italian, Chinese, Japanese, Swedish, German, Russian, Hawaiian—any nationality that could be scoffed at in speech, song, and pantomime, was. Space was made for drag "yaller gals" to serve as gender-bent foci for desire, not ridicule, and for romantic tenors to dish out the usual parlor sap and operatic corn—the kind of pap that the Virginia Minstrels used to make fun of.

This process really got into gear after the Civil War. Companies grew until the audience would be presented with a semicircle of twenty or more musicians, dancers, and singers, with only Mr. Bones and Mr. Tambo blacked up. Musically, the shows ended up in a land of syrupy, orchestrated Antebellum fantasy: "Plantation Melodies" are what they advertised, but by 1890, when commercial recording started, those mythical lazy plantation days were as long ago as Woodstock is now as I write this.

As the nineteenth century draws to an end, even the instruments themselves begin to change. The fiddlers—if any—are either playing in sections or tucking their instruments under their chins like violinists and delivering a mess of concert-hall gimmickry straight out of Ole Bull (1810–1880; flamboyant Norwegian violin virtuoso who pried $400,000 out of the States during his 1843–45 tour). The old African banjo has picked up steel strings and frets, which means that you can thrash out loud, metallic chords on it, should you so desire, or play "real" music on it, should you desire to do that. Worse, the bones and tambourine are relegated to the margins of the music, providing the occasional merely symbolic percussive flourish. Worse even than that, Coon impresarios—following European innovations in the art—begin to bring in real musicians with their "clarionets" and "violons" and whatnot, who soon almost entirely drive out the old ragged-ass rhythms. And there are an awful lot of other instruments to be seen: miscellaneous furrin novelties like the Spanish guitar, the Neapolitan mandolin, the Austrian accordion (although this one has some antiquity as a minstrel instrument), and the Chinese-Scottish-German harmonica—not to mention sports like the Hawaiian ukulele and the dicty 'cello. The bones of the old songs may survive, but their flesh is become strange.

Regardless, minstrelsy itself soldiered on well into the twentieth century, and minstrel songs were a staple of the early record industry. But the Coons that Edison and Victor and Columbia recorded at the turn of the century had little to do with Dan Emmett's brand of backwoods spunk (see below). If the biz excluded black artists, it was just as thorough at excluding rural (or rural-sounding) white ones. The first real hillbilly record didn't come until 1922, two years after Mamie Smith's "Crazy Blues" and thirty years after the first records by a black vocal group (see below).

The Horrors and Delights of Blackface Entertainment

The classic minstrel show as invented by Emmett and perfected by Christy is refracted through just about every aspect of American entertainment since. As a ritual, the minstrel show was as formalized as an exorcism. Each of its set parts has its own afterlife, appears peeking through a different window in American culture like a leering, priapic idiot glimpsed through a heavily barred attic dormer.

They sat, and later stood, in a semicircle—"the line"—with the bones man—"Mr. Bones"—on one end and the tambourine man—"Mr. Tambo"—on the other. The end men were the key to a good minstrel troupe: they told the jokes. "If you have two durned good end men you'll do well," the advance man for a traveling troupe was told in one Michigan town, "but if you ain't got good end men our people won't patronize the show."

The end men would usually bounce their riddles, quips, malapropisms, puns, indecencies, Daffy Duck wisecracks, and irreverent asides off "Mr. Interlocutor," the troupe's emcee. Mr. Interlocutor was the classic, well-spoken, slightly pompous straight man. He was also the first to stop blacking up. Between the end men and Mr. I were the musicians and the specialty acts—light tenors, jugglers, baggy-pants Irish comedians, maestros of the glass xylophone, blackface drag queens (the double mask was quite popular), you name it. Minstrelsy fetishized novelty every bit as much as the nation that spawned it.

The show had three main parts. Originally, it would begin with a sheaf of songs. By the 1870s this evolved into a full-blown mock-orchestral overture, swerved only by the rather unsettling rattle of

Mr. B's bones. As this dies down, Mr. I steps to the fore and says, "Gentlemen, be seated."

Then come the jokes. Mr. I might feed Mr. B or Mr. T a line, or one of them might just break in with something while Mr. I's parading his pomposity. The jokes themselves were as corny as anything the whiteface hayseed Coons of *Hee Haw* could come up with. This bit of Bones & Tambo, from *End-Men's Minstrel Gags* (1875), is about as good as they got:

"Tambo, was you eber in lub?"
"No sir, I can't say that I ever was."
"Well, I used to be in lub."
"How did you act when you went to see the young lady?"
"I didn't know how to do or what to do, till arter I axed my
    mudder."
"And how did she tell you to act?"
"She tole me dat when I went to de gal's house, dat I must
    set down and look kind a lovin' to her and say sumfin' soft."
"And did you do as directed?"
"Yes, sir."
"What was it soft that you said?"
"*Mashed pertaters.*"

More typical is the following nugget, recorded for Edison by S. H. Dudley & Len Spencer in 1904:

Dudley: Hey Len, do you believe in dreams?
Spencer: Indeed I do; for instance, last week I dreamed that I
    was the father of twelve little pickaninnies.
Dudley: What do you think that means?
Spencer: That means that things are looking very *black* for me!
General laughter, and ride out on a slightly Coonified jig
    (Ed. 8672: "Georgia Minstrels").

They'd follow this up with some sentimental and comic songs
and some more jokes, perhaps interspersed with a little rapid-fire syn-
copatin' on the banjo (the fiddle, an ambiguous signifier, seems to
have fallen away far sooner than the unambiguously African banjo).

Then came the so-called olio, where all the specialty acts would
do their bits of acrobatics or musical mystification. This was pure
vaudeville, as varied as the energies and eccentricities of a growing
and far from homogeneous populace could make it. The olio would
end with a "stump speech," a holdover from the earliest days of the
Virginia Minstrels. One of the end men would stand up and speak
on a popular topic of the day, stringing together as many malaprop-
ismic Coonanities as his verbal imagination could deliver, putting
them across as pompously as a gasbag Southern Senator. A sermon
of Emmett's from 1873 gives a pretty good idea of the proceedings.
"Bredren an' sistahs—" it begins,

> I'm gwine to preach, I is: an spose dis am de fust time, tho' I
> come berry nigh it once 'afoa when I swept out de chuch. I'ze
> gwine to 'splain de troof to de nebberlastin' bressin' ob yoa
> poar souls. I doesn't mean de soles on yoa foot, de soles ob
> yoa boots, nor de corns on yoa heels; but, as de pote sez, "de
> soul dat lies widin de sarkumicklar ob de human frame."
>   ("Bressed Am Dem Dat 'Spects Nuttin',
>   Kaze Dey Ain't a Gwine to Git Nuttin'!
>   —a Negro Sermon").

And so on. Clearly, the kind of inane crap where delivery is everything.

The show would close with a one-act comic playlet. At first, these
were set on the plantation with everyone blacked up; later, anything
went—as long as it was funny. The skits tended toward parody and
slapstick of the lowest and most base kind—The Three Stooges meet
Amos 'n' Andy. But however they were executed, whomever they

pissed on, they would always end with what was called a "walk-around." Everybody would come out on stage and stomp about to as rousing a tune as they could find, a-singin' and a-wavin' and a-clappin' their hands and generally carrying on. In fact, the mighty "Dixie" started its career as a walkaround, introduced by Bryant's Minstrels, with whom Emmett was appearing, at New York's Mechanics' Hall (472 Broadway) on April 4, 1859; admission twenty-five cents.

By the late 1870s, the walkaround began doing something new: the cast started strutting around in pairs, male and "female," flinging their legs up in the air and throwing their heads back in wild abandon—rather like the stroll on Mr. Don Cornelius's *Soul Train.* This was the cakewalk. While the Coons were making with the abandon, the band—those same stiffs who had edged out the ol' banjo and fiddle—would play a march more or less like any other, with lots of brass and a set number of parts. But here's where they redeemed themselves, because in one important way their marches were not like the others—they were, in part, syncopated. Black music, thrown out of one door, was marching back in through another. But now we're tugging on another strand in the skein of American hot music.

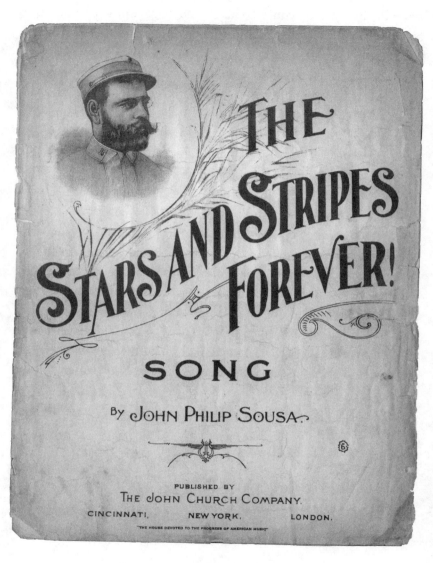

Sousa, or subversion from within.

PART II

Ragtime, or All Coons Alike

TRUMPET: an instrument of Wind Musick, used in publick Rejoicings, but especially in War.

—G. GUILLET DE ST. GEORGES,
The Gentleman's Dictionary (1705)

Ragtime's Buried Roots:
Brass Bands and the Birth of the Record Industry

There was another tradition of hot music in nineteenth-century America, one even more popular than minstrelsy, and far more respectable (to be sure, the temperature and the degree of respectability tend to vary in inverse proportion). Every town in America didn't plunk a bandstand down in the middle of Courthouse Square just to have a bunch of mooks in fleece wigs bang on tambourines and tell Coon jokes. What then were all those white picketfencers listening to? Horns. Minstrel music—country music—was string music; the brass drove the music of the towns.

In the mid-1800s, partly as a result of massive German immigration, partly as a byproduct of the Civil War, brass (aka military, aka marching) band fever began to infect the country. Every overeaten posse of weekend warriors, every town and hamlet, every tannery and grogshop had to have their uniformed marching band. (Except in much of Dixie, where folks weren't nearly as interested: an 1889 *Harper's* article claimed that good bands were unknown there, and indeed none of the famous ones were from the South—but they had their own music down there.) At the height of the movement's popularity, from around 1890 to 1910, there were some 20,000-odd bands in the country, each with at least ten members and usually more; the "standard" lineup was seventeen men or women (there were girl bands, too: Helen May Butler's Ladies Military Band was a turn-of-the-century hit). The greatest professional bands were much larger: eighty to a hundred pieces, a juggernaut of sound driving all before them. In 1869, Patrick Gilmore (1829–1892)—the country's leading bandsman and composer of "When Johnny Comes Marching Home"— organized the National Peace Jubilee in Boston, where he presented an orchestra of 939, with soloists such as Ole Bull himself, a chorus of 10,000, and a hundred firemen with anvils and two batteries of artillery to supply the necessary oomph to Verdi's "Anvil Chorus." In 1872 he led the World Peace Jubilee, and doubled everything. Noise and spectacle.

Band music at the end of the nineteenth century was like rock at the end of the twentieth—it was everywhere, worldwide, a least-common-denominator pop orthodoxy with just enough heat to keep the kids interested but not so much as to give their parents a rash. The top bandleaders—Gilmore, John Philip Sousa, Arthur Pryor, Giuseppe Creatore—were stars, their soloists targets of adolescent fantasy and aspiration. They toured constantly, and, through the mass-marketed sheet music with which the huge New York publishing houses were papering the nation, their music made it to those few places where they didn't. In a world where all music was live, in a country where almost everybody played *something*, folks actually knew enough about music to appreciate its instrumental varieties, to be dazzled by flamboyant virtuosity.

This being pop, flamboyance in general was often rewarded: uniforms were flashy and facial hair was lush. Creatore, a Neapolitan (a surprising number of band stars were foreign-born), was famous for conducting with his whole body—tossing his long, dark hair around, leaping back and forth, singing along at the crescendos, hamming it up in a most satisfactory way. "WOMEN ON TABLES IN HYPNOTIC FRENZY" was the New York tabloid headline in 1902; women, I suppose, had precious few other opportunities to experience sexually charged entertainment. Bohumir Kryl, whose name I covet, was another character typical of the outré wing of the music. With his piercing eye, his "wonderful mass of tangled flaxen hair," as the *L.A. Examiner* put it in 1905, and his unmatchable technique on the cornet—the Stratocaster of the band era—he was unforgettable. He'd hold impossible highs for a whole minute, dive down to lows of which the instrument was technically incapable—trombone notes, bass clef stuff (he created them through skillful manipulation of harmonics), and fly back up in a blur of fancy fingering. Sensational.

Spectacle was part of the band movement in America almost from the get-go. At the beginning of the nineteenth century, it was basically folk music, nothing more than the semi-organized and indifferently equipped bands of the new country's indifferently organized and semi-equipped militias. Their music was functional. Brass horns had been used since Roman times to signal the troops above the din of battle and raise their general level of violence; the European armies of the eighteenth century took these venerable instruments, tech'd them up, arranged them in arrangements—it was the century of close-order drill—tacked on some of the drums, cymbals, and reeds that the Sultan used to rile up his janissaries and give their enemies the wigglies, *et voilà!* The only difference between our bands and the European ones is that theirs were better. Much better. But there's not much point in getting into detail here; suffice it to say that it took a Frenchman to come over here and turn the whole thing into showbiz. Antoine Jullien (1812–60), aka "the Monsieur" alias "the

Mons," was a piece of work. Dandified, fastidious, deeply in love with his genius, he was the *maestro di tutti maestri*. He kept a white, crimson, and gold throne on stage into which he would subside between numbers, seemingly exhausted by his exertions with the baton—the hardest-working man in the industry. When Beethoven was on the program, he'd stop the show while a liveried flunky bearing a silver salver brought him a pair of kid gloves and a jeweled baton.

When he came to New York in 1853, Jullien staged unprecedentedly spectacular programs loaded with elaborate descriptive pieces—one was the musical recreation of a fire, featuring real firemen putting out real fire (and real panic in the audience)—and quadrilles and polkas, forms of pretty hot dance music that were new and physical enough to get the music-as-intellectual-art crowd opining to the effect that "he makes a colossal toy of the orchestra." But the Mons could turn around and, with a "Tut me no tuts, *mon vieux*," do a night entirely of "serious" music—Mendelssohn, Mozart & Co.—and better than it had ever been played in America. When he returned to Europe the next year, a much richer man, he left a musical culture transformed. He died six years later in a Paris insane asylum; somehow one isn't surprised.

It wasn't until after the Civil War that bands caught up with the Mons, when Gilmore started mounting his extravaganzas. Then things really started picking up steam, bands popping up like lawyers at a train wreck. The mountain of surplus horns lying around from all those regimental bands didn't hurt—cheap instruments meant everybody could take a crack at forming a band. Some of them were even good.

The problem, from our hot perspective, is that bands tried to be *too* good. In the 1870s and '80s, class was the name of the game, at least among the pros. Sure, the popular bands would play some pop numbers and marches—*faute de mieux,* people even danced to these—but the real dough went to the ones who could tear off a nice-sized march one moment and then turn around and squeeze out some

Brahms, and preferably without blasting your wig off. The fact is, like most pop phenoms, the bands had an inferiority complex: they wanted the average Joe to like them, but they also wanted respect from the Henry James crowd. The stuff they were playing was real music, right? In practice, of course, this meant moving indoors from the parade ground to the concert hall and presenting a mass of light classics, arranged—or rather eviscerated—for wind instruments, with plenty of flashy solos and variations grafted onto them. The overall effect must have been not unlike (shudder) Emerson, Lake, and Palmer. There was an entire repertoire of pretentious dreck, with titles like "Carnival in Capri" and "Danse Banale," that has thankfully vanished with the snows of yesteryear. The bands had drive to spare, when they were of a mind to use it, but precious little swerve; they were as predictable as liver and onions. If they were American in their scale and execution, they were still essentially European in their outlook and their music. But sooner or later they were bound to rub up against real American music, find some software as hard as the hardware.

In the 1860s and '70s, bands would occasionally cross paths with minstrelsy. During the war years, Gilmore's band was known to throw "Old Dan Tucker" and "Oh Susanna!" into his sets, and after Appomattox everybody played "Dixie." And there were all those horns and woodwinds infiltrating into the minstrel show orchestras. By the last decade of the century, minstrels and bandsmen were on the same track and closing fast. Minstrel shows started carrying full-sized marching bands with them, behind which they would parade into each new town. W. C. Handy, at one time bandleader for a company of the popular Mahara's Minstrels, later testified to the excitement this could drum up in a Bentonia or a Cutter's Corners, as "the procession circled on the public square, and the band played a program of classical overtures plus a medley of popular airs for the throngs that assembled there in the open." Inevitably, the bands started working up more and more Coon material; as Handy recalled, "*Brudder Gardner's Picnic* (a selection containing the gems of Stephen

C. Foster) was always in order." But now we don't have to conjure up ghostly images of the music, reconstruct it with our mind's ear. When the brass band express slammed into the minstrel caboose, they got it on record.

♪

The American record industry started in 1889 or 1890, when a certain distributor of Edison phonographs—whose name is unfortunately lost to posterity—began quietly attaching coin boxes to the devices, which the Great Man was marketing strictly as a primitive sort of Dictaphone. This unsung genius then arranged to have professional musicians—their names too are lost, the first recorded pop groups—do their thing for the wax cylinder, over and over again (there was no way of duplicating the early cylinders—every cut an original, although soon they started using multiple machines). He then put these ungainly devices in places guaranteed to have high pedestrian traffic, chiefly saloons and drugstores. Even though the selections were limited, the sound was atrocious, and you had to listen through rubber ear-tubes like those things they used to give you on airplanes (and still do on Delta), it caught on pretty much instantly; but then again, in America, novelty is always preferable to perfection. One New Orleans drugstore took in about $500 a month from theirs, and that's in *real* money, when a nickel would buy you a schooner of beer as big as your head and you could get a lever-action Winchester delivered to your doorstep for twelve bucks. The cylinders wore out so fast they had to send a boy on a bicycle around to change them three times a day. The other distributors got the hint quickly, and by 1891 Thomas Edison was in the music business, willy nilly. The catalog of his most enthusiastic subsidiary, Edward Easton's Columbia Phonograph Company of Washington, D.C., was already ten pages long.

Unfortunately, the first thirty-five years of the recording industry are the undiscovered country from whose bourne no traveler returns. We're kind of fuzzy on exactly what got recorded and by whom, and haven't an earthly idea how much of it still survives. There are discographies for the major labels, at least, if often sketchy ones, but there were lots of small labels whose activities have yet to be documented. Until recently, record collectors weren't much interested in this whole area of music, which means that many, many records have perished forever. Since Edison's early wax cylinders couldn't be copied except through a kind of pantograph system (they came up with a way to mold them in 1902), many were produced in minuscule quantities, and those five or ten or fifty copies have since all been broken, erased (you could scrape a wax cylinder clean and record over it), or eaten up by mildew. Many discs were melted down in World War II, ostensibly to coat shell-primers and varnish tommy-gun stocks and whatnot: in 1897, the Berliner company, pioneers of the flat disc, switched from vulcanized rubber, which tended to lose its grooves, to a shellac/filler mix (it remained the medium of the 78 pretty much until the bitter end), and the sources of shellac were under Japanese control. Many others just plain broke—shellac discs are brittle.

Small wonder then that, until recently, hardly anything from the period was available on CD or LP: even now, after a boom in home CD technology that has allowed collectors to start their own record labels with no more than an afternoon's work, I'd be very much surprised if there were more than two hundred CD's worth—five thousand or so selections—reissued (that's not counting opera and the like). Probably the total is significantly less, especially since many of the same records keep turning up over and over again. A random statistic: the French Pathé company's 1904 catalogs listed "some 12,000 different recordings," according to phonograph historian Roland Gelatt; Pathé was by no means the largest producer. Another: in 1909, over twenty-seven million disks and cylinders were manufactured in America alone. This improportion has made for a lot of bilge: when writers talk about the-birth-of-the-blues or New-Orleans-cradle-of-jazz, you'll find forty-seven out of fifty just plain ignoring anything recorded before about 1914; it's a pain to get ahold of, y'see, and besides everyone knows that stuff is strictly from squaresville, so why bother. Of course, this means that they'll tell you stuff like "military bands couldn't play ragtime," "nobody slid the trombone before Kid Ory," "Mamie Smith made the first blues record in 1920," and "Louis Armstrong invented scat singing when he dropped his cheat sheet." No. Fortunately, the CD burner and the MP3 are slowly eating into this unknown territory: diligent Web searching, and perhaps a little networking, can yield a surprising number of acoustic recordings.

Unfortunately, in its raw form this stuff sounds pretty scaly to modern ears. While the 78 rpm shellac disk and the wax cylinder had their advantages, clean sound was not one of them. Of course, the usual exceptions and exemptions apply—a mint-condition well-recorded performance can sound startlingly vivid if played on good equipment, more so than anything on LP and especially CD; but most of the fun records were recorded quickly and cheaply and then got played over and over again, and 78s wear out faster than toddler togs (cylinders are worse). The first time you hear one of these recordings, it sounds like it's playing on some mook's headphones half a subway car away, with the train running express on steel wheels down old tracks through a trash-filled tunnel and twoscore field-tripping little schoolies between you and him indignantly whispering to each other about how lame their teachers are. Perhaps I exaggerate. But not by much—the so-called "acoustic" recording process works on the same principle as the two condensed-orange-juice cans and a string the geezers among us are held to have played with when they (OK, we) were young, back in the dreary days before Nintendo. (It wasn't replaced by an electric process, with microphones, amplifiers, and all the rest, until 1925, or later for the cheap labels.)

You speak, sing, strum, blow, buzz, whatever, into a horn. This vibrates a membrane. Attached to the membrane is a needle. This needle cuts a groove into a soft surface that revolves beneath it. To play back, repeat, but in reverse. It's elegant in its simplicity; it barely works. Theoretically, with a horn big enough, a membrane flexible enough, and a medium deep enough, you could capture everything from a gnat's fart to the collapse of the Roman Empire. In practice, seeing as the whole apparatus has to fit on somebody's tabletop, you can capture the *idea* of a voice or an instrument—the notes, the rhythm—but its true sound, its timbre, is far more elusive. And if the instrument happens to do its best work in the bass clef, *sayonara*.

The best acoustically recorded 78s had a frequency response of about 168–2,000 cycles; compare this to the so-called "full frequency response recording" we've had since World War II, when British anti-submarine researchers expanded the capturable range to 20 to 20,000 cycles. It's not much. To make matters worse, many of the most interesting records are badly worn. The various digital denoisifiers and processing technologies available in the Data Age have helped some of the music emerge from its veil, but you can only do so much even with the silkiest sow's ear.

But if you spend enough time with all but the worst of them, you can learn to listen through the smutch and turn that narrow little band of dull sound into music as we know it—it's like those annoying fuzztone pictures of nothing that you stare at until a 3D image suddenly pops out at you. The recording may be quaint, but the music isn't. And a certain amount of intellectual comfort may be taken in the fact that, should you be listening to this music on an original gramophone or phonograph (*nota distinctionem*: phonograph = cylinders; gramophone = flat discs), you'd be hearing the original wave: the actual echo of, say, King Oliver's band, trapped, frozen, and brought down to you. No electrons, no bits, just that one sound. Practically, this makes not a bit of difference, especially if you're listening on CD, but food for thought, what what.

What was the saloon crowd dropping its nickels for—what was a pop record in the Gay Nineties? Easier to say what it wasn't. No jazz yet, of course, and the blues was still lurking in the obscure copperhead swamps where it was spawned; matter of fact, since the new industry was rigorously Jim Crow, almost no black music at all (the occasional swing-low jubilee quartet, but that's about it). And hillbilly music was too embarrassing: the thoroughly citified folks who organized the biz didn't think anyone would pay cash money to listen to *that* old crap unless it was given a thorough scrubbing. The politest elements of the rural repertoire may have passed muster, but only if detwanged or played strictly for laughs. On the other end of the spectrum, symphonies were out and opera was iffy: the sound was so atrocious that artistes of the better class basically wanted nothing to do with the medium (it's their loss, so screw 'em; nobody will ever know what they sounded like). Piano music in general was tough, since the left half of the keyboard wouldn't record right—but then again, neither would anything else that plays in the bass clef, and for that matter violins didn't do too well, either.

What's left? A grab bag of kickshaws and whatnots, determined largely by the resolutely middlebrow tastes of executives like Edison and Easton. Third-rate operatic tenors wading manfully through ghastly parlor ballads of the barbershop quartet variety. Comedy routines, usually at the expense of the hyphenated American. Recitations from Shakespeare and others less august. A chap named John Yorke AtLee [sic, God knows why], who whistled; he was enormously popular, especially when he did birds. Instrumental duets and trios on hot numbers like "Pop Goes the Weasel." And there were brass bands, and lots of them, doing what they do, and banjos. Gussied up banjos, but banjos nonetheless.

In 1891, then, there were suddenly two worlds of American music: the one that made it on record and the one that didn't. The former—let's call it Topworld—was Northern, civilized, white (there was a black Topworld, too, but the only people who recognized it as such were other blacks). It was overwhelmingly middle class, a world created by shopkeepers and senior clerks, people with fine penmanship and clean collars and a knack with machines; people, who, as the contemporary humorist George Ade put it, "said 'Whom' and wore Nose Glasses" and "never had been known to call Anybody by his First Name." It was, in short, a forward-looking world of skill and professionalism, of taste (according, as always, to prevailing standards) and restraint and deep sublimation. Topworld's music was polite and asexual—but in no way intellectual, mind you (I'm leaving the intellectuals out of this; in American culture, they're Third World). It was also boring, and its adherents knew it.

The latter, the one that didn't make it on record—let's call it Underworld—belonged to those whom Thomas Pynchon's dissident William Slothrop calls the "Preterite," the "*second Sheep, without whom there'd be no elect*." The passed over, the left out, the not catered to. People with callused hands. People who were being replaced by machines. People who couldn't or wouldn't get with the program. Later, when the Preterite finally made it on record, a producer tried to get the Tennessee banjoist Uncle Dave Macon to moderate his singing. "Now, Cap," Uncle Dave explained, "I can sing any way I want to and still be heard. I've got a lot of get up and go. And I've got a smokehouse full of country hams and all kinds of meat to eat up there in Readyville. I've got plenty of wood hauled up, and I don't have to be bossed around by some New York sharpshooter just to make a few records, 'cause I've done my part on the record making anyway." Not every second sheep had all that meat to fall back on, but they all had a lot of get up and go. Too much of it, in fact; it made the citizens nervous.

Southern, rural, colored, poor—from the perspective of the parlor gramophone, same-same. Their music sweated roughness, unease, wrath. And sex, of course. It was dangerous. But it wasn't boring, and folks on top knew that too. Each world wanted some of what the other had. Underworld craved respect, legitimacy, be-somebodyship;

Topworld craved the freedom to be nobody special, just another human animal with all the needs and desires appertaining thereto and no obligation to maintain one's precious dignity. The border between them was porous—if you were white, anyway—but everyone knew more or less where it was; often it ran right through them. In any case, it was well patrolled. One of George Ade's patented "Fables in Slang" concerns "a Certain Mrs. A." whose husband was constantly making "Bad Breaks": "When he bought Striped Shirts of the Georgia Minstrel Pattern she told him that he had the Sartorial Instincts of a Crap-Shooter [that's code, by the way]. She asked him why he wore his Hat on one side of his Head, just like a Common Rough. She toasted him on both sides."

The women patrolled the men, the men patrolled the women, everybody patrolled the kids, and yet these worlds still couldn't—can't—keep away from each other. The story of the American record industry's first hundred years or so is the story of them grinding up against each other, drawn inescapably together by the force of their mutual attraction (B.G., critics will someday call it—Before Garth; Mr. Brooks must certainly be the avatar of the assimilated Preterite). And friction like that produces heat.

The first recorded sign of this is in the bands. The industry began to take shape just as the band craze was getting well and truly out of hand. And just as the usual forces of social order—concerned parents, stiffnecked educators, politicians, and other professional busybodies—began to harrumph about it (all that blaring brass, you know—roils the blood), roughnecks like John Philip Sousa gave them something *really* scary.

♪

John Philip Sousa. It's hard to see him fresh, as his contemporaries did. All ramrod spine and whiskers, spectacles and baton, he's a Mount Rushmore head. In his day, though, he was something more vital—composer, bandleader, librettist, public intellectual, novelist (he wrote three: one good, one bad, one in between), Sousa was one of those energetic, thrusting types who defined America at its youthful best. Sousa was born in Washington, D.C., in 1854; his father, a Portuguese immigrant, was a trombonist in the United States Marine Corps Band. Twenty-six years later, young J. P. was appointed director of that very same band; he was that kind of guy. He was proficient on violin, clarinet, trombone, and drum; he could conduct, compose, and run a business. He took a band of slack, demoralized lifers and turned them into the musical equivalent of Navy Seals. When, after twelve years of "Hail to the Chief" and general governmental chickenshit, Sousa left the Marine Band, he had no trouble founding his own (it included thirteen men from his recently deceased idol Patrick Gilmore's crew).

Now, Sousa was no dummy. For one thing, he hated recording, recorded music, and records. Not because he was a stiff, but because he was perceptive enough to hear beyond the Beta version of the technology with all its bugs: this crackly, dim-sounding device was trouble, and he knew it. He wrote a famously crotchety essay about it in 1907, called "The Menace of Mechanical Music": "Sweeping across the country with the speed of a transient fashion in slang or Panama hats, political war cries or popular novels, comes now the mechanical device to sing for us a song or play for us a piano [he hated the player piano too; I'm with him on that one], in substitute for human skill, intelligence and soul." Why pay a gang of local tune wranglers every time you want to hear a song when you can buy it once, played by musicians a hundred times better than your neighbors'll ever be? And why learn to play an instrument—a royal pain in the ass, as anyone who's ever practiced their scales can attest—when you can toss a disc in the machine that will put musicians a thousand times better than you'll ever be right there in front of you? No amateur musicians equals no local bands; no local bands equals no sheet music sales and not much interest in touring bands.

Nobody'll give a damn about instrumental music, except for dancing. And you can dance to records. "Canned music," as Sousa called it, was going to put him and his kind out of business. It took a little longer than he thought, but he was of course absolutely right; just try to make a living as a musician these days.

For a man who hated records, Sousa sure made a lot of them. Or rather, his band did. Of the twelve-hundred-odd records credited to Sousa's Band, he was in the studio for only a few: three sessions out of some two hundred. But if his employees wanted to pick up a few extra bucks cutting some records, using his name, his arrangements, and his songs, far be it from him to stop them (he even let them moonlight in the major labels' house bands). In Washington, they call this "plausible deniability." Beginning in 1893, the year after the band was formed, under various directors—Arthur Pryor, cornet star Herbert L. Clarke, Walter B. Rogers (who also conducted the orchestras on several Caruso sides), and a handful of others—its members recorded if not constantly, then at least it seems that way. Unfortunately, as of this writing there has been no comprehensive effort to collect and reissue the works of the Sousa Band, especially in its youth. That said, relatively early versions of three of his most famous marches—"El Capitan," "Stars and Stripes Forever," and "The Washington Post"—are available for inspection, all recorded by Berliner in 1897. It's not easy in the mind to separate these antediluvian performances from the thousands of other performances of these numbers that lurk in there (trust me, you know these songs—maybe not by name, but you do). Yet even with the stripped-down ensembles used for making band records at the time, even with the absence of the master's hand on the tiller, they reveal a band capable of generating an effortless, brisk drive, if not a lot of swerve. Perhaps in the second strain of "El Capitan" there's a hint of swing, of rhythmic looseness (Berl. 42 ZZ), but on the whole the fellas play things pretty straight.

But the Sousa Band didn't confine its repertoire to marches, either in concert or on record. For one thing, they did did arias, solos, even whole concertos, either original or cut out of somebody else's orchestral cloth (think bits of *Tannhäuser*, arranged for military band). Besides mangling the classics, they did waltzes, polkas, quicksteps, galops, mazurkas, patrols, and dances otherwise unspecified. And, more importantly for our purposes, they did, and recorded, a precious few Coon songs, cakewalks, and rags—thus slipping a little Preterite swerve into their mechanized brass drive.

♪

Ragtime mythology holds that the music first reached Topworld notice at the Chicago World's Columbian Exposition of 1893 (it was supposed to be timed to coincide with the four-hundredth anniversary of Columbus, but things began running late and you know how it is), when what seems like half the country, elect and Preterite, dutifully trooped to Chicago to view the gargantuan beaux-arts confection of plaster pilasters and inch-deep reflecting pools, cavernous sheds full of the latest technological whatsits and theme pavilions representing the world's diversity. It drew almost thirty million people in the six months it was open, among them—according to the myth—every cardsharp, pool hustler, and whore in the Midwest. Along with the whores came the so-called "whorehouse professors," the gentlemen whose métier it was to tickle out a soundtrack to the sporting life. And it was largely these gentlemen who, in the year of Dvořák, ensured that his prophecy would come true, for when they poured in from rough towns like Sedalia and St. Louis, they brought ragtime with them, and ragtime was something new—at least to the solid Topworld butter-and-egg men who (presumably) slunk off from their families to spend a little time in the parts of town where the day's work begins at the other nine o'clock.

The truth of this may be of the symbolic variety. There exists precious little hard evidence to corroborate it. Not that there necessarily would be—the annals of the demimonde are written in condensation and smoke. This we do know: John Philip Sousa's new band was one of the featured attractions of the Exposition, and it made a huge hit with two very different numbers, Charles K. Harris's parlor weeper "After the Ball" and a sanitized—but still jaunty—little whorehouse ditty named after (and still sung in schoolyards because of) its infernally catchy syncopated refrain: "Ta-Ra-Ra Boom-Der-Ay." It might be syncopated, I hear someone in the back row objecting, but is it ragtime?

There's more than one ragtime. Like jazz, it's not so much a kind of music as it is a way of playing it. The so-called "classic" ragtime is that Scott Joplin stuff we all know from "The Sting," supermarkets, and Tastee-Freez trucks—jaunty, jangly piano music with a lot of tricky fingering. This appears to be a sophistication of the simpler and funkier "folk rag," a tantalizing, mostly string-based music that didn't really make it onto records until the mid-1920s, when the music was in its sunset years. Then there's the "ragtime song," a catchy pop number with a bit of syncopation in the vocal line. A ragtime song such as "Ta-Ra-Ra Boom-Der-Ay" or "Alexander's Ragtime Band" usually bears pretty much the same relationship to a classic rag such as Tom Turpin's "Harlem Rag" (the first piano rag by a black man to be published) as "Rock-A-Hula Baby" does to "That's All Right, Mama." Many of these songs are aka Coon songs—raggy pop numbers with lyrics in Broadway Ebonics about the lives ("I lives in de State ob Alabam'") and loves ("I loves dat chicken!") of watermelon-eatin' ragtime-raggin' Coons—the virtual Negro of the minstrel stage updated and adapted to Tin Pan Alley mechanisms of mass marketing. What all these have in common is a commitment to drive-through syncopation, through playing repetitive treble rifflets off against a steady, strong-stepping two-beat bass. Ragtime is rhythm music. And you can play it on anything—despite what modern classic-rag chauvinists insist, a piano is not essential equipment. In its heyday, ragtime—classic ragtime, Scott Joplin ragtime—could be heard on everything from solo accordion to seventy-piece brass band. That said, it would be foolish to deny that the piano is its signature instrument, just as the cornet is for early jazz, the clarinet for swing, the Telecaster for rockabilly.

What ragtime's precise, historical relation to minstrel music is, we don't know. Like Christianity and the chili size, it was created away from the direct eye of history. Most everyone then and now agrees on who started it: ragtime was black music. But nobody's precisely sure about the when, the where, or the how. Back when it hit, theories abounded—it was Latin American, it was pure African, it was backwoods fiddle music, it was Kentucky barrelhouse music, it was Southern or Western or from right here in New York City; it was invented at Shake Ragtown, a village near St. Louis, by "a left-handed fiddler, a Frenchman named Tebeau."

All in all, however, the popular consensus can be found summed up in the semi-grammatical little preface to an early ragtime song sheet—"Syncopated Sandy," by Ned Wayburn and Stanley Whiting: "RAG-TIME...originated with the negroes and is characteristic of their people. The negroe in playing the piano, strikes the keys with the same time and measure that he taps the floor with his heels and toes in dancing, thereby obtaining a peculiarly accented time effect which he terms 'RAG-TIME.'" Ragtime was black piano music, just like minstrel music was "black" banjo music. The only difference is the quotation marks.

Considering the question without anger or partisan zeal, it's not too difficult to explain ragtime as a natural development of the Africanized jigs and reels the minstrels were exploiting in the 1840s; as a recuperation and elaboration, as bebop to minstrelsy's swing, funk to minstrelsy's soul. Take the simple syncopations of the minstrel tunes and complicate them, redouble them, play the cross rhythms off against each other, and you get something like ragtime. Of course, the story's more complicated than that. There's the whole question of the so-called "Spanish tinge," for instance; of the influence of Latin American, and specifically Cuban and Mexican, music on the emerging genre. Ben Harney, about whom you shall read more below, dropped the following little bombshell in his pioneering *Rag Time Instructor,* in 1897: "RAG TIME (or Negro Dance time) originally takes its initiative steps from Spanish music, or rather from Mexico, where it is known under the head and names of Habanara [sic], Danza, Seguidilla, etc." There's something to this, to be sure; far be it from me to call Ben Harney an idiot. For example, the basic rhythmic cell of Cuban music (whence that Habanera) is eighth note, sixteenth note, eighth, sixteenth, eighth / eighth, eighth, eighth, eighth (dat-da-dat-da-dat / dat-dat-dat-dat). You'll find plenty of ragtime tunes with precisely the same syncopation. Whether this is due to direct influence or parallel development, there's one crucial, characteristic difference: in America—North America, that is; English-speaking America—the whole shebang is played in double time, and with that hard Celtic edge.

In any case, the basic rhythmic characteristics of ragtime were already present in embryo in the music of Dan Emmett and his contemporaries, in the percussion and particularly in the banjo playing. As has often been pointed out, ragtime's staccato flurries of unsustained notes, its swift triplets, and its steady bass counterrhythm provide a perfect aural footprint of the banjo. Since you can't hold a note on the banjo (the drum-head gives plenty of snap and pop but hardly any resonance), to get lots of sound you need to hit lots of notes, and the banjo's short drone string was added so you can automatically pick out a steady counterrhythm with your right thumb, leaving the other fingers free to pick accents. But ragtime was nurtured at the piano and grew up taking full advantage of the harmonic and melodic possibilities that having ten notes at your disposal instead of five offers. What's more, the early professors wasted no time in working every Franz Liszt, music-school piano trick in Christendom into their playing, especially if it gave them a little something with which to dazzle the punters and cut their cronies. You can hear this process in full ferment in "The Banjo," an 1854 composition by Louis-

Moreau Gottschalk, the New Orleans–born Creole piano virtuoso. Designed as a pianistic portrait of the instrument, it's a rather stiff-legged affair, a series of flashy, disjointed treble variations on a basic theme out of Foster and Emmett laid over a clunky bass. If it doesn't hang together like a rag, it at least shows that you can play this new American music on the piano without ill effect (American audiences ate "The Banjo" right up).

Another angle: whoever put ragtime together, when it came to taking this new wiggle and turning it into actual songs, reached out to both traditions of hot music—minstrel and brass—and ran them together like the two halves of a zipper. The early rags, you see, aren't breakdowns or ballads, they're *marches*. Joplin's "The Entertainer" and Sousa's "Washington Post" are the same under the skin. Not only do rags and marches share basic meters—generally 2/4 time, but sometimes 4/4 or even 2/2—the "conception of form and tonal design is identical," as ragtime musicologist Edward Berlin points out. That is, rags follow the same general sequence of parts or strains as marches, develop in the same ways. "The parallels are so close that significant distinctions can be found in only two areas: meter and rhythm": if it's unsyncopated, it's a march, otherwise, "the march becomes a rag." (And if it's half syncopated and half not, it's a cakewalk.) No wonder the bands picked up on them so quick. The march was the prevailing form of instrumental music in post–Civil War America; people were even dancing to it, *faute de mieux*—imagine, if you can, shaking a leg to the *Monty Python* theme (aka Sousa's "Liberty Bell March"). Early ragtimers like Louis Chauvin were known to play ragged-out versions of Sousa marches; indeed, a Berliner record survives from sometime in the late 1890s of ragtime "Banjo King" Vess Ossman doing "Stars and Stripes Forever," with a definite raggy lilt (Berl. 470 Z)—not to mention the one that ragtime alumnus Jelly Roll Morton cut for the Library of Congress in 1938; it swings like mad. From this to writing your own, tunes where you can really let the ragtime loose, is a pretty quick step. Ultimately, folk ragtime seems to be a case of post-minstrel black banjo rhythms (perhaps touched with a little Latin lilt) grafted onto brass band marches and played on the parlor piano.

Although ragtime didn't start filtering into Topworld culture until the late 1880s, it was probably bubbling under in black circles for a long time before that. The basic building blocks for a recuperation of minstrel music must have been there in most black communities. The comfort with cross-rhythms, with syncopation. The new familiarity with the piano. The training in European concepts of composition and harmony newly available in the black colleges that had been founded since the end of the Civil War. The occasional name has been preserved—John Baptist in New Orleans, Hatchett and Bad Hooks in Memphis, Pluck Henry in Chicago, No Legs Cagey in Philly, Abba Labba and Jack the Bear in New York, a handful of others. But the place it seems to have come together most strongly is in the semi-frontier area just west of the Mississippi, specifically the bit between St. Louis and Kansas City. Joplin's hometown, Sedalia— a dusty railhead town in western Missouri—may have been ragtime's cradle; at any rate, it had a lot of whorehouses, and where there were whorehouses, there were pianos, and where there were pianos, there were "professors" to play them. Ragtime's metropolis was St. Louis, no slouch itself when it came to sporting establishments.

When the collective faculty of the Missouri brothels descended on Chicago in 1893 (if that in fact is what happened), it was with a finished music, one consistent and widespread enough to cause people to take notice. Not for the first time, black musicians were in a position to turn that notice into cash. But unlike the black purveyors of minstrel music, which was also held to "originate with the Negroes and be characteristic of their people" (as Wayburn and Whiting would say), black ragtimers managed to retain some kind of control over where the music was going, at least for a while. The biggest hit of all hard-core—that is, instrumental—ragtime was Joplin's 1899 "Maple Leaf Rag"; it sold over a half-million copies in its first ten years. The efforts of Georgia minstrelsy and of Reconstruction-era black song-writers such as James "Dem Golden Slippers" Bland and William Shakespeare Hays had gained black musicians a wobbly perch on the edge of the biz.

♪

Ragtime first broke into Topworld in the form of the cakewalk. Back in plantation days, the slaves would don ragged finery and prance around in parodic imitation of the folks in the big house, and which-ever couple was most over the top would win a cake. That's the myth, at least; *de veritate fabularum non disputemus.* Starting in the late 1870s, minstrel shows started staging the walkaround as a cakewalk. The music that made it onto the stage was a snappy march, gener-ally unsyncopated, and, as one expects from mainstream (i.e., white) postwar minstrelsy, without much "black" character. Soon, however, some strains of these marches began to be cautiously syncopated, the beat stretched and snapped a little—ragged, in other words (I shall pass with head averted the hot and unresolvable debate over the origin of the "rag" in "ragtime"). Whether this reflects "authentic" black practice or the minstrels' attachment of Coon signifiers—synco-pation, repetitive riffing—to standard marches is obscure, since nobody seems to know very much about "real," folk cakewalks. In any case, by 1892 they were staging cakewalk contests at the old Madison Square Garden in New York. Before long, the cakewalk went nation-wide, tipping over into a craze. As it tipped it pulled ragtime with it.

But it took a couple of years to fall, as if everybody had to roll up their sleeves, tighten their shoelaces, and take a few deep breaths before they could shake a leg. Or maybe it's just that the Panic was on and nobody had any of the quibus to throw away on dance music. In any case, the first ragged-out cakewalk to be published was "Ras-tus on Parade" (the title describes the genre), by Kerry Mills; it came out in 1895. Mills was a white, classically trained violinist. He also knew a killer groove when he heard one, as he proved with his 1897 "A Georgia Camp Meeting" (rewritten in 1899 as "At a Georgia Camp Meeting")—nobody wanted it, so he published it himself and sold a quadrillion and a half copies.

The first song with ragtime accompaniment labeled as such— "Oh, I Don't Know, You're Not So Warm!" by Antigua-born Georgia minstrel Bert Williams (see below)—had come out the year before, but 1897 was the year that "pure" (i.e. instrumental) ragtime surfaced. William Krell published the "Mississippi Rag" and fellow ofay Theodore Northrup did "The Louisiana Rag," subtitled "Description of Louisiana Niggers Dancing (The Pas Ma La Rag)"—which was an 1895 composition by the phenomenally, wickedly talented black-in-blackface Ernest Hogan, of whom we shall be hearing more; "La Pas Ma La" has a pretty good claim to being the first ragtime song published. Also in 1897, a massive and unruly black St. Louis publican published "The Harlem Rag." Tom Turpin was the real thing— an Underworld champ, a star in the Life. His Rosebud Bar was *the* place for hot music in St. Louis—well, the Rosebud and Mme. Babe Connor's Castle Club, a swank black whorehouse where Turpin had once been the professor. Mama Lou, the Castle's resident singer, is credited with originating (which isn't precisely synonymous with writing) not only "Ta-Ra-Ra Boom-Der-Ay," of Sousa fame, but "A Hot Time in the Old Town," "Frankie and Johnny," and "Bully of the Town"—all deathless classics, and in her versions all perfectly filthy. The girls danced to them on a mirrored floor, if that helps to set the tone. Mama Lou never recorded, and neither did Turpin. At least Turpin managed to publish a few of his compositions.

In fact, none of the first wave of folk/classic ragtimers made actual records, not for market-leader Columbia—the 1898 catalog was thirty-two pages long—not for Edison, who stepped into the market directly in 1896 and was soon second only to Columbia in size, not for Berliner, whose gramophone, playing flat, one-sided 78 rpm discs, was introduced in 1894, and not for any of the other dozen-odd companies

The greatest of all cakewalks.

in the biz. Scott Joplin never made a record in his life, and he lived until 1917. (He did make a few rolls for the player piano, as did several other of his Underworld colleagues; see below.) But if the Topworld wasn't interested in Underworld performers, it was certainly hot for Underworld music.

By the end of the century, the bands had gotten hip to the new beat—from marches ragtime came, to marches ragtime returned. Despite their striving for class, their Beethoven and their Brahms, the bands had never really got the ultimate respect that their dicty repertory was aiming at. For all that Sousa might maintain that "there is no hierarchy in art" and that, if musicians still thought that a brass band was inferior to a symphony orchestra, "inferior it is not; it is simply different," there was an inescapable, albeit often faint, odor of vulgarity to everything they did. They were the beat of the petite bourgeoisie, not of the intellectual establishment. One fastidious critic summed up what they were up against when he said that as far as he was concerned, practically every brass band sounded like "a threshing machine through which live cats are being chased."

If you can't beat 'em, screw 'em. Ragtime was the distilled, filtered, and refined essence of vulgarity, if you considered it vulgar to acknowledge that America isn't Europe, that the miscegenated pot likker that we call a culture can actually amount to anything. In this, Sousa—March King, most popular musician in the world, etc.—was a vulgarian at heart. At any rate, by 1898 he started cautiously programming cakewalks. Arthur Pryor, his young Missouri-born trombone ace, took to smearing his notes in a most unconventional way and coming up with super-funky arrangements of tunes like "Smoky Mokes" (Glossary of the Vulgar Tongue: *moke* = person of color), "Creole Belles," and "At a Georgia Camp Meeting." It's as if Sinatra had hauled Scotty and Bill into the studio one day in 1955 and cut "That's All Right, Mama." The cakewalks were Sousa's bird, discreetly flipped to every fancy uptown antimacassar who ever sniffed at the balance of his endlessly drilled reeds in his interpretation of Handel's "Largo." By 1900, he was even throwing in a couple of all-out rags, if only a couple; others were less cautious.

Ragtime gave the bands what they lacked: funk, snap, swerve. All those massed horns blasting on the beat had already guaranteed that their marches would have drive, but the added syncopation transformed the bands from bulldozers to M1 Abrams tanks: fast, mobile, deadly. A record like the Peerless Orchestra's 1904 "Smoky Mokes" (Ed. 712) rips out of your speakers with an urgency that ten decades have done nothing to abate. Some bands, such as Thomas Preston Brooke's Chicago Marine Band, began to specialize in the new beat (something of a pistol, Brooke—the putative "King of Ragtime"—was also the first to feature a female cornet soloist; he never recorded), others drew the line and held onto the dicty dream, and many, as usual, sat on the fence.

Sousa approached syncopating with his usual rigor. At his new band's first rehearsal, Sousa told them, "I want this band to play with the precision and polish of the finest symphony orchestra." He was dead serious, even when they were playing "fun" music. Not a lot of room for them to screw it up—or swerve it up. On the other hand, when applied to the right material, this kind of discipline can make for tremendous drive. James Brown used to fine people for a single wrong note.

Consider "Whistling Rufus," cut by the band (or at least a pocket-sized version of it—maybe a dozen men out of sixty) in 1900: 1:43, all drive (Vic. 361). Nary a speck of improvisation, all instruments in tune and in tone. Like all cakewalks (except of course the ones that don't), "Whistling Rufus" has three strains, only the first of which is heavily syncopated, and that only in the melody line. After a couple of bars of introduction that are mostly lost in the groove noise, out of the smutch emerges a fat, rock-solid bass, strutting beneath the perfectly blended cornets and reeds as they kick out the herky-jerky riffs characteristic of the cakewalk. Everything is broken down into units; there's no flow. What you get instead is a tense, nervous energy:

the syncopated four-bar riffs kind of oscillate in place until, just as it's getting on your head, the whole thing tips over into the B part, a straight-ahead unsyncopated march. (The switch between syncopated and unsyncopated parts is not unlike switching between funk, all tension, and stomping hard rock, all release.) Then another quick taste of the syncopation, then *another* part, the so-called "trio," somewhere between A and B in feel. This grooves along nicely until the band, probably conducted by Arthur Pryor, rides out on that first march, blasting louder and louder each go-round yet perfectly in control.

It's interesting to compare the Sousa Band's "Whistling Rufus" to a 1904 version by Edison's resident hot music specialists, the Peerless Orchestra (Ed. 704). The Edison announcer (early cylinders were announced; there was nowhere to stick a label), sounding slightly fed up as usual, gives out with " 'Whistling Rufus,' played by the Peerless Orchestra, Edison Records." Then a tin whistle skirls off the beginning of "Believe Me, If All Those Endearing Young Charms." Enter the Coon: "Weyah, hah hah, mark my soul, yonder comes Rufus now, a-whistling his favorite tune! Whaah-hah-hah, Lawd!" And now the song. In case you still haven't been able to summon up the proper context, they stick a set of bones right next to the recording horn, so that it practically drowns out everything else (or maybe it's rimshots on a snare; the effect is the same). The cakewalk is comedy, it's minstrelsy, it ain't white. Sousa treated it just like everything else, with the same mechanical precision, the same attention to detail, the same seriousness. Wagner or "Mammy's Little Pumpkin-Colored Coon," it was all music to him, and all good. The Peerless Orchestra wasn't that high-minded.

Still, although the bass doesn't quite have Sousa's snap and the B strain, the march, is on the flabby side, the Peerless Orchestra's got verve, and the rat-a-tat of the bones drives everything along to good effect—lacking the Sousa Band's control over dynamics, they may have to fall back on them to punch up the end, but it's punched up all the same. It's a great record, looser and in some ways funkier than the Sousa Band's, but I suspect that, live, Sousa's men would grind the Peerless Orchestra into powdered milk.

Kerry Mills, who wrote "Whistling Rufus," is also, you may recall, the character responsible for "At a Georgia Camp Meeting," a mainstay in Sousa's band book. His band took a few cracks at it in the studio, including a couple conducted by Pryor. Of these, the version from October 23, 1908—unfortunately after Pryor had struck out on his own—is available for inspection (Vic. 16402). Like "Whistling Rufus," it's a cakewalk. But while WR is a pretty catchy number, AaGCM smacks of the satanic—the A melody, the raggy one (pinched more or less from the Civil War hit "Our Boys Will Shine Tonight"), is one of those aggressive, springy little things like "Dixie" that will, once entered into your brain, reserve the right to echo through your cranium and extrude itself through your lips at any momentary lapse of concentration. You *will* hum it, whistle it, sing it, remember it; you must.

Sousa's law stated that "a march should make a man with a wooden leg step out." The way the band pushes through this one, he could leave the peg home. They've learned a thing or two about funk in the eight years since "Whistling Rufus." It's still as tight as a hungry boa, of course, but now the sections have learned to stretch their notes a little, just enough to pull the music forward as well as push it. It swings—not like Count Basie, but nonetheless. There's even some call and response section work in the B part: the brass lays out a funky riff—a syncopated little thing ending in a note that's stretched just a little too long to be legit—and the piccolos and clarinets answer it with a springy little jiggle of their own. Under it all there's a sort of strong, dark pulsing, the dimly recorded echo of the thundering rhythm: trombones, sousaphones (named after your man, of course), drums. Like "Whistling Rufus," the dynamics build to a controlled climax, the sound getting heavier and heavier as the band drives it on home. The total effect is anthemic, like Led Zeppelin without all the squiggly guitar. If you played the song at halftime, State would disembowel Ag (or Ag State), strutting all the way.

The main thing that the modern, post-jazz listener will miss here is solos—the squiggles. When the band's forging ahead at full speed, there's nobody to take the wheel and jerk it, to bring in the element of surprise, of danger. Sousa's Band had soloists, all right, but they played set pieces: themes and florid variations all composed and pre-arranged; sheet music. These would be set against a minimal, often-muted backing, so as not to detract from the magnificence of the solo. Free improvisation isn't part of the vocabulary. Here the Jesuit lurking among the readership intrudes: "How, my son, is that any different from the jazz trumpeter or rock guitarist who steps into the spotlight and plays the exact same solo, night after night?" This, I believe, is a philosophical matter, and *quae supra nos, nihil ad nos*—what's above us is nothing to us. Let's say it's not different—a point to the Jesuit—and move on, with but a quick glance at Herbert C. Clarke.

First cornet in the Sousa Band on and off from 1893 to 1915, Clarke was a desperate man for blowing the horn. Consider the two takes of his own "Caprice Brillante (The Debutante)" Clarke recorded with Sousa's Band on October 21, 1908 (take 1 = Vic. 31721; take 2 = Vic. 35090-B). A few bars of fast waltzing from the band and Clarke unleashes a stupefying set of runs and trills, spinning up and down the scale, soaring and diving. The band punches him up to a cadence, and then lays off entirely as he flies solo, with more of the same. His tone is perfectly even and articulate from lowest low to highest high, his speed is speedy, his fingering fleet, his caprice *très brillante*. He never misses a note, and he's pitching them out by the bushel. Take two is identical. Clarke's solos are meant to dazzle, and they do. What they aren't meant to do is surprise, and they don't. The trills and runs all start somewhere logical and end somewhere logical, making entirely logical steps in between. Clarke never tries to drive the express off the tracks. There's no swerve here.

But Clarke wasn't Sousa's only star soloist. Our friend Arthur Pryor (1870-1942) was another. The premiere trombonist of his day, Pryor recorded a goodly amount of the same kind of cabbage that Clarke was pushing, if slower and lower. But unlike his bandmate, Pryor also cut scads of rags and cakewalks, many of his own composition—including one of the greatest and most popular cakewalks of them all, "A Coon Band Contest" (both Edward VII and the Kaiser loved it). And as early as 1904, Pryor was recording Tom Turpin's "St. Louis Rag."

Not that Pryor needed ragtime to get hot. To hear the heat a good band could generate even without syncopating, track down his record of "Falcon March" (Vic. 5798) from 1910. W. Paris Chambers's composition is a particularly dicey one to play, with chromatic runs dive-bombing here and blasting off there, crisscrossing and playing tag. This kind of thing requires perfect intonation and microprocessor timing to pull off, and only someone with Sousa's symphonic precision could do it. Which Pryor has—not only does he pull it off, he makes it swing. The band has some of that loose-limbed flow for which the Territory bands—the jazz bands from K.C., St. Louis and points west—of the twenties and thirties would be so celebrated. This is a great band: if Sousa is the March King, Pryor is the Count (of course, since no black brass bands from the period recorded, we'll never know who the real Count was; could be Pryor's just Charlie Barnet in a stiff collar). Ask not whom I would kill to hear them live; ask rather whom I wouldn't.

Not only is it a great band, it's a great record—Pryor was one of the first to experiment with arranging for recording, reinforcing the main elements of the music and tossing out many of the irrelevant and unrecordable subtleties. Take the bass. When Pryor left Sousa in 1903, he took his friend Simone Mantia with him. Mantia, an ex-Gilmorite, was a demon soloist on the euphonium, or baritone horn—sort of a midfielder between tuba and trombone. Mantia stayed with Pryor for twenty years, and it must be he who is driving the band on

Arthur Pryor, Trombone Soloist of Sousa's Band.

The audiences that have attended Sousa's concerts from Maine to the Pacific Coast, have listened to the playing of this famous artist with wonder and delight.

His appearance as a soloist for the evening is always greeted with a burst of applause. Although Mr. Pryor is still a very young man, prominent musicians say that he is the greatest trombone soloist the world has ever heard.

Read what Mr. Pryor writes us about Gramophone Records.

"The records that I have made for your company are both a pleasure and a surprise. The reproductions are loud and yet not harsh or squeaky; and the tone is pure and smooth in quality. I believe the process which you have is the only way a very loud record can be made without distorting the natural tone of the instrument used. The reproductions of my playing to the Gramophone are certainly better and more satisfactory to me than any records I have ever made on the Phonograph or Graphophone."

Yours truly,

ARTHUR W. PRYOR,

Trombone Soloist, Sousa's Band.

Trombone Solos by Arthur Pryor.
3300 Sweet Lorina Rae
   (A beautiful waltz song, composed by Mr. Pryor)

3301 Polka, Exposition Echoes
   (A very brilliant polka, written by Mr. Pryor at Chicago during the World's Fair)

7

From the land of rag: Arthur Pryor on a page of National Gramophone Co.'s 1899 catalog.

COURTESY OF ARCHEOPHONE RECORDS

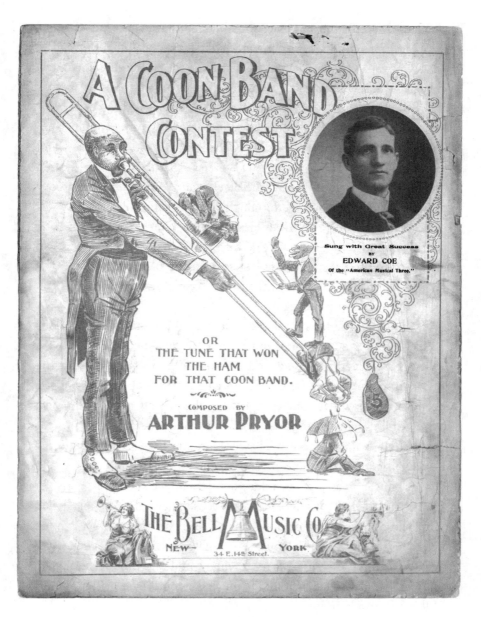

His magnum opus.

"Falcon March": the bass switches between fast, tense pulsing and ripping runs without losing the groove. It's an amazing performance, and you can actually hear it: the arrangement clears enough underbrush so that Mantia can walk tall.

But what about the ragtime? Luckily, enough of his key records can be stitched together from various reissues to give us a pretty good picture of Pryor's talents in this direction. Of these, "A Coon Band Contest" (more on which below), "Yankee Shuffle" (1908), "Frozen Bill Cakewalk" (1909), and "Mr. Black Man" (1910) are nice, groovy cakewalks, if conventional (although "Yankee Shuffle" does have its kinks). "Trombone Sneeze: a Humoresque Cakewalk," however, is something different (Vic. 1223). It's Pryor's own thing; he recorded it in June 1902, at one of his last sessions with Sousa's Band. The composition itself isn't much, but in Pryor's arrangement you can hear a revolution building.

The most seditious bit is the four-bar riff on which the A part is built. In the first two bars, you have a typical syncopated cakewalk riff, except everyone, lead and rhythm alike, is knocking out the clipped, choppy accents; there's no steady pulse under it—Sousa's got a brand-new bag. The cornets keep the accents going in the next two bars, the answering half of the riff. But here Pryor introduces something major in the way of swerve: rather than go along with the groove, his trombone *smears* its part, and smears it bad.

A "smear" was ragtimese for what jazz musicians call a "slide" or a "gliss" and their dicty colleagues a *glissando*—which is just Italian for "sliding" a note up or down the scale. Pryor doesn't just use the gliss, he shoves it right in your face. A gliss can be gentle, serene, lyrical; these ain't. On the smears, Pryor's trombone produces a harsh, farting sound that no symphonic musician could ever call euphonic. I'll bet Sousa hated it.

Pryor doesn't stop there. "Trombone Sneeze" breaks so many Topworld rules it's hard to know where to start: besides the scuzzy tone, the call and response, and the sliding, there's the improvisation—Pryor

cautiously varies a couple of his smears; the blue notes—he deliberately stretches some of his smears just a little bit out of tune and
hangs them there just a little too long; and the sneeze. Here's where
things get really wild: toward the end of the record, after a couple
of nondescript march parts, the band cuts out. Trombone to the fore—
BLAAA-AWWWWWWWW-AAAAAP! The band, in ragged uni-
son: *'Tchoo!!!* Trombone: *BLAAAAA-AWWWWWW-AAAAAP!*
Band: *'Tchoo!!!* Key change, repeat, fanfare, ride out on the A. This
kind of hokum was exciting when Count Basie did it on "Do You
Wanna Jump, Children?" thirty-six years later, and it's exciting here.

Those smears don't show up on "Love's Enchantment" or "Little
Nell" or any of Pryor's other dicty solos. He didn't learn them from
his bandmaster father. They had to come from somewhere. In fact,
though there's no instrument as glissable as the slide trombone, the
effect is practically unknown in real music (Rimsky-Korsakov might
have played with it a little, but not so as you'd really notice it). It took
four-hundred-odd years for someone to make use of this peculiarity
of the instrument. It took minstrels. As Rick Benjamin, historian of
the ragtime trombone, writes in the *Ragtime Ephemeralist*:

> ... the use of this playing technique was ... occasionally docu-
> mented in magazine and newspaper reports of minstrel shows
> dating back to the 1870s. In this setting, white performers in
> blackface used the slide trombone as a raucous noisemaker
> to somehow assist in their "evocations" of plantation life. Curi-
> ously, there is no known evidence that real Negroes on real
> plantations (either before or after Emancipation) ever had
> access to the instrument. Nevertheless, late minstrel perform-
> ers for decades relished [the] comic possibilities of the slip-
> horn—undoubtedly as a condescending extrapolation as to
> what [a] typical Negro would do with one if he stumbled
> across it.

Condescension was undoubtedly a part of this, but I suspect that, as usual, there's more to it than that; that the smear also gave players the ability to capture parts of African-American music (as they understood it, of course) that were otherwise unreproducible. That certainly seems to be Pryor's intent, anyway.

Pryor, who was only two years younger than Scott Joplin, was from St. Joseph, Missouri, close to Kansas City and not far from Joplin's Sedalia. This was prime ragtime country. It wasn't just the professors and banjo trios who were playing the stuff, either. There were black brass bands, too (none of which recorded, needless to say): Sedalia's Queen City Cornet Band, a popular local institution, used to play "Maple Leaf Rag" and other Joplin numbers; in fact, Joplin himself played cornet in the band for a while. The QCCB used to compete successfully with other black bands in statewide contests—which brings us to "A Coon Band Contest."

Pryor recorded dozens of versions of "A Coon Band Contest," both with Sousa's Band and his own. The one that's available for inspection dates from 1906 (Vic. B 793-6). It's a standard cakewalk, nowhere near as odd as "Trombone Sneeze." The band takes the A and the B at a comfortable, funky lope, Mantia supplying the rhythm oil. Then come the smears: the end of every phrase in the C just kind of rips apart as Pryor's trombone slides out from under it (Pryor's published arrangement has a trombone solo here, but he leaves it out). Did Pryor base this on black bands he actually heard? Were the black bands of Missouri smearing their trombones? It's a good bet, anyway. Black music has never been too interested in the scale as Western Europeans think it should go: it likes plenty of notes you can't hit from the "standard" slide positions on the trombone; that take some pretty radical poking around to find (see below, on the blues).

What comes after the smears really sets "A Coon Band Contest" apart from his old boss's stuff. Right before the final ride-out, Pryor's boys ritard the rhythm, slowly winding the tempo down to a stop. Then they pitch themselves headlong into a final eight bars of the C—

smears and all—at a greatly accelerated tempo. Now, one of Sousa's real rigidities was tempo—an old military bandsman, he prided himself on never varying it; it was simply not negotiable. Pryor was more flexible. All this pulling and pushing the beat would have driven Sousa ape. Problem is, that stretch is at the heart of real ragtime.

By the mid-oughts, bands had begun recording flat-out rags, where *all* the themes are syncopated, and the syncopations are layered much more thickly than in the relatively simple cakewalks. Here, too, Pryor was ahead of the pack (in 1902 he wrote and recorded a number called "The Passing of Rag Time," but he seems to have changed his mind). He did, among others, some real classics, including Turpin's "St. Louis Rag," white K.C. ragtimer Charles L. Johnson's famous "Dill Pickles Rag," and Henry Lodge's enormously popular "Temptation Rag." These are fine, and the last (Vic. 16511) is positively torrid, but hottest of all is Pryor's own "Canhanibalmo Rag" (Vic. 16883), from 1911. The way his band bites this one off is a caution. Compared to the cakewalks, it's faster, nimbler, and the smears are better integrated; compared to Sousa's players, Pryor's are stone syncopators. As Pryor himself said, "The regulation bands never got over being a little embarrassed at syncopating. The stiff-backed old fellows felt it was beneath their dignity and they couldn't or wouldn't give in to it." By the sound of this record, he didn't hire any of them.

The B part of "Canhanibalmo Rag" features a particularly funky bit of tempo manipulation: the first time around, the band stretches each riff out just a bit too long over a steady bass; when the part comes around again at the end of the song, even the bass stretches the beat, slowing it down as the clarinet (or clarinets, or piccolos—something trebly, anyway; it's very hard to tell on these recordings) zips fast scales up to the rest of the band just in time to nail the next strong beat, where there's a sexy group bump and grind. Playing with time like this, setting rhythms against each other—that's the real ragtime; that's Africa. It's also the first thing that the Tin Pan Alley crowd had pitched overboard: straight syncopation, like in the cakewalks, was easy enough for a Topworld, notes-on-the-staff musician to get; this wasn't. By 1911, "Canhanibalmo Rag" was an anachronism.

♪

Sousa's and Pryor's weren't the only good bands, or the only bands to dig into ragtime. I've been able to inspect rags and cakewalks from at least a dozen others, including the Metropolitan Orchestra, the Victor Military Band, the Victor (Dance) Orchestra (both featuring moonlighting Sousa men), Prince's Band/Orchestra (with Bohumir Kryl, who does nothing to call attention to himself), Conway's Band, and two different Peerless Orchestras, the Edison one and a later British one. Taken collectively, there are few surprises among them and a goodly number of small pleasures: the way the Peerless Orchestra struts through its 1904 "Smokey Mokes" (Ed. 712). Frank Schrader's serpentine trombone smears on the Victor Military Band's 1911 "Slippery Place Rag" (Vic. 17006). The savage intonation of the brass on the Edison Military Band's "Hot Time March" (incorporating "Hot Time in the Old Town," natch; Ed. 103) and their "Southern Smiles Two-Step" (Ed. 8549), both from 1904. The funky little woodblock tickle on the A part of Prince's Orchestra's 1912 "Black Diamond Rag" (Col. A-1140). The trombone solo—right off the sheet music—on mustachioed nonentity Maurice Levi's heavily smeared 1909 "Coon Band Contest" (Ed. 10128); who cares if the guy's just reading notes: it's fast and loud and at least it sounds spontaneous. There are others.

The brass bands were Topworld's musical front line. They were respectable: they played Wagner and Beethoven. They wore uniforms. "The military band," Patrick Gilmore maintained, "may remain like a rough street tramp, or he may undergo a polishing that will make him equally fit...to occupy the concert-room with his more sensitive sister [the symphony orchestra]." Their reach into ragtime, as timid as it may have been, was a step back to the street. It was radical.

For the first time, Americans who should know better were turning to the Underworld. What's worse, they were playing black music without blackface: *you couldn't tell who the Coons were!* They were blacked up inside.

And yet, in the greater scheme of white musical Coondom the bands were rarely more than high yellow; others got darker. Ragtime was string music and then piano music (and what's a piano but a box of strings?); it sure as hell wasn't horn music. That is, you could play it on horns, but you couldn't really cut loose on it. Ragtime is about rhythm, about overlapping beats; it's vertical, as Gunther Schuller would say. You can do that on a banjo or a piano, spin out the staccato notes in endless strings and intricate webs; you can't do it on a horn, where all the notes come out in a horizontal row and the limited capacity of the human lung imposes its own rhythms; you need to overlap lots of horns, and all that blare dulls the edges of the beat even in the sharpest band. What's more, the best band musicians had all those years of constant rhythm marched into them at one hundred and twenty beats per minute (the Marine Band's official tempo), no more and no less.

Every once in a while you stumble over the traces of someone who breaks free and makes ragtime play on his turf, bends it to the expressiveness and vocal power of the horn—e.g., Pryor's smears. Usually, though, nothing for the professors to sweat over. Too bad you couldn't get their instruments properly on record. Occasionally they tried: Victor let their studio accompanist C.H.H. Booth cut loose with "Creole Belles"—see below—in 1901; it seems to be the first recorded piano rag, but I've never heard it and I don't know anyone who has (it's on Victor 1079, if that helps). Usually, though, the record companies were content to resign any interest in the instrument for uses other than accompaniment to their competitors in the canned music racket, the makers of the player piano.

This is unfortunate indeed. Consider the case of "Maple Leaf Rag." In 1916, Scott Joplin, then almost fifty and in the terminal stages of tertiary syphilis, cut seven piano rolls. To make one of these, you would play your songs on a regular keyboard and the machine would mark the notes you hit on a roll of paper. Then somebody with an X-acto knife (or current equivalent) would cut little holes in the paper. Essentially, your performance was being digitized, the void and solid of the paper functioning as the 0 and 1 of the byte. In fact, as you may recall, computers used to be programmed with punch cards—essentially little slices of piano roll. Like digital music, the data on the roll was easily manipulated. First off, that somebody would make sure all the marks were in the right places—if your timing was off or you hit a clam or two, he could see that and move the holes accordingly. He might also add extra holes of his own— harmonics, runs, flash, and gingerbread. What would come out of this collaboration would be not unlike your original performance, but it wouldn't be it. Not only are the little imperfections that make us human gone, but nuances of volume, pedal work, all the little flutters in time and force that make a machine like a piano come alive. The result is something between sheet music and recording, but I fear closer to the former.

In any case, I'm not going to deal with them here, beyond noting that Joplin cut rolls of his masterpiece for two different companies, to particularly poor effect. He was no longer the professor of his youth; he was barely a T.A. Still, listening to them you can catch a faint echo of funk lurking in the denatured, freeze-dried jangle; a blue harmony, a delicate swerving of time, a polite chord-burst coming slightly after it's expected. This whiff of a more human art gives us a pang for what might have been, had the player piano fad not sucked all the oxygen out of the market for canned pianistics. The pang is particularly strong when we compare Joplin's halting "performance" to the United States Marine Band's 1909 record of the song (Vic. 16792). The gyrenes storm it like it was the Halls of Montezuma—bugles ringing, bayonets fixed, determination grim. It's exciting, *mais le ragtime, ce n'est pas la guerre.*

Banjos, Coon Songs, and Vocal Groups

Thank God for the banjo. Ironically enough, just as ragtime hit, the old banshaw, newly fangled up with steel strings, frets, mechanical tuning pegs, head-tighteners, and whatnot, was enjoying a vogue among the parlor classes. There were associations (Topworld's first instinct is to associate; that way, nobody's out on a limb), clubs, and amateur orchestras. It wasn't long before all these clean-living young Christian gentlemen (and not a few young ladies) were cautiously ragging it up. From the banjo ragtime came, and to the banjo it returned—but only after traveling from Underworld to Topworld through the piano and the music folio (of course, black banjoists were most likely syncopating all along, but see below). And since the steel string banjo was one of the few instruments that recorded reasonably well, it also wasn't long before the record companies began capitalizing on the banjo craze. Any piece of music could be cut into a banjo record, from Wagner to "Walkin' for Dat Cake." The old banshaw's Coon roots were submerged deep enough that a so-called "operatic" banjo soloist like the Brit Joseph Bell could move units with selections from *Tannhäuser* and *Il Trovatore*.

Studio banjoists such as Vess L. Ossman—another "King of Ragtime"—and Fred Van Eps recorded literally thousands of sides (including, however, scads of repeats and overlaps) from the late 1890s to about 1911, when the ragtime craze began abating, or rather transforming itself. In 1896 or '97, it was Ossman's privilege to make the first ragtime record of any kind, an unnumbered Columbia cylinder titled simply "Ragtime Medley." In general, the banjoists' technique was phenomenal and their music was warm, especially when Vess teamed up with a mandolin and harp-guitar to form a kicky little string band. Like good session men, real musicians, the banjo experts played what they were told and didn't put too much of an individual stamp on it, swerve it too much. Everybody bought their records.

The Banjo King in 1907.

COURTESY OF DARRELL LEHMAN

To listen to Ossman is to understand why. In 1907, he cut a version of "Maple Leaf Rag," backed by Prince's Orchestra. While the orchestra lumbers away behind him, Ossman snaps out a blistering take on the song. The descending bits careen, the rising bits rocket, the picking patterns throughout are intricate and syncopated. Cross rhythms abound. It's a million times trickier than the jarheads' version and hotter than any piano roll (Col. A-0228).

Yet Ossman still can't help but play it at transwarp speed. Now, Joplin had attached a warning to the sheet music for his 1905 "Leola": "Notice! Don't play this piece fast. It is never right to play 'rag-time' fast." The faster you play a rag, the less all that pulling and bending of time registers on the ear; from funk, you retrieve jangle. Typical ofay jive. What saves Ossman is that there's also a looseness to his playing that slews the music around to face its Underworld roots even as they recede into the distance—a fluffed note here, an accent not quite nailed there, a discreet slide or two on the bass string (or maybe they're bends; at this speed, it's hard to tell), some improvisation in the pattern-picking. If the tempo were slower and the band were funkier, or better yet sitting things out in a Bierstube somewhere, it would be a truly hot record. Still, it's easy to see why, far more directly than the brass band or the rhythmically challenged player piano, it was the banjo record that shot the swervy new rhythms into the heart of the middle-class home, like an arrow straight from Underworld's loins.

How does Ossman compare to the black banjo wallahs of his day? Of course, since the great Horace Weston, the one black banjoist likely to have been allowed to make a significant number of records, had died in 1890, before the industry got off the ground, and this comparison has to be based on a single record, Cousins & DeMoss's 1897 duet of "Pour [sic] Mourner" (Berl. 3010), the only black American banjo record from the ragtime age to make it down to us. There were a few others made: occasionally—once in a Coon's age—someone would get an idea to ask the *original* banjo experts to tickle the strings for the recording horn. As early as 1891, the Louisiana Record Company, an Edison subsidiary, secured the services of one Louis Vasnier. Only one of his cylinders survives, "Brudder Rasmus" from 1892, and he doesn't play the banjo on it (or if he does, you can't hear it; the sound quality is horripilating). Nobody else's efforts have survived in any form. There may have been a few more put out by some of the other regional companies—George and James Bohee made a few in England—but none have turned up. So: "Poor Mourner." Alas, it's hardly a banjo record at all: after five seconds of intriguingly bluesy picking, Cousins and DeMoss just strum simple chords on the damn things to accompany their gospel singing (for which see below). Nothing to see here, no ragtime. Move along.

This leaves Vess holding the ragtime title. And why not? After all, he did make the first ragtime record. Luckily, it's available for inspection, along with more than a dozen of his other rags floating around out there in reissue. Unfortunately, in Uli Heier and Rainer Lotz's bio-discography of banjo records (wondrous the works of man &c.) his entry extends to twenty-six pages in eight-point type. But if a dozen records is short of a truly representative sample of his work, it'll have to do; it helps that a lot of those pages are eaten up by repetitions—if Ossman recorded a song once, it's a good bet he recorded it five times, for five different companies, in five different formats.

"Rag Time Medley of Coon Songs," to give it its full title, is a cylinder Ossman cut for Columbia sometime around 1896, some three years into his recording career (Ossman also did one of the same for Edison around then). In less than two and a half minutes Ossman plinks his way through Ben Harney's "Mr. Johnson, Turn Me Loose," "All Coons Look Alike to Me," and "A Hot Time in the Old Town," all huge hits. Granted that it's the first ragtime record, with all the burdens and uncertainties that being first implies; it's still underwhelming. The accompanying pianist doesn't have the foggiest idea how to play this music, and Ossman doesn't sound much better. It's practice, anyway.

It didn't take him long to get it down. Born in 1868 in grimy Hudson, New York (later known, like Sedalia, for its whorehouses), Sylvester Louis Ossman—"Plunk" to his cronies—grew up in respectable Topworld surroundings; he had a work ethic. He picked up the banjo at twelve and claimed to have practiced ten hours a day for the first three years and four hours a day forever after that. He could and did play anything, from Wagner to you-know-what; it was the you-know-what, however, that spread the butter on his toast. Ragtime was what he did best, and by the turn of the century he was cutting bales of the stuff, with all kinds of accompaniments from studio orchestras to piano players to nobody at all.

Vess's skill and determination paid off: he was a star. His records sold, his gigs were packed, he played for Roosevelts and royalty. Still, he was a bit of a stiff: he was given to windy pronouncements like "You have to pick hard and keep the same volume of tone all throughout a piece, combined with absolute accuracy; [this makes] a superb foundation on which to put light and shade for concert work" and "I am...addicted to grace notes and *appogiatura*" (Glossary of the Vulgar Tongue: *appogiatura* = skipping up to a dissonant—to European ears, anyway—note and then falling quickly back to a "correct" one; slipping in a fast blue note). He even told the British interviewer who elicited these opinions in 1903 that banjoists shouldn't neglect the metronome, since "it is the playing of marches, two-steps, cake walks, etc. in unsuitable time which makes them sound ridiculous"—see comments on "Maple Leaf Rag," above. In fact, his playing is rarely as mechanical as his words suggest, especially when compared to that of his younger competitor Fred Van Eps or twenties banjo king Harry Reser.

If Vess Ossman wasn't exactly an Underworld character, at least he could fake it on the banjo. His funkiest rags were done with the Ossman-Dudley Trio, with Audley Dudley on mandolin and Roy Butin or George Dudley on harp-guitar (that thing they play in Scorsese's *The Last Waltz*). Formed around 1900 and recording intermittently for most of the next decade, the Ossman-Dudley trio was the first successful string band to record. At a typical session, on January 24, 1906, they cut: "St. Louis Tickle," "Koontown Koffee Klatsch," "Dixie Girl," "Fantana," "The Mayor of Tokyo (Selections)," and "It Happened in Norland: Al Fresco—Intermezzo." Unlike the hayseed string bands who succeeded them in the twenties, these guys had options: they could play it rough or they could play it real real nice. Typical Topworld musical schizophrenia: half parlor recital, half Coon show. All three of the Ethiopic numbers have been reissued. "Koontown Koffee Klatsch" and "Dixie Girl" are cakewalks. The latter is by Danish-born songwriter J. Bodewalt Lampe, famous for the killer cakewalk hit "Creole Belles"—note the typical European obsession with the precious flower of our Southern womanhood—which was recorded several times to stunning effect by Sousa's Band (Vic. 17252 from 1912 is especially hot); it's a fine record, gentler than the brass cakewalks but still swinging (Vic. 16667). The antiphonal interplay between the banjo and Dudley's dimly recorded mandolin (the Neapolitan instrument was just then being introduced into American music) has a fine delicate drive to it. "St. Louis Tickle," however, is the real thing.

The song had a 1904 copyright by Barney & Seymour, about whom ain't nobody knows nothing—but that's only part of the story. Some say they stole it from the white Missouri pianist and mandolin-band leader Theron Catlen Bennett, but his title wasn't much better than theirs. Some attribute it to cornetist Buddy Bolden, the unrecorded founder of New Orleans jazz, others to others. In fact, nobody really wrote the "Tickle": it's a folk rag, three simple and swervy strains plucked out of the whorehouse air and stitched together; whoever did the needlework, the cloth was found goods. The B strain is of especial pungency and interest: of great antiquity in the Mississippi Valley, it's, as one ragtime book puts it, a "notorious bit of musical low-life." People knew it as the "Funky Butt" (Glossary of the Vulgar Tongue: *funky* = stinking; *butt* = butt, as in dog-end, fag-end, roach), and the words that went to it were filthy. Singing it could supposedly get you thrown in jail in some of the better-churched settlements in the area; just whistling it could get your face slapped. And whistle it folks certainly did: it's a catchy sonofabitch, so catchy that Scott Joplin worked it into the chorus of his song "Sarah Dear," ragtime popularizer Ben Harney drew on it for his "Cakewalk in the Sky"—a somewhat anemic 1905 version is available, done by the Victor (Dance) Orchestra, including various Sousa vets (Vic. 31412)—and, a third of a century later, Jelly Roll Morton cut it as "Buddy Bolden's Blues," mingling so much of his heart and labor with it that it will be forever his.

In Ossman's hands, the "St. Louis Tickle" is a jaunty, simple rag, shot through with intimations and echoes of the blues, whose crows' nest was just beginning to peep over Topworld's horizon. Ossman, front and center on all of three strains, feeds his *appogiatura* jones as Butin fills in bass and harmony and the atrociously recorded Dudley for all intents and purposes lies doggo. The drive Vess generates is both delicate and intense—it's like he's carving these venerable riffs into your head with a tattooing iron—and he swerves the tempo enough on the "Funky Butt" to get that feeling of pre-orgasmic suspension of time that is the very essence of hot. He even flubs a few notes, brave soul. The song was a huge hit, although it seems way too funky to have much appeal for the manyheaded. Times change. [Warning: Ossman's lame 1909 version of the "Tickle," cut with Prince's Band (Col. A-937), is to be avoided like the Panamanian cholera; but by then, rumor has it, he was devoting most of his practice time to mastering the whiskey-jug.]

Ossman tackled other folk rags, his clear favorite being Tom Turpin's "Buffalo Rag," a zippy little number that kicks like a back-firing chainsaw; he cut it about a half-dozen times (e.g., Vic. 16679, from 1909), but never with the Trio. There's also a kicky take on "A Coon Band Contest" out there. When he was bad, he was superbad. Now, writers who address the matter of the rag splash a good deal of ink about, bemoaning the dearth of piano records from the days of the craze. Sure; it is to weep. But most of them are all too happy to leave you with the impression that this is the only "real" ragtime, that anything else is a pale imitation that should be smiled at weakly and tossed back into the water. Bullshit.

♪

Vess Ossman was one of those thick-necked types who make a starched collar look like a bondage device. You can't say the same for his pupil, competitor, and successor Fred Van Eps, whose pencil neck and pinched, narrow face—like Sgt. Carter of *Hogan's Heroes*—are emblematic of his playing, and of what was happening to ragtime banjo and ragtime in general. Compared to Ossman, Van Eps, born in 1878 (in Somerville, New Jersey), was faster, cleaner, and more precise. Conversely, he lacked Ossman's "rhythmic facility," as Van Eps himself conceded—his swing, his groove, his funk. But as ragtime began fading from America's pop brain, it started turning into an art music, and Fred Van Eps was the man on the spot for that.

Van Eps, having taught himself to banjicate from Ossman records, started recording himself at age twenty with numbers like "Koonville Koonlets" and "Nigger in a Fit"; it didn't take long before the race was on. At first, Ossman's five-year head start kept him in the lead. But once ragtime began stiffening up, Van Eps pulled into the lead.

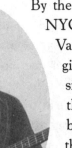

*Fred Van Eps, from a 1916
Victor Records catalog,
still trying to keep ahead.*

COURTESY OF ARCHEOPHONE RECORDS

By the time Ossman soddenly decamped from NYC to the middle parts of America in 1910, Van Eps had pretty much taken over his gig: he was the one accompanying the hot singers, doing the latest hit rags, etc. When the masters wore out to some of Vess's biggest hits, Victor didn't call him back into the studio; they used Fred instead—they got around to the "St. Louis Tickle" in 1920. When Vess died in semi-obscurity in 1923, Fred was still recording regularly. I'd go into more detail here, but all but one of the dozen-odd Van Eps cuts reissued are from 1911–23, and that one's a rube number, without a trace of ragtime.

Unfortunately, if the god of reissues (Hippolytus? Aesculapias?) has smiled but weakly on Ossman and Van Eps, he has displayed a stern face indeed to their competition. There are a couple of very early duets by Cullen & Collins, about whom very little is known, including a nice, if brief, 1898 duet on "Eli Green's Cakewalk" (Berl. 485). There's a fine, funky "Whistling Rufus" by Olly Oakley from 1903 (GC 6374)—a Brit, no less, Oakley must have been the Jimmy Page of his day—but precious little else.

♪

If we find ourselves deprived of archaic recorded evocations of negritude, the general public in the Gay Nineties and the Unepithetical Oughts, when they were anything but archaic, was not, for that is when Coondom caught its second wind.

And a foul wind it was. From 1890 to 1910 there were about 2,000 lynchings in America—many executed with a public savagery that is, from my comfortable seat at the exhausted end of the twentieth century, almost unbelievable. An Atlanta grocery window displayed what you and I would call human knuckles; they used another adjective. Reconstruction was dead and Jim Crow laws were coming in everywhere in the South. Not that things were much better in the North—de jure and de facto are only one little Latin word apart, and in this country at least Latin words have never been worth much more than the spit it takes to say them. We've always had types who think that white culture in America has nothing to do with black culture; that you can neatly separate them—I'm sure we all know a couple. But the farther Topworld pushed actual black folks to the margins of society, not without the all-too-willing assistance of white Underworld (we never have managed to get that class solidarity business straightened out), the larger Coons loomed in the pop culture.

To supplement the nostalgic, sweetly comical Old Plantation darky of the minstrel stage, the nineties saw a new-model Coon. His English was still Ebonic and his fatal weakness for the fruit of the watermelon vine was unabated—and he sure could dance. But he was a coke-sniffer. Crap-shooter. Razor-toter. Chicken-stealer. Trick-procurer. Flash-roll-flasher. Cop-dodger. Cop-killer. He was wise. He was the bully of the town. He was Stack O'Lee, he was Railroad Bill, you best not fuck with him. He was the Bad Nigger of every cracker's nightmares. His bowler hat was cocked over one eye, his boxback checkered suit was tight, and his rap was as up-to-date as the typewriter, the horseless carriage, or the phonograph.

His home was where the mechanized jangle of ragtime kicked American pop into the twentieth century: the so-called "Coon" (more politely, "ragtime") song. The average mainstream—i.e., Topworld—pop song around the turn of the century was a waltz-time confection of treacly sentiment and ormolu morality, occasionally spiced up with a dash of English music hall pluck and a dram of vaudeville Ireland. "After the Ball" (1892), the "Sidewalks of New York"

(1894), "Sweet Rosie O'Grady" (1896), "In the Good Old Summer-time" (1902)—all million-sellers. This was not threatening music. "With the moral import of our songs," wrote an anthologist in 1894, "no fault is to be found.... The tenor of their verse is in the direction of strictly permissible reminiscence and affectionate expostulation.... These American songs are commendable for sobriety of statement and worthiness of purpose."

What he means is this:

> I've really come a long way from the city,
> And though my heart is breaking I'll be brave,
> I've brought this bunch of flow'rs, I think they're pretty,
> To place upon the freshly moulded grave;
>
> If you will show me, father, where she's lying,
> Or if it's far just point it out to me,
> Said he, "she told us all when she was dying,
> To bury her beneath the apple tree."
> *Chorus:*
> In the shade of the old apple tree,
> Where the love in your eyes I could see,
>   When the voice that I heard,
>   Like the song of a bird,
> Seem'd to whisper sweet music to me;
>
> I could hear the dull buzz of the bee,
> In the blossoms as you said to me,
>   With a heart that is true,
>   I'll be waiting for you,
> In the shade of the old apple tree.
>   —"In the Shade of the Old Apple Tree,"
>   H. W. WILLIAMS AND E. VAN ALSTYNE, 1905

And possibly even this, especially if his definition of "permissible reminiscence" extends to worlds that never were:

A camp-meeting took place,
By the colored race,
Way down in Georgia.
There were coons large and small,
Lanky, lean, fat, and tall,
At this great coon camp-meeting.

When church was out,
How the "Sisters" did shout,
They were so happy,
But the young folks were tired,
And wished to be inspired
And hired a big brass band.
Chorus:
When that band of darkies began to play
Pretty music so gay
Hats were then thrown away—
Thought them foolish coons their necks would break
When they quit laughing and talking
And went to walking,
For a big chocolate cake.
        —"At a Georgia Camp Meeting (A Song in Black),"
                                    KERRY MILLS, 1897

But he sure as hell doesn't mean this:

I went out to a Nigger crap game
It was against my will;
The coon took all my money I had

Except one greenback dollar bill.
There was a hundred dollar bill upon the table,
The nigger's point was nine
Just then the copper stepped through the door—
Chorus:
But I got mine,
   I got mine, boys,
   I got mine;
I grabbed that hundred dollar bill,
Through the window I did climb.
Ever since then I've been wearing good clothes
And living on chicken and wine.
I'm the leader of society
Since I got mine.
     —"I Got Mine," J. QUEEN AND C. CHARTWELL, 1901
       (as performed by Collins and Natus, 1903 [Canadian
                      Berliner Concert 5206])

As sociology, this may be quite as vile; as ethnography, quite as revolting, as Mills's foolish, cakewalking Coons—but as entertainment...I got mine. The modern ragtime establishment, if you want to call it that—all those conservatory piano-tinklers and such—has tended to take one look at the Coon song and quietly close the door on it, whistling softly to itself and hoping that nobody will notice. Not that you can blame it. It's pretty hard to defend a song with a title like "All Coons Look Alike to Me" or "Coon! Coon! Coon!" And most of the songs—including "I Got Mine"—were written by white guys anyway, most of them working in that bastion of real folk culture, New York City. But. While many Coon songs aren't much different in essence or purpose from the skinhead slatherings available on the Internet—heavyhanded racial jeers, the lynch mob's song—others absorb the Coon persona and use it subversively in much the same way that gangsta rap uses the nigga. Many of the more popular Coon songs were by black songwriters like Ernest Hogan, Irving Johns, and Bert Williams. And a surprising number of Coon songs, Topworld evocations of black Underworld, were absorbed into the Underworld musical tradition. When Underworld finally makes it on record in the 1920s, performer after performer, black and white, spits out as his (or, of course, her) own a digested and folkified—and usually much improved—version of a song that was originally thought up by some guy sitting in an office on West 28th Street with garters on his sleeves.

The first Coon song to hit, "New Coon in Town" by J. S. Putnam, predated ragtime by a good ten years; it was really just another dialect song like "My Mariuccia Take-a Steamboat" or "Is That Mr. Riley?" and not particularly hot. But once ragtime became a musical signifier of blackness, it was the work of a moment to slip some of it into the Coon dialect song. To be sure, some serious tinkering had to be done: classic ragtime, with its subtle, lacelike funk, was too delicate for mass tastes, and far too complex rhythmically for the average white parlor pianist, who experienced music as notes on a page (funk—the slippage or swerve of time—is notoriously hard to notate). Hell, it was too difficult for most of the songwriters. So they regularized it; cleaned it up. And goosed it up. Powered it up. More drive and less swerve. You can find the same moves in the Original Dixieland Jazz Band, Benny Goodman, the Rolling Stones, Kid Rock (but not Eminem). Black, the thinking goes, equals wild. P-R-I-M-I-T-I-V-E. So to make it black, make it *loud*—regardless of the fact that black music, certain carefully staged vocal rituals aside, is characterized by subtlety and restraint (see below, in the discussion of the blues). American music—white American music, anyway—has a tendency to aim for the black and hit the green (as in "The Wearin' of..."—you know, that wild Celtic strain). "Authentic" or not, in the case of the Coon song the results were satanically catchy: the syncopation, often confined to the vocal line, drove the simple, repetitive melodies along. The lyrics, tales of violent love and lost poultry, were unsentimental and colloquial; inelegant to be sure but not boring. It was a caricature, but it rocked.

♪

The song goes like this:

Announcer: "All Coons Look Alike to Me," sung by Arthur
   Collins with banjo accompaniment by Mr. Vess L. Oss-
   man, Edison Records.
[VLO: brief display of banjo prestidigitation]
Talk about your Coons having trouble,
I think I have enough of ma own;
It's all about my Lucy Janey Stubbles,
And she has caused my heart to mourn.
There's another Coon, a barber from Virginia,
In society he's the leader of the day.
And now my honey gal's gwine to quit me,
Yes, she's gone and drove this Coon away.
[VLO: dramatic cut-time chords]
   She'd no excuse
   To turn me loose
   I've been abused
   I'm all confused
[VLO: wild chromatic ripple]
   —Uhyeugh, Lawd! [spoken]—
   Cause these words she then did sing:
[chorus, whomping on the caps]
ALL COONS look aLIKE to me!
I'VE GOT another BEAU, you see,
AND HE'S just as GOOD to me
As YOU
   —Nigger [spoken]

[94]

—ever TRIED to be,
HE SPENDs his MONey free.
I KNOW we CAN't agree,
So I don't like you no how—
All Coons look alike to me.
[VLO: a couple of lines of banjo chorus.]

There's another verse, but this should be enough to establish the kind of racist trash we're dealing with here. (A sense of academic propriety prompts me to acknowledge that I didn't achieve the impressive degree of accuracy with which these lyrics are transcribed without recourse to a cheat-sheet; ten years of playing bass in punk bands didn't leave my hearing unmarked. The song was, however, recorded in 1899, and it is rock 'n' roll, and as far as I know the Rock and Roll Hall of Fame has no current plans to induct Professor Henry Higgins as a forefather. Even after listening to Collins's Cooning *ultra nauseam*, all my naked ear could get out of the third line of the verse, for instance, was "It's Alabama loose in hagabubble." But go and do thou likewise.)

Problem is, it was written by one Ernest Hogan, and his vaudeville tag was "The Unbleached American" (his real name was Reuben Crowders or Crowdus; "Hogan" was either an attempt to butter up the notoriously negrophobic Irish or a sly jibe at them— or both). Not only was he black, he was a bit of a song thief. What Hogan did here was take a particularly catchy Chicago barroom ditty, clean up the words, and tack on a verse setting up the situation— a certain young lady is equally indifferent to all other suitors now that she has a new beau. The "Coons" of the title and chorus, went his reasoning, was an improvement over the original "pimps." "All pimps look alike to me"—in the era of the "ho" and the "byotch," inoffensive and almost sweet; back in the day, unprintable. "Coons" and "niggers," however, could flit through the mouths of Topworld without provoking intake of breath or slantendicular glance.

The "Unbleached American."

COURTESY OF CHRIS WARE/*THE RAGTIME EPHEMERALIST* MAGAZINE

In spite of the improvements, Hogan's song didn't endear him to the black intelligentsia of his day any more than, say, Luther Campbell's too-live Coon act did in the 1980s ("all boys look alike" was the PC substitution). The ofays loved it, though—when Jack Johnson defended his heavyweight title against Jim Jeffries on Independence Day, 1910, the good bleached Americans who trooped out to Reno to see white mastery reasserted sang along lustily when the band struck it up as Johnson stepped into the ring. History is silent as to what they sang when Jeffries threw in the towel in the fifteenth.

Unfortunately, nobody thought to shove the Unbleached American's face into a recording horn before TB enrolled him in the choir eternal in 1909, at age forty-four (but see below). At least we've got Collins. Arthur Collins (1864–1933) recorded in almost every context imaginable—cylinder and disc; talking, singing, talking and singing; solos, duets, quartets; with piano, with banjo, with band. He was a professional Coon, Mick, Yid, Wop, Hayseed, and even sometimes Yankee; blacks weren't the only figures of Topworld fun (e.g., Ed. 9463, "Good-A-Bye, John": "you come-a da home when you was-a drunk / you cut-a da string, he lose-a de monk [=monkey, in the vernacular of the day]"—John the organ-grinder might be a Dago, but there's more O'Sullivan than "O Sole Mio" in Collins's cadences). Still, it was Collins's Coon act that got over the most—he was America's ace Coon.

Going by the tiny sample available, this massive body of work seems to be largely—how do I put it—crap. Not this one. "All Coons" is a thoroughly modern record, much more so than any of those delicate "pure" or "classic" rags—so modern that the first five notes of

His magnum opus.

The King of the "Coon Shouters" in 1907.

COURTESY OF DARRELL LEHMAN

the chorus riff are in the same rhythm that, sixty-six years later, the Rolling Stones would use to kick off "Satisfaction." Like "Satisfaction," the tempo is fast but not too fast to stomp. And it's short—in and out in two minutes and four seconds.

Ossman's banjo is unleashed, rampaging—the way he pitches chords in on the whomps and stitches them together with ripples and tickles is the quintessence of hot. Drive. Swerve. Collins's voice, low in the mix in classic r&r style, is rough-edged but not grotesque, unwhite but not undignified. For someone who grew up with Elvis and Mick Jagger and Gregg Allman, it's difficult to hear the Coon in it; it just sounds—dare I say it—normal. It's the "white" voices, all those ee-nun-see-yating parlor singers, that sound weird. Thanks to Collins—and Jolson and Bert Williams and Bessie Smith and Louis Armstrong and Bing Crosby—everyone sings like Coons now.

Zoom in for a moment on the way Collins tosses that odious "Nigger" into the chorus. It's the most intelligible word on the record, because he steps outside of the song—swerves out—to just say it, plainly and clearly. No hagabubble here. You can hear contempt in his voice, Topworld white to Underworld black, but there's also a surprising dignity there. He breaks song, but not character, and his Coon is no shuffling, mush-mouthed plantation darky—he's a tough son of a bitch. To appreciate Collins's craft, track down a copy of "May Irwin's Bully Song," recorded for Victor in 1907—which is none other than her version of "Bully of the Town," of Mama Lou fame. When La Irwin, a Scottish-Canadian blonde of the creamy, zaftig variety, proclaims in her clear, slightly fruity soprano that she's

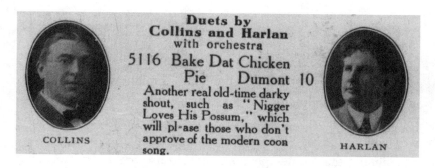

Collins and Harlan, from a 1907 Victor catalog.
The most popular duo act of their age.

"a Tennessee nigger," it's impossible not to laugh at the ridiculousness of it all. She's Vanilla Ice in a whalebone corset. (And yet the song itself is infernally catchy, with strong beats and lots of vintage gangsta slang).

A few of Collins's other Coon songs are available for inspection, but the doubleplus-unhot backup really drags them down. A piano, a couple of horns, maybe a fiddle, all stiff and no swerve. No fun, although the crazed "Whoa, Bill!" (Col. 1463) he cut with Byron G. Harlan is worth a spin, if you can find it: men shouting, drums bashing, cymbals crashing, trombone smmeeeaarrring. What kind of music is it? Minstrel? Western? Damdifino, but it ain't polite. (Harlan, by the by, played "Mr. Whop Flop, a nice young man" opposite W. C. Fields' "Si Flappum, a regular playactor" at the Great One's New York stage debut in early 1899.) There's also a very hot twenty-eight seconds of "Cohan's 'Rag Babe'" from 1908 where the band skirls about like mad while Collins calls out the names of various scandalous Coon dances: "Pasmala! Bombashay!" (Vic. 5483). Other than that, Collins is supposed to have cut more songs by black songwriters than anyone at the time, but good luck finding 'em, and no guarantee of any heat if you do.

♪

Collins was on the pop end of the minstrel rainbow; he was skilled and pliable enough to do anything to keep his feet firmly planted in the treacherous soil of Topworld. There were plenty of others who were less adaptable—Coons through and through. The ragtime era saw almost the whole spectrum of Reconstruction-era minstrelsy (minus the Georgia variety, of course) committed to record, from the thoroughly up-to-date Collins to thoroughly ossified Emmettoids like banjo-picker Harry C. Browne, who cut "Old Dan Tucker" in 1916 and Foster's "Oh, Boys, Carry Me Long" two years later. Edison, the chief offender here, captured the middle ground with a string of truly lame minstrel-shows-in-miniature perpetrated by the likes of Collins, Harlan, musical comedy star Billy Murray, Len Spencer, and S. H. Dudley (not to be confused with the sepia S. H. Dudley, who worked with Bert Williams). In general, the jokes stink and the music is brief and sappy and very very white.

Rag specialist Len Spencer, from a 1907 Victor catalog.

COURTESY OF DARRELL LEHMAN

Len Spencer, at least, redeemed himself here and there for the crap he cut on Edison. The version he did in 1902 or 1903 of Ben Harney's "You've Been a Good Old Wagon" for Lambert records is one of the hottest of all Coon records, complete with romping ragtime piano breaks (Lam. 989). "The Cake-Walk in Coon Town," by the Victor Minstrels (Vic. 1828), is still racist trash, of course, but at least it jumps. Its premise is a cakewalk contest, with Spencer making Mr. Interlocutor over as a badass razor-toting MC: "I'm just as good as a regiment of razors," he warns the

Darktown 400 before they start gamboling for the gateau, "an' if any of you baaad Coons cuts in an' pesters me, I'm a-gwine to cut you down in the flower of yo' youth." A stereotype, sure, but a butch one. Then the band rips into a quick medley of current Plantation hits—"At a Georgia Camp Meeting," "Cakewalk in the Sky," a couple of other faves; the minstrels spit out the nostalgic, happy-darky lyrics with machine-age clangor and the band tacks them on down. Couple #3 takes the cake (the scenario and dialogue, I should point out, are swiped from the *Witmark Amateur Minstrel Guide and Burnt Cork Encyclopedia* of 1899). According to jazz/blues historians Samuel Charters and Len Kunstadt, the "five-piece band—two clarinets, cornet, trombone, and piano" displays "an unmistakable jazz style." I wouldn't go that far, but their ragtime is definitely on the loose and swingy side. In any case, the whole thing's only two minutes and forty-four seconds, but they're worth Edison's entire minstrel catalog.

With one exception. Unlike Spencer, Collins, Greene, and most of the pop minstrels, Polk Miller was as Southern as grits and motor sports. He came from a slave-owning family in Virginia and claimed to have been the one to furl the rebel flag at Appomattox—can't get more Southern than that. Can't get more Southern than this, either: Miller led the first mixed-race group to tour and record, was a good enough "darkey dialectician" (his tag) for Mark Twain to "personally endorse" him, and banjicated to such perfection that Joel Chandler "Uncle Remus" Harris thought there was a "live nigger" hiding in his instrument.

'Course, there was. Like Harris himself, and Southern culture in general, Polk Miller internalized the Coon. If, the reasoning seems to go, these newfangled Negroes aren't near as deferential and accommodating as that mythical plantation darky upon whose broad, dumb shoulders our whole culture stands, we have to both force them to be so by law and brutal custom and—here's the beauty part—supply them (and us) with a model and example with which they can contrast their behavior. This means, learn to talk black, walk black, sing and dance and strum black (or at least, what you want "black" to be). Own them on the inside. (Just make sure y'all don't let them do the same to you.) This serves chiefly to demonstrate the deficiency of Southern scriptural education: "He that toucheth pitch shall be defiled therewith," Ecclesiasticus warns, and the pure practitioners of racial superiority through condescending imitation were more defiled than they could ever realize. When Miller took the stage with his "employees" the Old South Quartette—all "genuine darkies of the 'Sunny South,' trained in music by Mr. Miller," as Edison advertised them—he didn't black up. He didn't have to; everyone knew he was a Coon; he even billed himself as "The Old Virginia Plantation Negro."

Miller and the Quartette cut seven cylinders for Edison in late 1909, "real 'darkey' plantation melody," according to the Edison house organ. Just to make sure folks knew where he was coming from, Miller started things off with a rousing version of "The Bonnie Blue Flag" [of Texas], which just happened to be the Confederacy's second-favorite anthem (after you-know-what); one wonders what the poor bastards in the OSQ thought about this one. It couldn't have helped that their record company singled Miller out for his efforts "to bring the ruling race an appreciation of the characteristics of the Negroes." Yassuh, boss. I'm shakin' 'em, boss.

Credentials established, Miller went straight for the Coon songs— "The Laughing Song" (aka "Oysters and Wine at 2 A.M."), "Watermelon Party" ("Watermelon's nice—hurry up and cut a slice / Watermelon's fine—hurry up and give me mine")—and spirituals. Forget the former; the latter are the real Tabasco. Take the old spiritual "What a Time" (Ed. Amb. 391): as on the others—"Rise and Shine," "The Old Time Religion," "Jerusalem Mornin'"—Miller strums the guitar (the banjo only turns up on "Bonnie Blue Flag") and lines out the lead; the Quartette answers him. The fervent call and response sets up a strong pushme-pullyou drive. As for the

Old Virginia Plantation Negro's lead: he's good, really good. Collins and Spencer and the Yankee Coons blacked up their voices by putting a little growl in them, dissing their thisses and datting their thats. The way Polk bends his voice, stretches it, pinches it into his nose, shows a hipness to the African swerve that puts him at the cutting edge of Ethiopian delineation. And we have proof. We can check up on ol' Polk, you see.

There were a few other quartets who recorded in the period 1890–1910 doing similar material, with one key difference. They were black. Except for Bert Williams, who seems to have slipped quietly into the next part of the book while my attention was directed elsewhere, and George W. Johnson—a rather pathetic figure who recorded countless versions of his two specialties, "The Laughing Song" (complete with copious bellylaughs) and "Whistling Coon" (yep, whistling)—the only black musicians acceptable enough to Topworld to be let within shouting distance of a recording horn with anything approaching regularity were the harmonizers of Negro spirituals. If from time to time a black street singer or vaudeville type might push through the permeable borders of Topworld long enough to cut a few records, try as they might, collectors haven't been able to turn up more than a sparse and oddly sorted handful of their relicts—not a bad rule-of-thumb indicator of their original popularity. But the Colored 4s (and 3s, and 5s, etc.) sold.

Problem is, most of them were too respectable. Groups like the Fisk University Jubilee Quartet/Singers—elevating minds on disc since 1909 and in person for thirty-eight years before that—and the Tuskegee Institute Singers (recording since 1914) were fine-voiced and dignified. The spirituals they peddled were the kind of stuff that even a fancy Fifth Avenue cake eater could recognize as art. What the concupiscent humours cry out for, however, isn't art and dignity; you gotta put some of the old mohoska into it. As Polk Miller pointed out proudly in one of his publicity brochures, the Quartette's singing "is not the kind that has been heard by the students from 'colored universities,' who dress in pigeon-tailed coats, patent leather shoes, white shirt fronts, and who are advertised to sing plantation melodies but do not."

Laying aside his pathological Southern discomfort with blacks who "try to let you see how nearly a Negro can act the white man while parading in a dark skin"—i.e., demonstrate that they can be more Topworld than any cracker can ever hope to—Miller was onto something. The various Jubilee singers were no more an authentic representation of African American folk gospel than the minstrel shows were of, well, anything. They were authentic American showbiz, presenting a music made up and whited up to fit Topworld ideas of the Negro noble in his suffering. George White, the original faculty advisor and leader of the pioneering Fisk group, completely reharmonized the old plantation hymns in an impeccable, trained European style. Many of them were even created from whole cloth by professional songwriters, black and white. Smelling salts all around. In fact, it wasn't long before minstrel companies started working some of these "genuine darky spirituals" into their acts, further cooling off the proceedings.

But harmonizing wasn't just for Sunday, not just for the church choir. Topworld and Underworld, black and white, everybody did it; it was the easiest route to music—you could sing it by ear and didn't need an instrument. The quartet—a lead and tenor, baritone, and bass harmonies—was the usual small unit, and their number was legion. Louis Armstrong's first gig was in a boys' quartet, fishing for pennies on the streets of New Orleans. He didn't wear a pigeon-tailed coat or any kind of shoes at all.

This is one of the most neglected areas in American pop. Books are few and records have only recently been reissued, but it's well worth a quick detour—two stars, if not three. About the white quartets, there's not much for the likes of me to say. Based on a brief but not untedious sampling of a few cuts by Henry Burr's Peerless Quartet (big hits: "Sweet Adeline," 1904; "Let Me Call You Sweetheart," 1911) they worked the sweet and sleepy barbershop/parlor/ church axis. Dreck. But the Peerless were Topworld: Arthur Collins was their second tenor and Burr was Canadian (and thus by definition Topworld, although Hank Snow might kick against that); no real hillbilly harmonists seem to have recorded before the twenties.

As for the black groups. I balk at generalizing about a tradition that runs unbroken from the Edison days and before—hell, much of it reaches straight back to Senegambia—through the Mills Brothers and the Four Tops to Bell Biv Devoe and Destiny's Child, but I'd take 5-2 that any given black vocal quartet (or trio, or quintet) record has at least a shot of funk in it and often a good deal more. Still, most of the few who recorded in the earlies stuck to gospel, much of it ecstatic and hot, but just as much as careful and clean and dull as the music of the Jubilee choirs. Some sang smut—Coon songs and such. And a few did both.

The first black quartet to record was Edison's aptly named Unique Quartet, beginning in 1890. Columbia answered them the next year with the Standard Quartette. Both made a bunch of records (exact numbers are lost), probably at least fifty each, and both stopped recording in 1896 (the year of Plessy v. Ferguson, when Jim Crow was tightening up and lynchings becoming a common amusement of broad elements of white society). The known titles are a mix of spiritual and Coon, with the Edison group (natch) heavier on the latter. A tiny, precious clutch of cylinders have been recovered, of which I've heard two by each group. The Standard Quartette's "Keep Movin'" and "Every Day'll Be Sunday Bye and Bye," from 1894–95, are straight gospel and lukewarm at best—the lead-against-riff antiphony is there, but tempos are somnolent and fervor is lacking.

The Edison group's stuff is hotter and uglier. On the earliest survivor, "Mamma's Black Baby Boy" from 1893 (Ed. 694), Joseph Moore's lead soars and quavers with remarkable vividness against the simple, dark harmonies of the Quartet as it lines out a stupid little tale of black juvenile irresponsibility. The second verse is typical:

Moore: She gave me ten cents to buy me some gum
Quartet: I'm my mamma's black baby boy
Moore: I slipped in a saloon and I bought me some rum
Quartet: I'm my mamma's black baby boy
Moore: I staggered and stumbled all over de place
          and the mud he did splatter all into my face
          And de people all say I was a disgrace
          I'm my mamma's black baby boy
Quartet: I'm my mamma's baby boy
          I'm my mamma's baby boy
          Alllllll dayyyyyy...

Although the tempo is slow, there's a certain drive in the refrains and Moore swerves his intonation a little; warm enough, but there's no regiment of razors here. You can counterbalance some of the racism and caricature in a song like "All Coons &c." with its subversive realism and toughness. Not here; this is pure watermelon music. Quartet Coondom, at least on the early records, was strictly of the plantation variety. It sold well in the Confederacy.

The second relict, "Who Broke the Lock," is a version of a song later beloved of quartets and gutbucket jazz/blues/hokum bands alike, who recorded it variously as "Who Broke/Stole the/de Lock/Latch (on/off the/de Hen Roost/House Door)." On their 1895 cylinder (cut for either The U.S. Phonograph Co. or Walcott & Leeds, two indies of great obscurity and short duration) the Uniques give out with the Coons and purloined poultry, but their call and response sets up some real swing and the words are a lot less lugubrious than "Mamma's Black Baby Boy," if only because they zip by faster. In fact, put a rhythm section under them and you've got the Coasters.

There's the irony: the unaccompanied, often raw sound of the early quartets is more backward (whatever the hell that means) than the delicate intricacies of ragtime, yet their simple antiphony turns out to be the shape of the future. Ragtime becomes jazz, gospel harmony becomes rock 'n' roll. Which becomes of course that poly-mer they use to sell cars, snack foods, and eighty-dollar concert tick-ets. The stone which the builders refused is become the head stone of the corner. As the anonymous Coon quartet (white? black?) who cut "Camp Meeting Jubilee" for the piratical Little Wonder label in 1910 says, "rock me and roll me in your arms." 'Course, they make sure to add "in the arms of Moses," but it takes them a while (LW 339).

At least since Empedocles in the fifth century B.C., people have suspected that the universe is made up of polarized opposites—love and strife, black and white, hot and cool, plain and chunky, sacred and smut. But for just as long, people have recognized that these opposites tend to run together. Take the Dinwiddie Colored Quar-tet, out of the John A. Dix Industrial School of Dinwiddie, Vir-ginia. The DCQ, although they once toured with Ernest Hogan, were ostensibly a pure gospel group; at least, the six titles they cut for Victor in 1902 are all jubilee boilerplate. And yet on a couple of them—"Down on the Old Campground" and especially "Poor Mourner"—they can't help but slip the bacon in.

On "Campground" (Vic. 1714), the basic setup is the same as for all the close-harmony gospel fours: call and response, a refrain of three repeated lines and a capper, a simple—even monotonous—harmonic structure. Yet Sterling Rex's lead tenor cuts and the har-monies are close and thick and rich as bone marrow; a superior group. "Coon shout by the Dinwiddie Colored Quartet," says the announcer, and then it's all hypocrites and Jesus until the last verse:

Down in the barnyard on my knees
I thought I heard that chicken sneeze
he sneezed so hard with a whooping cough
†argle† sneezed his head and tail right off.
[About that 'argle': I've listened to the sumbitch about fifty
   times, but without a cheat-sheet, argle it shall remain. I've

staked it off with the so-called *crux desperationis* (†); it
means I give up.]

I hope he was kneeling in prayer, but I cannot silence the voice of
doubt. The Unique Quartet and the Standard Quartette may have
switched back and forth between sacred songs and Coon songs,
but here they're run together, interlaced, contaminated, corrupted.
And out of corruption comes life—anyone who has left a porkchop
lying around too long in the summer heat can attest to that.

"Poor Mourner" (Vic. 1715) is the same song Cousins & DeMoss
cut four years earlier. It was something of a standard—the Standard
Quartette seems to have cut it in 1894, when one Ed DeMoss is
listed as a member (no reason not to believe that he's the same guy),
Pete Hampton did one in London in 1904, and it was the first disc
cut by the great Frank Stokes in 1927 (as "You Shall"); there were
others. In C&DM's hands, the song has drive—their banjo strumming lays down a beat and they push it along nicely with harmony
riffs, but the antiphony's on the bony side what with only the two
of them to sing the responses. And the verses—what you can discern of them—are the usual gospel Adam and Eve stuff.

The Dinwiddies take it with wings swept back and afterburners
on. The refrain is a titanic, churning, almost incomprehensible catch
of "poor mourner"s and "you shall be free"s. What's more, the snap
they put into the "you-shall" is the same snap Ernest Hogan heard
in "all-pimps"—pure ragtime. The verse—harmonized, for a change—
picks up exactly where "Campground" lets off, with the knees and
the sneeze, just about word for word. The chicken is as much a
leitmotif in black Underworld music as in white Topworld imitations of it—here it even comes back again in the third verse:

> I got the gal, she's workin' hard,
> Workin' right over here in the white folks' yard,

Cookin' them chickens and servin' the stuffing;
Thinks I'm working but I ain't do nothin'.

Rhythm and blues—for Topworld, this last verse was like the strange blip that darkened the edge of Pvt. George Elliot, Jr.'s Oahu radar screen at 7:06 A.M., December 7, 1941. The gal in the white folks' yard makes up one of those set verses that pop up over and over on blues records from 1916 (George O'Connor's "Nigger Blues"; see below) through the thirties. That means that this is the first recorded trace of the blues, which would soon surface to change all American music (with certain unutterable exceptions) into something strange and wonderful.

In the meanwhile, while putting down black citizens, the Coon song spread their beat everywhere—the music of the Missouri whorehouses became the pulse of Tin Pan Alley. In the first decade of the new century, the syncopated skip of ragtime broke out of the Coon song ghetto and started popping up everywhere. Irving Berlin used it—in fact, you might consider his 1911 "Alexander's Ragtime Band" the official requiem for ragtime and the Coon song; see below. By then, ragtime had gone through the whole cycle of American hot music: an Underworld—usually black—music of obscure origins gets accepted by one part of mainstream culture and used to define itself against and annoy the other part until the other part comes to tolerate it, at which point it is thoroughly co-opted, its distinctive Underworld features almost lost and its Underworld roots denied, and it has come to resemble as a son to a father the wishy-washy crap that it replaced. Ragtime, jazz, swing (if you consider it not jazz), rock 'n' roll, honky-tonk, folk, blues (a special case; but think about Eric Clapton), rock, funk/disco, and now even hip-hop have played out or are playing out this scenario.

Although ragtime and Coon songs never completely replaced the respectable strains of the parlor song, they made much deeper inroads into mass culture than any other hot music since before the Civil War. We won't get much into the furious (and perennial) debate they sparked among the chattering classes. Some patriotic intellectuals picked up on ragtime quite soon as a perfect representation of the fauve part of American culture, the part that was like European culture on steroids. Other intellectuals of both races, guardians of all that is decent, felt that ragtime had undone fifty years of careful and tireless gentilification. "How can we regard this invasion of vulgarity in music other than a national calamity," one Arthur Weld wailed in 1899; "this cheap, trashy stuff could not elevate even the most degraded minds, nor could it possibly urge any one to greater effort in the acquisition of culture in any phase."

He was right, of course. Two years later, the American Federation of Musicians ordered its members to cease and desist from ragging forthwith; as if. What was passed over—suppressed—had broken loose, never to be caged again. To favor a music that "savors too much of the primeval conception of music"—Weld again—"whose basis [is] a rhythm that appeal[s] to the physical rather than to the mental senses" (sound familiar?) was to attack the system of sublimation driving American industrial achievement. At least the bands, vulgar as they may have seemed before, were European—at least they tried to play Beethoven, claimed to respect real art. Ragtime sneered at it. People were even ragging the classics. "Avaunt with ragtime rot!" another bluenose was still urging in 1914, "let us purge America and the Divine Art of Music from this polluting nuisance!"

He was a little slow. By 1908, ragtime was fading. It wasn't quite dead yet, but that didn't stop Sousa from playing coroner: "Ragtime had dyspepsia or gout long before it died. It was overfed by poor nurses. Good ragtime came, and half a million imitators sprang up. Then as a result people were sickened with the stuff. I have not played a single piece of ragtime this season because the people do not want it."

He was talking about the real stuff, of course, the tricky instrumental dance music. What he didn't realize was that it wasn't just
pure ragtime the folks were sick of; that the bands who had helped
to spread it were being set up for the gold watch as well. American
culture calls out for the new, and the new must yield to the newer.
Even as ragtime and ragged pop were reaching deepest Ohio, black
musicians and white were working on a new wiggle, and you
couldn't play it on seventy-six trombones.

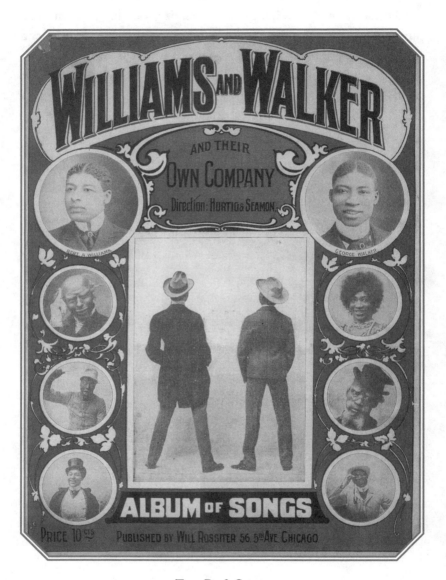

Two Real Coons.

PART III

Black Folks' Opera

Krazy Kat: I dun't sim to reckinize this "sinnery"—Offisa
              "Pupp"—do you?
Officer Pupp: Can't say that I do.
Krazy Kat: S'kwee.
Officer Pupp: Very queer.

Blues into Jazz

The twentieth century began Saturday, January 27, 1917, at the south-west corner of 8th Avenue and 58th Street, New York City, right off Columbus Circle. Now, some may say it began as early as February 15, 1898, in Havana harbor, when the battleship *Maine* kicked off the American Century with a mighty bang. Others may plump for December 17, 1903, atop a hill not far from Kitty Hawk, North Carolina. Still others, the first of July 1916, on the muddy banks of the Somme. And others otherwise. You used to be able to turn up plenty who would put it toward the end of 1917, in St. Petersburg. (There are even a few mechanical souls who insist on January 1, 1901—as if history and chronometry are confixed at every point.) With mine, at least nobody got hurt.

That Saturday night, the Original Dixieland Jass Band opened at the 400 Room on the second floor of Reisenweber's enormous and swank restaurant/nightclub multiplex—dancing until 6 A.M.—and exposed jazz to New York and the world. (The dates are a little tangled here, mostly because Reisenweber's seems to have booked a jazz band of some kind to spark up the dead third-floor Paradise Room starting on the fifteenth, while the ODJB—first acronym in jazz!—was back in Chicago where Reisenweber's found them, holding out for more money. If this is the case, this band failed to titillate and their name is lost to us.) As I write this, Wynton Marsalis's Lincoln Center Jazz Orchestra is slated to move into an elaborate new concert hall going up on Columbus Circle, within pissing range of where Reisenweber's once stood. And so jazz, which forced European art music to retreat into the concert halls, withdraws to a concert hall of its own, not fifty yards from where it launched its first assault. *In girum imus nocte*—we go in circles through the night; I can't for the life of me remember who said that, but he was talking about moths. Still, he knew something about the ways of the world.

They must have been something to see, the ODJB. There were just five of 'em—Nick LaRocca on cornet, clarinetist Larry Shields, and trombonist Eddie Edwards up front, with Henry Ragas on piano and Tony Sbarbaro's drums backing them up—but they made enough noise to get noticed. Within a week, they were pulling in unprecedented crowds of rubbernecks and looky-loos. And first thing Monday morning, they got a note from Columbia Records inviting them to their fourteenth-floor studios in the Manufacturer's Trust building, a block away from the club at 59th and Broadway; they wanted to see what all the fuss was about. The audition was on Wednesday. The band set up; the sharpshooters in charge were distinctly dubious. They didn't even bother to tell the carpenters who were building shelves in the studio to knock off. LaRocca and the boys cut loose with one of their originals. Columbia passed. Noise. Crap.

No matter; on February 26 the ODJB went up to Victor's studio on the top floor of the nondescript brown brick loft building that still stands glumly at 42 West 38th Street (no plaque). The ensuing record—two originals, more or less—hit the stores on March 7 and promptly sold a million and a half copies. (When Columbia looked upon this they began to think the boys may have had something there, after all; on May 31, they had them back over to fake up a couple of current pop numbers.)

Suddenly, jazz was everywhere. If history is, as Hegel maintained, "the march of God through time," then the ODJB was its marching band. Five white kids from New Orleans (their average age was just under twenty-five), by later standards a bunch of mediocrities, they had nonetheless an impeccable sense of just where to be when Clio was looking for new kicks, and—more important—how to act when a goddess smiles upon you. With the pugnacious and far from stupid LaRocca at their head, the boys unshrinkingly spearheaded a blitzkrieg of hot music and hype that took Topworld by assault: no slow percolation here, as with ragtime, no gradual infiltration of Topworld's marches and mains. One minute there's ragtime, the next—jazz. Invented in New Orleans, perfected in Chicago, metastasizing in New York, whence infecting the nation and then the whole goddamn world.

That was—and still pretty much is—the party line, at any rate. The real story, of course, isn't quite that simple. The ODJB was just a thread in a tapestry that can't be unwoven. But it was brightly colored enough to get noticed, like a thread of blaze orange in a fine Tabriz. Just about everyone who has looked into the matter concedes that the boys cut the first records to be explicitly marketed as "jazz." (The obligatory exception: Columbia slipped out a disc labeled as by Borbee's "Jass" Orchestra while Victor's disc was still gestating. But this was mere cashing in: the band's real name was Borbee's *Tango* Orchestra.) The problem is, like the Zapruder film, these discs show everything and nothing—the music is there for everyone to see, but not those shadowy figures who set them up to play it that way. This has allowed a thousand flowers of crank historiography to bloom. Some ofay critics have waved the records around as proof that white boys invented jazz, period—so H. O. Brunn, the ODJB's chronicler; others, black and white, have tagged them as evidence of an attempted robbery of the black man's music that failed only because of the extreme incompetence of the perps. Most of the expertocracy inclines to the latter.

Everyone this side of Brunn would at least agree that Nick and the boys weren't irreplaceable; that even without them, sooner or later Topworld was going to notice that ragtime was mutating in a thousand places into something even worse—looser, faster, noisier, more sexual. Jazz bands (or "jaz," or "jas," or "jass," or even "jasz"—however you spell it, the word seems to have been related to "jism," and, in certain Underworld circles, meant "fuck") had been showcasing this mutation in vaudeville for over a year when the ODJB did their thing. And in fact, weeks before the ODJB's Victor date, the white Coons Collins and Harlan (their hit: "Alexander's Ragtime Band," 1911) had already cut versions of a pretty standard ragtime something-or-other called "That Funny Jas Band from Dixieland" for two different companies, Victor being one of them. But none of that stuff lit the fuse.

The scene in the teens was kind of like that of the mid-seventies, when, against the background of a form of music that was grown old, bands as diverse as the Ramones, Pere Ubu, the Talking Heads, and even the veteran Stooges and New York Dolls were all working on pieces of something new, but nothing really knit them together. It took the Sex Pistols and the name that was pasted on them for people to notice the punk that was there all along, thus exposing big rock's Underworld pretensions as the pathetic sham they had become. Thus the ODJB and ragtime.

Unfortunately for the enquiring mind, the immediate roots of the ODJB are buried far deeper than those of the Sex Pistols, and in the absence of a Rough Trade or a Sire Records to get them on wax and a *Creem* or a *New Musical Express* to cover the honky-tonks, social clubs, barbecues, whorehouses, turpentine camps, and suchlike soil where they were growing, back around the turn of the last century, scholars have had to rely on codgers' memories and the spottily preserved ephemera that Underworld culture tends to throw off—small ads in the back pages of obscure local papers, business cards, ledgers, etc.; even the occasional condescending squib in the national media, such as it was. Fringe stuff, and almost all of it from outside the scene. *Variety*'s bit from November 1916 is uncharacteristically informative:

> Chicago's claim to originating "Jazz Bands" and "Balling the Jack" [a dance with a particularly nasty hip-grind] are as groundless, according to *Variety*'s New Orleans correspondent, as 'Frisco's assuming to be the locale for the first "Toodolo" and "Turkey Trot" dances [equally hot; see A Brief Digression on the State of Vernacular Dance in Progressive America, below]. Little negro tots were "Balling the Jack" in New Orleans over ten years ago, and negro roustabouts were "Turkey Trotting" and doing the "Toodolo" in New Orleans as far back as 1890, he says. "Jazz Bands" have been popular there for over two years, and Chicago cabaret owners brought entertainers from that city to introduce the idea....

Yet even this doesn't help us much—what's the link between jazz bands and ballin' the jack, if any? If jazz bands have been around for only two years, precisely what kind of groove were these "negro tots" and "roustabouts" twisting to back in the day? And just who is this New Orleans correspondent? The questions multiply, and definitive answers—if such can exist in matters human—have gone to the grave with the generation born in the years just after the Civil War. When all is said and done, we're still left holding that record, two songs by a band that called itself "Jass."

As far as enigmatic documents go (e.g., the Rosetta Stone, the Second Amendment), the first jazz record's a live wire. Like your standard fifties R&B 45, Victor 18255 features a fast side and a slow side (well, a slower side). "Dixieland Jass Band One-Step" tears out of the gate like a nitromethane-fueled funny car. Its frame may be ragtime, but somebody has done some serious chopping and channeling, and the engine is definitely not stock. The other side, something openly calling itself "Livery Stable Blues," sounds kinda like the blues we know—the standard changes are dimly discernible (in one of the song's parts, anyway) and there's a good deal of blue tonality being thrown about throughout. But the energy seems all wrong: too frenetic, too driven. (The ODJB were, in part at least, accidental punks: both of their songs were too long to fit on the standard 78, and rather than cut them they speeded everything up. Of such accidents are revolutions made.)

But it's not just a question of drive. Where a ragtime record such as Sousa's "At a Georgia Camp Meeting" is close-order drill, all discipline, precision, and snap, the ODJB record, no matter which side you approach it from, is more like a boardinghouse biscuit-scrum, everyone grabbing at the same time and devil take the hindmost. Now and then—mostly at the beginnings of the verses—you hear all five instruments playing together in the old Sousa and Pryor way, generating a tremendous amount of brass-driven punch. But then Shields's clarinet will tear loose with an unpredictable squeal—at the same time LaRocca's pushing his notes into bleats, Edwards is running his trombone all around the changes and stitching everything together with little smears, and Ragas and Sbarbaro...well, they're pretty hard to hear, save for the occasional snatch of romping piano and some unidentifiable thumping here and there from the drums. For the first time on record, we can hear what happens when you promote the swerve from a means of coloring notes and phrases to an organizing principle—and it's not pretty. All blaring and braying, at first acquaintance these are loud, ugly records that defy easy conceptions of musicality. They're ragtime gone feral. They're rock 'n' roll.

Whatever this music is, it's certainly not jazz as we often hear it today—a couple of guys noodling around in the foreground while a bass player and drummer hold their coats and wait for their own turns to noodle. Here there's no noodling at all. Everyone's phrases are short, punchy, and rhythmic, and they seldom stray far from the business at hand; there are no real solos (in fact, there's no real improvising beyond what occurred when they came up with the tunes: every repeated chorus and verse is played the same way). But neither does anyone hold anyone else's coat. Provided he doesn't step on anybody else's toes, each man's free to construct his part as he sees fit, with nobody telling him different—especially not some guy who wrote a bunch of notes down on paper.

Those little black crotchets and quavers caused the boys a little legal trouble that neatly illuminates the revolution that they ushered in. In fact, *both* sides of Victor 18255 saw them in court. One of the three strains of "Dixieland Jass Band One-Step," it turns out, was lifted from black ragtimer Joe Jordan's 1909 "That Teasin' Rag." He sued and won. That at least was pretty straightforward. Not so the courtroom wrangling with Alcide "Yellow" Nuñez, the band's former clarinetist, over the ownership of "Livery Stable Blues." After much amusing (to the press, anyway) back and forth about who could and who couldn't read music—the band's official position was that reading music was for squares—the judge threw the case out. As far as he was concerned, once you stripped away everybody's improvised parts, there was no tune left to fight over. Ragtime was music, all right; the blues were something else.

♪

The Origins of Jazz. Even the most half-assed and cavalier thumb-through of the voluminous literature on American music will show you that this perennial head-scratcher is inextricably intertwined with that other famous head-scratcher, The Birth of the Blues. Everyone more or less agrees on that. But then the theories—blues came first, jazz came first; all jazz is blues, all blues is jazz (that should of course be "are," but what do you want, good grammar or good English?—besides, Robert Johnson says "the blues *is* a lowdown shakin' chill," which is good enough for me); jazz is American, blues is African (few get further into the Dark Continent than that—as if a Yoruba prince, a Mande gold trader, and a Hausa woodcutter are all going to have the same music in 'em); jazz is African, blues is American; blues is country, jazz is city; blues is black, jazz is creole—or even purely white—and so forth. All of them are right—well, all except the last one, which is patent bullshit no matter what Mr. Brunn may say. The problem lurks in the whats—what is jazz, what is the blues, what's the difference between them.

One of the deepest-clinging foundations of historiography is that, when presented with a complex phenomenon about which there exists a large body of conflicting theories, you whiffle. Punt. Pass the buck. Just toss 'em all on the table and let the poor bloody reader sort 'em out. Maybe afterward you can cautiously venture a well-hedged opinion or two of your own—"the consensus of the best authorities seems to indicate that the blues is one of the formative influences on jazz, but solid evidence for this is sparse and sometimes contradictory." Rather than perpetuate such pudding-livered waffle, I'll take my stand here and now: when you strip it naked, jazz = ragtime + blues. No blues, no jazz, it's that simple. Nothing new here, certainly; the only oddity is that some gents can be found to deny it, but that's their misfortune and none of my own. And so, the blues.

♪

Everyone pretty much knows whence the blues: slavery's first child, conceived in the miscegenation between field-holler and big-house hymn, born in a cotton field, raised in a juke joint, nursed on knife-drawn blood and cheap corn whiskey, as old as the swamps and young as last Saturday night, rough and tough and bad to the bone—you know how the tune goes. But as for *what* it is, well...it's a slippery sonofabitch. Unfortunately, that's a question you just can't dodge: when it comes to finding the hot in American music, the blues is so high you can't get over it, so low you can't get under it, so wide you can't get around it. There's at least a spoonful of it in just about every record I'll be talking about from here on.

The first problem is, when we say "the blues," we're really talking about two different things: a certain kind of song and a musical mode (basically, a particular way of tempering the scale—although the musicologists might quibble with this). Usually where you find one, there's the other, but not always.

One thing that seems clear, to me at least, is that it all begins with the mode. When folks insist that the blues is as old as the hills, that it goes back to Africa, this is what they're talking about.

In 1853, Frederick Law Olmsted (the guy who built Central Park) heard a South Carolina railroad gang singing on the job: "One raised such a sound as I had never heard before, a long, loud musical shout, rising and falling and breaking into falsetto, his voice ringing through the woods...like a bugle call. As he finished, the melody was caught up by another, and then another, then by several in chorus."

That "rising and falling and breaking into falsetto" is the mode of the blues. Harvard archaeologist Charles Peabody heard it in the Mississippi Delta in 1901, when he heard a lullaby that was "quite impossible to copy, weird in interval and strange in rhythm; peculiarly beautiful." White observers always had trouble notating black American music, as we saw with ragtime. At least ragtime tended to follow straight European harmony, Arthur Pryor's smears and whatever unrecorded geniuses from whom he filched them notwithstanding. The blues mode, its scale, has too few notes, and the ones it does have tend to get mangled: *do-re-mi &c.* becomes something like *do*-(no *re*)-almost *mi-fa*-almost *so*-(no *la*)-*ti* flat, more or less-*do*. It's neither major nor minor. You can't play it on the piano without recourse to trickery.

Furthermore, none of these notes are really stable: they have a tendency to bend, to flutter, to slide into each other or stretch away. Ragtime, stretching as it does back—however indirectly—to the dances slaves used to temporarily forget the shittiness of their lot, is at heart drum music, rhythm music. It's all about setting up patterns— drive. The blues comes from the songs they sang the rest of the time, and it belongs first and foremost to the human voice. And it's all about avoiding patterns—swerve.

Ever since Plato, the thought gang has recognized that different harmonies have different emotional effects on the listener. The Greeks, being rational almost past the point of reason, parsed these quite precisely. The scale characteristic of the Ionians (essentially a C major) was hard and prickly, that of the Phrygians (a distinctly Oriental E minor with flat 2nd and 6th) wild and exciting; of the Dorians (D minor 7), sedate, sober, manly; of the Lydians (F major with augmented 4th; weird), soft and sad, etc. (of course, try to find two Greek writers to agree on the details of this scheme...). At any rate, if you got the harmony right, you could inspire your pha- lanx to crush the next town's; wrong and you ended up chained to an oar. This scheme isn't as eccentric as it seems; even now, the major scale is sunshine to the moonlight of the minor (= the Aeo- lian mode, which the Greeks thought pompous; hard to find some- thing more culturally variable than the meaning of music).

So what are we supposed to feel, listening to this mode's (to Western ears) off notes and unstable harmonies? What's the char- acteristic effect of the... "Senegambian" mode, let's call it, if only because the area between the Senegal and Gambia rivers was the first to send its unwilling sons and daughters to the New World. (I don't mean to suggest that the blues is African; the way it turned out, mode and song together, it's American, through and through—

let's say the mode it embodies calls up a synthetic memory of African music rather than being anything an individual back in West Africa would be able to pin down as the music she grew up with.) At any rate, it sounds better than "Mississippian mode." But back to our question. The vernacular hands us a big fat clue.

"The blues" as slang for depression goes way back—at least to 1839, as the following bit of fictionalized Coonspeak from the New Orleans *Times-Picayune* illustrates:

Sam Jonsing: I feels bad—I'se got what de white folks calls de bloos, and de wos sort at dat, dat's what I has...
Pete Gumbo: De what you call 'em, Sam?
Sam Jonsing: De bloos—de raal indigo bloos.

Mr. Jonsing then proceeds to define the blues in various terms, including a man's feeling bad when he gets up in the morning, and "wusser" when he goes to bed at night, and thinking that "his body is made ob ice cream, all 'cept his heart, and dat—dat's a piece ob lead in de middle." (Easy to turn this into a blues: "Oh, my body's ice cream and my heart is made of lead"—see below.) So the blues is the mode of the lowdown ache—a harmonic gloss on Jeremiah's lament, "Wherefore came I forth out of the womb to see labour and sorrow?" Loneliness, abandonment, disenfranchisement, rejection, exploitation, pointlessness, boredom—all the Prozac emotions, plus horniness.

But, as we all know, there's more to the blues than that. The blues is like Leviathan, in the book of Job, in whose "neck remaineth strength and sorrow is turned to joy before him"; its tonality isn't minor or major, neither pure sorrow nor pure joy, but something partaking of both. The carefully cultivated instability that's at the heart of the blues, the seemingly random (but actually willed) swerve—a moment of sickening tonal freefall, but contained—can somehow turn that sorrow into joy or, to be more precise, ecstasy: be it religious, sexual, terpsichorean, or even destructive and violent.

The Senegambian mode is tough to rope into European classical theories of music—if music is, as Samuel Johnson defined it, the "science of harmonic sounds," then the blues ain't it. Since antiquity, European music theory has been based on the assumption that music is mathematics in action. Numbers, however, don't improvise; making it up as you go along has always been a part of the European tradition, sure—the so-called "figured bass" of harpsichord music is the classic example—but it's always been marginal, something you do but don't talk about. The blues calls for a new kind of science, one that can deal with the same process turning out differently every time you run it. A chaos theory, in short.

If classical music is math, the blues is English. It's like an animated conversation, where every word's timing, accent, intonation is variable with the speaker, and every variation carries meaning (e.g., that old Benny Hill riff on the title of "What Is This Thing Called Love?"—"What Is *This* Thing Called, Love?"; "What *Is* This Thing Called, Love?"; et cetera). Every note is vocalized, turned into surrogate words, and every musical phrase can carry that same burden of meaning. What makes all this even more difficult for the dicty musician to pin down is that this swerve is often very subtle, a matter of split-second timing (as in ragtime) and infinitesimal harmonic hanky-panky. Easy to shoot for, easier to miss.

There's something else. When we think of someone singing the blues—or gospel, or soul, for that matter—there's a voice attached to that thought. And it's gruff, rough, tough, and anything but pretty. One thing the many discrete musics of the Dark Continent have in common is an abhorrence of the "pure" unmodified tone. Take the banjo, for example, where the pure vibrations of the strings are corrupted by the drumhead's snap. The European way with a string is to isolate its tone and enhance it; give it as much resonance as possible. In Africa, lyres have rattles tied to the ends of the strings, drums have rings of little bells around the heads, some dancers' masks have kazoos hidden in the mouth-holes, while "other masked singers," as Palmer remarks, use "deep chest growls, false bass tones produced in the back of the throat, strangulated shrieks, and other deliberately bizarre effects." This obsession with tonal weirdness is no more odd than the European obsession with tonal purity—nothing in African music could be as strange as the castrati—but its results are certainly less predictable, even after generations of bubbling away at the bottom of the melting pot.

It's not that the blues is entirely without system. Like any kind of music, with the possible exception of the more yowlerific and unlistenable products of the twentieth-century avant-garde, it's a language, and like any language the blues has ways of saying things that make sense and ways that don't. You can jiggle the words and phrases, twist them, recombine them. But you can't just wrench the grammar around at random. In practical terms, this means that the Senegambian mode is articulated through a whole crazy quilt of stock figures, patterns, riffs, licks. Traditional ways of saying things, each with just enough spin to make it new.

Now, at the cusp of the blues' third calendar century, it's difficult to hear these licks with fresh ears. There's a tendency to just boot up hazy images of Woodstock, of Alvin Lee playing *all* of them— every blues lick ever conceived—in about eighty-five seconds flat, and then doing it over and over again. All the swerve has been drained out of them; they're carved in granite like a Maya Lin memorial. I won't launch into a rant about Eric Clapton, bluesman; or the irony of superannuated black performers singing about shotgun shacks and cotton fields for audiences of J. Crew–clad yuppies. In "I Got Mine" days, the blues was alive and strong and not at all respectable, and all those bendy, twisted chains of notes actually meant something.

♪

By the turn of the twentieth century, the blues as mode had completely permeated the so-called "Negro Spiritual" (with certain exceptions for the pigeon-tailed coats, patent leather shoes, and white shirt fronts that so pissed off Polk Miller; see Part II)—had been there for generations, was nurtured there, and through it become ubiquitous in Underworld black song—without ringing Topworld alarms; as religious music, it seemed pretty nonthreatening, and the intellectuals liked it, in a patronizing sort of way (remember Dvořák?). And threads of it were woven through ragtime and minstrel music before that (the "St. Louis Tickle" is a prime example). But it was only when the Senegambian mode found a secular genre entirely of its own that black vernacular music started to get recognized as something different in essence from the music of the American cracker. It took a song to trigger this, one that brought all the free-floating blue riffs together into something Topworld could recognize as separate from the old hymns and the mangled little jigs of the slaves and their children: "The [Fill-in-the-Blank] Blues." In fact, this catchy and malleable old chestnut was probably based on a white hymn—the eccentric but brilliant blues researcher Stephen Calt nominates the English Methodist Charles Wesley's "Roll Jordan," which was kicking around the backwoods of America by 1801, if not earlier. One day, the theory goes, instead of "I want to go to heaven, I do / I want to go to heaven, I do" somebody somewhere (where? see below) sang something like "I want to drink turpentine and die / I want to drink turpentine and die." And then she (just as likely as he) rhymed it off with a capper like "I'll see my little baby by and by." Somebody else added a verse here, another there, and you know the rest. The farther it grew away from Wesley's hymn, the more it picked up from the pool of West Africanisms that lay just beneath the surface of black American music—call and response, whoops, bends, and so forth.

Like any good underground music—jump, rockabilly, funk, you name it—this knot of blue was easy to teach to the musically illiterate homeboy and a bitch for the musically literate (i.e. Topworld) outsider to bash out convincingly. At first glance, there isn't much to it. Twelve bars long, more or less (there are also eight- and six-teen-bar blues—particularly favored by jazzbos—but twelve is the standard), thus: I / I / I / I / IV / IV / I / I / V7 / V7 / I / I. Those are the standard chord symbols, the conventional way that musicians harmonize the blues. What they break down to, for any-one who's never picked up a guitar or blown a harp, is this:

- two bars (plus one beat): a vocal line, starting and generally ending on the keynote, *do*, with accents on the two and four— "The blues ain't nothin' but a good man feelin' bad" (/ I / I /)
- two bars (minus one beat): an instrumental fill, also on *do* (/ I / I /)
- two bars (plus one beat): the same vocal line, but often moved up the scale three steps to *fa*, although still ending back down on *do* (/ IV / IV /)
- two bars (minus one beat): back to *do* for another instrumen-tal fill (/ I / I /)
- two bars (plus one beat): a different vocal line, starting four steps up at *so* and rhyming with the first one, capping it off— "Oh! That's a feelin' that I've often had" (/ V7 / V7 /—or / V7 / IV7 /)
- two bars (minus one beat): a final fill in *do* (/ I / I /)

And that's it: no verse/chorus metastructure, no bridge, no three themes as in marches, cakewalks, rags; just those twelve bars, over and over and over again.

To balance out the monotony, there's headspace built into every part of the structure. If that business of the plus and minus one beats doesn't throw the sheet-music crowd (which, just to compli-cate things, occurs in the vocal/lead line, and not in the accompa-nying harmony), this is pretty much sure to. The fills can be one or two notes or a hundred. Or none at all—silence. Or you can take up the space with words, repeating the first phrase, commenting on it, adding to it, responding to its call. Or you can just moan. The fills can be two bars long, three bars, three-and-a-half bars, one-and-a-half bars, whatever. They can be all the same, or cleverly varied. You can add instruments, get whole sections of them ad libbing the fills or riffing them out in lockstep. The tempo can be a jaunty lope, a flat-out tear, a bone-weary stumble, almost none at all. You can substitute chords in various places, make it elegant with a gussied-up harmony and some smooth chord voicings—up to a point. You can also say to hell with harmony; just set up a simple riff on *do* and hang on to it while your voice does the moving—see John Lee Hooker. But at root, no matter how you play it, it's just one song—provided you stay within the Senegambian mode. If you did everything I just said but used, let's say, major seventh chords throughout—those soft, jazzy chords that America (the band) strummed into oblivion on "Horse with No Name"—or even plain old major chords, or minor ones for that matter, you'd get music, but it would be nothing like the blues.

As for the words. These, too, tend to be improvised, and there's a sackful of stock phrases that singers tend to throw in without paying overmuch attention to English 101 concepts like "thematic coherence" and "rhetorical structure." What they have in common is their selfishness: when I sing the blues, it's my problems that make me sing, not yours or those of the fellow down the street who bagged his wife indulging in a bit of how's your father with the UPS guy. The blues song is all about me. If I sing about you, it's only to emphasize how you treated me like shit.

There was always a healthy strain of egocentrism running through the American musical vernacular—"Dixie," "Camptown Races," "All Coons Look Alike to Me," "In the Shade of the Old Apple Tree"— to choose but a few random examples out of a multitude—are all in the first person. But the blues takes this to an extreme: those four songs, as is general in nineteenth-century American music, weave the "I" into a story, a narrative about other people, places, events.

The blues shrinks this circle of experience to a hula-hoop; the blues singer's world spins tightly around her or him, never beyond arm's reach. "If I feel tomorrow like I feel today / I'll pack my suitcase, make my getaway" (traditional); "I asked for water, and she gave me gasoline" (Tommy Johnson); "I was up this mornin', my blues walkin' like a man" (Robert Johnson); "I was once a married woman, sorry the day I was" (Mary Johnson); "I cried and worried, all night I laid and groaned" (Bessie Smith). The most important word in the blues is "I," in all its inflections. When Dan Emmett sings,

> I come to town de udder night,
> I hear de noise an saw de fight
> De watch-man was a runnin roun,
> Cryin, Old Dan Tucker's come to town
> So get out de way!
> Get out de way!
> Get out de way! Old Dan Tucker,
> You're too late to come to supper.

the "I" is there, but it's just an observer, watching. The real badman is in the third person. Same with non- or pre-blues black songs like "Stagger Lee" and "Railroad Bill," "John Henry" and even "Frankie and Johnny."

Now take, for random example, Jelly Roll Morton's "Winin' Boy Blues," cut for the Library of Congress in 1938 but composed back in the oughts, when he was a whorehouse professor in New Orleans:

> I'm the Winin' Boy, don't deny my name.
> I'm the Winin' Boy, don't deny my name.
> Pick it up an' shake it like sweet Stavin' Chain,
> I'm the Winin' Boy, don't deny my name.

No hero here but Jelly Roll (Dictionary of the Vulgar Tongue: "Winin' Boy" = "Windin' Boy," where *wind = grind*).

𝅘𝅥𝅮

The blues may have been personal, but it sure as hell wasn't nice. In both song and mode it was pure Underworld, and—unlike ragtime—determined to stay that way. Even in the Senegambian mode's most "elevated" form, the spiritual, it isn't triumphalist (whites sing hymns, blacks sing spirituals; that's the way the ofays saw it, anyway—best to keep the hymns uncontaminated, what what). The most ecstatic evocation of Glory Land still tends to contain a memory of melancholia. As Lucretius says,

> ...*medio in fonte leporum*
> *surgit amari aliquid quod in ipsis floribus angat* (IV, 1133–4).

> ...amid a fountain of delights
> there's always something bitter welling up
> that vexes us among the very flowers.

Even in the sweetest black gospel records I know, the six songs cut for Okeh in 1923 by the two anonymous women and one anonymous man calling themselves the Kentucky Trio—things like "Mother's Religion" and "Shine for Jesus"—the *amari aliquid*, the something bitter, is there in the way the voices ever so slightly bend and thicken as they blend together.

In the mode's least elevated form, it's downright scary. Consider another blues Jelly Roll Morton recorded for the Library of Congress (discs 1669B–1672B), this one sung from a woman's point of view. It starts off like so:

If you don't leave my fuckin' man alone,
If you don't leave my fuckin' man alone,
You won't know what way that you will go home.
I'll cut your throat and drink your fuckin' blood like wine.
Bitch, I'll cutcher fuckin' throat, drink your blood like wine,
Because I want you t'know, he's a man of mine.

What follows is up and down filthy and unbelievably brutal—and
long. Seven sides, thirty-plus minutes, of *crime passionnelle* and pun-
ishment—a bloody, sadistic murder ("she pulled out a pistol, shot
her in the eye, / she said open your legs you dirty bitch I'm gonna
shoot you right between your thighs"), a swift trial, and a whole lot
of graphic jailhouse lesbianism. You couldn't play it on the radio then
and you can't now. But even the most pornographic parts of "The
Murder Ballad" are delivered with complete *sang froid*: as it goes on
and on, Morton spins out lines like "she said, I'm gonna get some
of this cunt, you bitch" without batting an eyelash or creasing a smirk.
What's more, Morton's weary, matter-of-fact drawl adds a dignity to
the story, restores the dimension of tragedy to it. Most paradoxical.
You could cut the smut and keep the hard-luck story, but the song
would actually *lose* its emotional punch.

The commercial record companies could never put out anything
as salty as "The Murder Ballad," but they came close—blues records,
once they start appearing in large numbers in the twenties, keep it real
more than any other music of the day. Back in the teens, however,
the blues was still a deep-cover Underworld thing. Ragtime seemed
unstoppable, invulnerable, even if it was conquering Topworld's
music in large part by accommodating itself to dicty norms. Everything was light and bouncy, everybody was happy. When the blues
began to filter up, it was Lucretius's something bitter. You can't
sweeten it up the way you could ragtime, almost out of existence.

There's no way to blue up an aria or a concerto and still have it
recognizable—the way the Senegambian mode shuns the pure, even,

tempered tone is a negation, a critique of European music, and you can't apply it to operatic melodies without transforming them utterly. The blues transforms not only the melody, but the rules that lie behind it. It's incompatible with European music in a way ragtime wasn't. Sure, you can write Senegambian-mode concertos—Ellington's "Black, Brown and Beige"—and even operas—*Porgy and Bess*—but you've got to start pretty much from scratch. So a blues *Rigoletto—Negroletto?*—nah. (One of the earliest black claims for the blues—it keeps coming up in the teens—is that it was "colored folks' opera." In other words, opera reconstructed on a Senegambian foundation. Perceptive.)

This stubbornness is heuristic, semiotic, hermeneutic, whatever. It means something. The blues is—was—a music of (oblique) resistance: like gangsta rap, it refused to aspire. For Topworld, this is the ultimate sin. Slackness. The blues stood for the utter lack of that "extraordinary gift for hope" that redeemed Gatsby (at least to Nick Carraway). You couldn't call Bessie Smith hopeful. Lively, sure, but not optimistic. Ragtime had hope; it aspired to integrate, admittedly sometimes against long odds. Scott Joplin poured most of his creative juices into *Treemonisha,* an ill-starred "grand opera" with syncopation (but don't, he insisted, call it ragtime). It was first performed in its entirety in 1972. Even Coon songs aspired, at least the ones by black writers. J. Rosamond Johnson—James Weldon Johnson's brother (together, they dashed off stuff like "Lift Ev'ry Voice and Sing")—used to perform "All Coons Look Alike to Me" as "All Boys &c." Much less offensive, and just as catchy. When James Weldon set to writing Coon songs, he kept the dialect and got rid of the trashy behavior. The result was, among other hits, "Under the Bamboo Tree"—you know, "If you lak-a-me, lak I lak-a-you / And we lak-a-both the same," that one. Cute stuff, no razors. In short, ragtime was starting to tone itself down. As our pop history has a way of demonstrating over and over, that's the cue for things to start jiggling again; for something Underworld to bob up. If you put American culture on the couch, you know commitment issues would come up, and soon.

♪

How did Topworld get the blues? A little where and when is in order. If you haul out your Rand-McNally and trace out an appropriately coffin-shaped irregular octagon around the points Memphis–Little Rock–Dallas–Houston–New Orleans–Mobile–Montgomery–Birmingham, you'll get where the song started. The when can be fixed at some time between 1890, when the codgers remembered first hearing the "earth-born music," as W. C. Handy called it, that they later identified as the blues, and 1908, when the first blues was published as sheet music. So: some 185,633 square miles—an area just about the size of Spain—and eighteen years to lose yourself in.

In a perfect world, now I'd talk about the songs that these old-timers witnessed—quote a verse or two, pin down precisely where and when. In this world, however, I can't do that. Basically, there's sweet Fanny Adams to go on until about 1902. Scraps—circumstantial and (slenderly) anecdotal. Topworld showed no interest in the history of the rural blues until the late fifties, and by then anyone who had been around the hood (or running away from it) in 1890 or so was tuning up for the choir eternal. And so all who write about this topic, specifics failing them, have recourse to Handy's sly and sprightly autobiography, which has a fat chapter on how he discovered the blues while leading a band out of Clarksdale, Mississippi.

In the heart of the Yazoo river delta—the tract of rich bottom-land east of the Mississippi stretching from just south of Memphis to just north of Vicksburg—Clarksdale was supposedly the site of Robert Johnson's crossroads (in case the devil keeps you waiting, you'll now find a Church's Fried Chicken there). Blues country. But Handy was a tourist in the Delta: born in the hills of northwest

Alabama, he had spent most of his adult life playing cornet with minstrel bands, from Montana to Havana. In other words, God knows what was going on down there before he showed up.

If, however, you had to pick a place and time off the top of your head for the blues to spring up, it would be the Delta in the 1890s. It's not that black suffering was more intense there than in, say, Georgia; nor that it had a monopoly on lynchings and other white mob violence. It's not even that such unspeakable sports were particularly frequent there. But the Delta had a despair of its own. It had been left largely untouched during slavery days, an unappetizing but virgin tangle of cypress swamp and thick, feculent forest broken only by the occasional isolated cotton plantation. After the war, the few white planters kept their freedmen on to sharecrop—which usually ended up as a form of debt slavery. The coming of the railroad in the late 1800s brought in more planters, and with them a host of rootless young black men and women to clear the forests and drain the swamps and raise the cotton. If these workers expected and hoped for a better shake—this was the New South, and everyone was starting over—they were doomed to disappointment.

Disappointment. And terror—the planters and the white townsfolk (who, truth be told, were often little better off than their black victims) ruthlessly put down by means illegal or legal (whatever "legal" means in a situation like this) any attempt to reshuffle the cards, no matter how trifling or symbolic. Between 1882 and 1903, white Mississippians lynched 294 black Mississippians, not counting the ones they did away with in massacres and (mostly one-sided) "race wars." There was nowhere to turn; no black middle class to aspire to, no way to reach an accommodation with the man. One Delta vet asked, "You know what it was like for the Indians, surrounded by fifty whites with rifles? Then you know what it was like in the Delta." There's no point in a dead Indian trying to get ahead, aiming for Topworld.

Maybe the oldtimer was exaggerating; maybe things weren't that bad. But I think not. When the record companies turned their attention to the hinterlands of the South, in the mid to late twenties, they cast their nets wide and hauled in a pretty good sample of what folks were digging on, black and white. Nowhere are the musics of the two races farther apart. In Tennessee, in Georgia, Alabama, Missouri, the Carolinas, Virginia, even elsewhere in Mississippi, you hear black musicians focusing on the blues, sure—it was hot, it was what the A&R men were asking for. But there's usually some reflection of the common—that is, Coon—musical style and repertoire of the turn of the twentieth century, a repertoire which the ofay songsters and fiddle bands were busy strip mining for the mike. You'll almost always hear a raggy guitar here, a jig-step there, a ruefully comic little ditty about a Coon who got over or a bad one who got cut down. None of that in the Delta. It's pretty much all blues, deep and dark and very, very intense. If the blues didn't first crystallize on the Delta's plantations, at least it found its most fertile soil there.

In any case, at some point, in some place, the various improvised riffs and verses that had been floating around the black South (like the ones the Dinwiddie Colored Quartet and their ilk were pulling together; see Part II) began to be perceived as separate, discrete songs. "The Funky Butt." "Alabama Bound." "Make Me a Pallet on Your Floor." "Sliding Delta." "Poor Boy Long Ways from Home." With the "new" songs came a "new" instrument. Visualize a bluesman. I doubt very highly he's picking on a banjo. That's because sometime around 1900, the venerable skin-box virtually disappeared from rural black music. Perhaps it was just too polluted, too laden with cotton bolls and headscarves, rolling eyeballs, black-dirt levees and—especially—burnt cork. Or perhaps the reason was strictly musical—the wider melodic spaces of the blues needed a guitar's ring to fill them. A banjo note speaks and it's gone; quick and loud. A guitar note lingers a while, lets you set up the next one without rushing and milk every bend and smear for its maximum emotional valence—especially if you use a slide, a trick at which many Delta players were adept. (As for that slide: as far as can be determined, the technique of fretting the guitar with a sliding metal or glass bar owes its central place in the blues to a nifty little land grab the U.S. pulled off in 1898, when it moved to annex the democratic constitutional monarchy of Hawaii, thus providing the proximate cause for a flood of guitar-sliding Hawaiian acts to wash through the nation's various vaudeville circuits and enabling W. C. Handy to encounter, sometime around 1903, "a loose-jointed negro" sliding a knife along the strings of his guitar as he sang the blues—"the weirdest music I had ever heard," as Handy recalled. It got under his skin, with momentous results.)

In the hot summer of 1895, a Georgia minstrel named Billy McClain rented out Ambrose Park, a private pleasure garden on the South Brooklyn waterfront, and staged "Black America," an outdoor extravaganza that attempted to do for its namesake what Buffalo Bill was doing for the West (perhaps the appropriate preposition is "to," but no matter). A photo from Black America entitled "Leisure Moments"—how black folk relax today—shows a group of well-dressed gents in their shirtsleeves sitting on a porch with a lady. The fellow in the corner is playing a guitar. A generation earlier, it would have been a banjo. As plenty of other pictures from the time demonstrate, when they were being professional Coons black musicians were still playing the banjo; when they were playing for each other, the guitar was the cutting edge. So total was this rejection that one white banjoist could opine, in 1891, that "the banjo is not of negro origin" and that "ten negroes play violins, harmonicas and guitars to one who plays the banjo—it must have started on the minstrel stage." (I should point out, though, that a four-string version of the banjo did remain standard in the rhythm section of black—and white—jazz bands through the twenties; it cut through the smutch better than the guitar. But those guys always sat in the back and wore tuxes. No danger of being taken for Coons. And see below, under James Reese Europe.)

In any case, music and technology walked hand in hand, as they tend to—in 1894, as Paul Oliver points out in *Songsters & Saints,* Gibson started making cheap guitars for the mass market. Competition followed. In 1900, both Gibson and Martin (the industry leaders) introduced steel string models, with a much louder, harder sound than the old gut-strung models. In 1908, Sears had a guitar with all the accessories going for $1.89. Even a field hand could afford that. (You could get them for less: around 1901, future bluesman Mississippi John Hurt's sharecropper parents bought him a guitar; it only cost $1.50.)

♪

By the oughts, folks were starting to take notice. When, down there in Clarksdale, W. C. Handy replaced some of the cakewalks and presentation pieces for which his dicty nine-man Knights of Pythias band was known ("they were all musicians who bowed strictly to the authority of printed notes") with simple arrangements of a few local favorites, rough stuff like the "distinctly Negroid 'Make Me a Pallet on Your Floor,'" he suddenly started pulling in all the good gigs. Political campaigns and whorehouses—where the real money was. That was in 1903. "The world is powerfully big, and a queer place," as he later observed.

A year later (she said it was in 1902, but '04 is much more likely), the eighteen-year-old Ma Rainey heard the blues somewhere in Missouri, where she was touring with a second-string tent show— the bottom rung of Georgia minstrelsy. (Hard to imagine her singing anything but the blues, but she did, and there's a hairy version of "At a Georgia Camp Meeting" she cut in 1927 to prove it.) Like Handy, she thought it was strange stuff when she heard it, but she added it to her show anyway. Down Home audiences responded mightily. And so she and Handy—and many another who catered to black Underworld's entertainment needs—started programming more and more of this new-old sound. Soon, by dint of the constant touring that low-level vaudeville required, they spread it through-out black America. Eventually, white folks—and respectable black ones—would have to take notice. But that would take sheet music or records, because respectable folk didn't attend tent shows or the theaters of the all-black vaudeville circuit, the TOBA (Theatre Owners' Booking Association, aka Tough On Black Asses). Mean-while, a generation of black stars rose and set who left their only legacy in the music of their imitators and plagiarizers: names like String Beans (né Butler May, aka "The Elgin Movements Man," aka "the blues master piano player of the world;" he died in 1917, age 23); John H. Williams ("The Original Blue Steel"); H. "Kid" Love; Johnnie Woods and his dummy, Henry (the earliest known act to sing the blues on stage); Willie and Lulu Too Sweet; Hop Hopson; and H. Franklin "Baby" Seals.

Out of all of these, Baby Seals actually got something on paper; in fact, he was the first black man to publish a blues, in 1912 (his only previous song was a certain "Shake, Rattle and Roll"—about shooting craps; New Orleans vaudeville Coon Al Bernard cut a version in 1919). Here, as everywhere, the black musician's alien-ation from the means of production held him back: Antonio Mag-gio, another one of those New Orleans Sicilians who keep inserting themselves into the Annals of Hot (cf. Nick LaRocca, Louis Prima, and Frankie "Sea Cruise" Ford, né Guzzo), got a four-year jump on him with an "up-to-date rag" called "I Got the Blues." But Mag-gio's number got no action. "Baby Seals Blues," arranged by black St. Louis ragtimer Artie Matthews, did a little better. Not a Top-world hit, it nonetheless went down well with Southern black audiences—in fact, it probably did as much to spread the blues as anything by W. C. Handy, at least among blacks. "Baby Seals Blues" eventually made it on record in 1923, when Louis Mitchell (an expatriate Philadelphian) cut it in Paris. By then, Baby Seals had been dead for eight years, long enough for his name to fade; Mitchell put his song out as "Sing 'Em Blues," the first words of the refrain. One other version later that year (again as "Sing 'Em Blues"), by the now-obscure TOBA star Charles Anderson—a drag queen/blues yodeler, no less—and fade to silence.

The next two blues out of the gate also came in 1912, and they made Topworld notice them. "Dallas Blues" by Hart A. Wand, a white fiddler/bandleader out of Oklahoma City (and hence the forefather of Western Swing), was a moderate hit and became a jazz standard. And then came W. C. Handy's self-published "Memphis Blues," an outgrowth of those early Clarksdale experiments with disciplining the blues. Big hit, even if not quite so huge as to make everybody fall out moaning "Oh, mama, could this really be the end." But besides selling a bunch of copies, the "Memphis Blues" had implications, which we'll get to below. The year 1913 saw the first straight twelve-bar blues published, "Nigger Blues," by the diminutive white Coon Leroy "'Lasses" White, then of Texas, later—twenty years later, actually—of the Grand Old Opry (and later still of Hollywood and B westerns). The epithet here is generic, telling the listener what kind of music he or she's going to get, and the song is the first collection of those free-floating blues verses that every bluesman knew, that every singer threw into a song when they couldn't think of anything else to sing. "The blues ain't nothing but a good man feeling bad" and such. "Throw your hands up in the air / and wave 'em like you just don't care," as the rappers say ('Lasses finally cut a version of his song for Victor in 1935; newly sensitized, they wouldn't release it).

One of the things the blues has in common with jazz is that they were both first recorded by ofays. The Victor Military Band cut the "Memphis Blues" on July 15 (Vic. 17619), 1914; Prince's Band covered it on Columbia nine days later (Col. A-5591; they also cut the first "St. Louis Blues" in December, 1915, on Col. A-5772).

That year also saw the first vocal blues—at least, the first vocal records titled and marketed as such—but these belong to the almost vanished world of vaudeville, and information on them is practically nonexistent. For the record, one Morton Harvey is generally held to have gotten there first with "Memphis Blues," issued by Victor in January, 1915. Eh. Marginally more interesting is a 1916 version of "Nigger Blues" by George O'Connor (Col. A-2064).

Like the ODJB, O'Connor was a bleached American of the white persuasion, but there the resemblance ends: if he was a Coon by night, when the sun shone he was a bigshot Washington lawyer and lobbyist (Nick LaRocca and Eddie Edwards, the ODJB's trombone man, were electricians). Nor was Mr. O'Connor just any Coon: he was minstrel to the White House for seven administrations, from Taft to Truman (some even tack on McKinley and Roosevelt the Elder). Comment would be superfluous. A blues singer, he's not—he's got a handle on the form, but the swerve escapes him. He knocks out the phrases like they were subsections of the Maryland Rules of Civil Procedure. But the "Nigger Blues" is a hell of a lot closer to our idea of the blues than Handy's composition. The song, not the singer.

After this, you can chart the blues' invasion of Topworld by the records it left behind. (To make things easier, most of these have been reissued.) The first black artist to cut a blues was probably clarinetist Wilbur Sweatman, who did Handy's "Joe Turner Blues" in April, 1917, with a saxophone sextet (modeled on the then-popular, now-lame Six Brown Brothers; Pathé 20167). That was an instrumental, as were the records Handy himself made later that year. A black person didn't sing the "proper" blues—the song; the twelve bars—on record until mid-1920, when Mamie Smith and her Jazz Hounds cut the epochal "Crazy Blues" (Okeh 4169; see below). Fletcher Henderson cut "The Unknown Blues," a good bet for the first piano blues instrumental, in 1921 (Black Swan 2026).

The first guitar blues by a black artist came in late 1923, when Sylvester Weaver accompanied the popular and frequently recorded Sara Martin (aka "the colored Sophie Tucker") on a couple of numbers, "Longing for Daddy Blues" and "I've Got to Go and Leave My Daddy Behind." The first *real* "country" blues record—where a rustic fresh from the backcountry moans lugubriously while spasmodically strumming a guitar; you know, the blues like its mama would recognize—didn't come until March or April 1924. That's when a certain Ed Andrews came before Okeh's field unit in Atlanta to cut "Barrel House Blues" and "Time Ain't Gonna Make Me Stay" (Okeh 8137); he never recorded again. (Sylvester Weaver had cut a couple of guitar blues back at that session in 1923, but they were instrumentals—fully realized, sophisticated harbingers of the next twenty years worth of blues guitar, but instrumentals.)

But the first blues to really freak Topworld out *en masse* was still "Livery Stable Blues." Whatever its exact relationship with that stuff Handy was digging on in Clarksdale and Tutwiler and Indianola and Hushpuckena, it's the first record to take the ferocious drive of the brass bands and swerve the bejeezus out of it. The military bands and their blues records were the inoculation, the ODJB—live virus. And—this is the part that appeals to me most—it scared a lot of folks (generally the ones you'd expect) witless. Others it left feeling that their lives had utterly changed forever. A lot of others—it did sell those million and a half copies. Whether it got its swerve directly or indirectly, through imitation or osmosis, it got it from the blues. And now that we've found ourselves back where we started, let's pause for a moment to ponder the historian Hugh Thomas's observation about firsts: "few occurrences thus named remain so after scrutiny." Then we'll look at what really happened.

The Pathology of an Infection:
The Blues in New Orleans and New York

*...par l'ordre de Nature, tousjours les jeunes succedent aux vieils,
et les vivans aux decedez.*

According to the order of Nature, the young always succeed
the old, and the living the dead.

—LOUIS LE ROY, *De la vicissitude ou variété
des choses en l'univers*, XII (1575)

Alone among known species, dead musical genres keep on breed-
ing—case in point, the thousands of two-guitars-bass-and-drums rock
bands formed in the 1990s. Looking at pop in the mid-teens, if you
aren't careful, you might think ragtime was still alive. The military
bands keep on pumping out versions of "Temptation Rag" and
"The Music Box Rag" and such; Gershwin's "Swanee" was pre-
miered by none other than the Arthur Pryor Band, in 1919. And
the piano ticklers tickle and the banjoists banjicate. Sure, Fred Van
Eps takes over for Vess Ossman as banjo king, but he spends a lot
of his studio time replacing the worn-out masters of Plunk's old
hits. You might even think that ragtime's growing, seeing as it's
pulling in dicty stuff like operas and concertos—e.g., Joseph Mosko-
witz's "Operatic Rag," which does to the great operas what Spam
does to pigs, or Conway's Band's pastiche of the *Hungarian Rhapsody*, "Hungarian Rag." And respectable folks no longer mind that
vulgar little hitch in the beat so much, especially when there's a
nice, catchy melody and some clean and clever words to sing. Of
course, that's the surest sign of musical necrosis. When my mom
told me she liked that "Beth," I knew I had to stop listening to Kiss.

The fact is, the leading edge of ragtime was busily downplaying
the unashamed Underworld physicality, display, and acting out that

got the music noticed in the first place, and touting up its precision, flash, "intelligence." They were turning it into America's first indigenous art music. You could already see the way things were heading in 1900, when the piano-jigging, doubletalk-spewing, leg-wobbling, cakewalk-rocking, white-passing (perhaps), and, alas, no-record-making Coon-song composer Ben Harney lost the *Police Gazette's* heavily promoted "Rag Time King of the World" contest to a certain Mike Bernard, who carried it away with cabbage like "Fantasy on the Pilgrim's Chorus from Tannhäuser and the Finale to Rubinstein's E Flat Concerto." By the teens, Bernard and his ilk—white folks, that is—were spinning out reams of written compositions in difficult keys, full of piano technique and flash and hardly any funk (when they weren't ragging Rossini and syncopating Schubert). "Try to pump glory into a pig and it will burst in the end," as the Good Soldier Schweik says. (Others, as always, were plain old cashing in, using a pinch of ragtime to spice up the parlor song and the music hall number to create modern pop.)

And so, in one form or another, ragtime—once cool and now rapidly becoming lame—was being clasped unto Topworld's narrow bosom like the estranged daughter who's just thrown over that loser she was seeing for the mill owner's son. It's the same old story: whenever some new, menacing beats pop up, the old menacing beats suddenly look real nice; given time, the mellow dinge of nostalgia can make anything look pleasant. Gangsta rap terrifies, punk rock sells tortilla chips.

Meanwhile, a new consensus was forming as to what was hot, away from the prying eyes of the timid. But making sense out of the hot scene of the teens and early twenties is ugly work, if any work you can do sitting at a computer in your bunny slippers can be called ugly. The history is confused, the players tend to the obscure and infrequently recorded, and what records they did make are rare and seldom reissued. Even worse, if by 1911 ragtime was a national phenomenon, its mutation into jazz was a local one.

There was a time when you could find someone who claimed to be the "inventor of jazz" in just about any town big enough to support a whorehouse. Thing is, they weren't wrong. They heard the ODJB and said, waitaminnit, I've been playing this shit—well, not exactly, but pretty damn close—since back in eleven, or ought-four, or even ninety-eight. James Reese Europe in Harlem; on Broadway, Bert Williams and Marion Harris, out of California and Kentucky, respectively; Wilbur Sweatman in Chicago; W. C. Handy in Memphis; Jelly Roll Morton in New Orleans and points west (and north, and east); Art Hickman in San Francisco; Ma Rainey in vaudeville (i.e., everywhere)—the list of people who more or less independently started amping ragtime's inherent swerve up into something new is long and nationwide. Yet none of them grew on just water and air and sunshine: in an age before radio, TV, or the Internet, before an integrated recording industry, each local scene had its own peculiar traditions, influences, demands, all of which had as much of a hand in shaping jazz and everything that came from it as the individual geniuses whose names made it into the history books.

To be sure, when it comes to the raw spunk that hardens into history, some scenes had more than others. Dubuque, for instance, was just about spunk-free, as were Bangor and Pasadena and even Boston. Then there's New Orleans. If anything, too much spunk—the myths and legends about the Crescent City in the days before jazz broke out are so thick and crusted that they've almost completely scabbed over what really happened down there. (Rather than pick at that scab, I'll send those who want fine detail to Louis Armstrong's *Satchmo: My Life in New Orleans*, probably the best book ever written by a musician, and Alan Lomax's *Mr. Jelly Roll*, a tantalizing torrent of talk from the Philosopher Pimp himself.)

♪

American mythology holds that, back in the day, the Big Easy was a big, fat, funky houseparty, where everybody—black, white, red, green, purple—sat around with everybody else eating red beans and rice, drinking hurricanes, and listening to lusty black folks with funny names like "Bunk" and "Satchmo" fart out that jolly Dixieland music until the milk wagon came. Sorta.

At least nine cultures—French, Cuban, other Caribbean, Yankee, Southern American, African American, Sicilian, Creole, a bit of German—ground up against one another in a narrow strip of bottomland sandwiched between the Mississippi and Lake Pontchartrain, squaring off in two main blocs: Southern and Creole, English and French/Spanish, new and old, hard-edged and soft-focus. (The Sicilians, recent and much-disliked immigrants, didn't really fit in with either group.) Both had Topworld and Underworld parts, white parts and black parts. The Anglos tried to keep these apart with the same Manichean finality as elsewhere in Dixie, not always successfully (they never did manage to get the working-class neighborhoods properly segregated). The Creoles viewed the whole thing with much more nuance and elasticity, but their way was fading. Before the Civil War, they ran the show; in the thirty years after Appomattox, however, more and more things went the American way. The hard way.

What does this have to do with hot music? For one thing, music has always been as good at setting people apart as bringing them together, and New Orleans, with its caste system, had a lot of folks who wanted to be set apart, as loudly and often as possible. In fact, turn-of-the-twentieth-century New Orleans was about the most musical town in the country. It had three opera companies; most American cities had none. It had music for every occasion, and every occasion called for music, from the most public to the most intimate—in the city's famous whorehouses, of which there was a preternatural abundance, "the customer picked out the girl and the piano player he wanted," according to veteran bass thumper Pops Foster, and "the piano player would play some slow blues" throughout the ensuing fucking and whatnot. Every social organization, club, group, circle, crap game, or powwow had a band of some kind. Even so, with all that demand, there were so many "musicianers," as they called them, that if one wanted to make a living he had to leave town or get a day job—a trade.

As you would expect, the Topworld Anglos had dicty brass bands and dance orchestras just like the rest of the country, while the Underworld blacks played it hot and lowdown: along with Memphis, New Orleans was the natural place for the blues to wash up, whether it came from east Texas, northern Louisiana, or, of course, the Delta. The Creoles—demon reed players—had their own special lilt that they brought to everything from opera to brass band marches to...to the point where things start to get interesting.

In the Creoles, New Orleans had a wild card. Ultimately, its French-Spanish elite was quite as racist as the Anglo South, there's little question about that. But where, say, a "respectable" Virginian would go by the "one drop" rule—one drop of black blood and you're a darky, period—his Creole counterpart would recognize gradations of color, each with its own class implications. The lighter-skinned descendants of the so-called "free Creoles of color" wouldn't associate with folks darker than them if they could help it, and for a long time they could. But in the 1890s, like the rest of Dixie, Louisiana started instituting Jim Crow laws and "the discrimination came," as jazzman Bunk Johnson later explained. The Louisiana legislature streamlined the whole delicate system of quadroons and octoroons and so forth by making them all, as I'm sure the legislators would've phrased it, "just plain niggers." Folks who had considered themselves pure (well, almost) French, Topworld, *white,* were suddenly typed together with illiterate turpentine-camp roughnecks and—worse—their own servants. Some left—the cartoonist George "Krazy Kat" Herriman's parents lit out for L.A., where they simply declared themselves white and put it all behind them. But most stayed and lumped it.

The older generations tried to maintain their separateness, their superiority. But the kids, adaptable as always, soon started hangin' with the homies. And, in New Orleans, hangin' involved music. Here's what happened when one young Creole clarinetist—George Baquet, who went on to play in several seminal jazz bands—rubbed up against the black cornet king Buddy Bolden (canonized in jazz lore as the first guy to play the blues on a horn):

> ...we went to a ball at the Odd Fellows' Hall, where Buddy Bolden worked. I remember thinking it was a funny place, nobody took their hats off. It was plenty tough.... Buddy held up his cornet, paused to be sure of his embouchure, then they played [proto-blues] "Make Me a Pallet on the Floor"...I'd never heard anything like that before. I'd played "legitimate" stuff. But this! It was somethin' that pulled me! They got me up on the stand that night, and I was playin' with 'em. After that, I didn't play "legitimate" so much.

"Plenty tough" is an understatement. A typical Bolden bit has him directing the band: "Way down, way down low / So I can hear those ho's / Drag their feet across the flo'," and then, with a shout out to the clientele—"Oh you bitches, shake your asses!"—grinding out another chorus of the blues.

Baquet's story, which must have occurred around 1900, was being played out all over town in joints such as the Animule Hall ("the patrons behaved like animals of the jungle once they entered"— Danny Barker), the Providence Hall, the Economy Hall, the Funky Butt Hall, Johnny Lala's Big 25, Pete Lala's, Toodlum's, the Pig Ankle, the Hot Cat, the Honky Tonk, the Fewclothes Cabaret.

Multiply Baquet's wild night by a few thousand (and it could have been pretty damn wild: one of the popular Underworld tipples was a mixture of cheap California red and cocaine, which cost a dime) and mix up the cast—sometimes it was the Sicilians (whom pretty much everybody looked down on) getting together with the Creoles, or the newly radicalized (to hang revolutionary language on an evolutionary time) Creoles jamming with the Anglos, or just about any combination save plain vanilla Anglos with pure chocolate blacks. It didn't hurt that they were all more or less living on top of each other—the poorer parts of town were still hopelessly mixed, so you find, for example, Buddy Bolden splitting a two-family house with the white Shields brothers, Harry, Eddie, and Larry. Larry, who played the clarinet, was one of the kids who later teamed up with Nick LaRocca to found the ODJB.

Pretty soon, in any case, a rough vernacular began to evolve, a swervy, "faked"—not read off a page—version of ragtime that owed a lot to the blues, but smoother and sweeter: just as the dicty players learned, not without difficulty, to bend things to the dark side—"you have to play real *hard* when you play for Negroes," Creole clarinet ace Sidney Bechet's brother later observed, "you got to *go* some, if you want to avoid their criticism"—the gutbucket ones began to work on their chops, learn to read a little, get more versatile—get "better." It didn't take the better players long to start blues-ragging everything from "Stars and Stripes Forever" (like what Vess Ossman had done, of course, but funkier) to *Il Trovatore,* turning a genre into a style.

Pops Foster's description of the "ragtime bands" (they didn't yet have a name of their own) that were down with the new groove could be applied more or less across the racial board: "...your trumpet, trombone and clarinet were your brass, then you had your guitars, drums [bass, Chinese snare, one cymbal, with maybe a cowbell or Chinese wood-block for color] and bass for rhythm. The fiddler usually could read and taught the rest of the bands the numbers...." The string bass in place of the more common tuba was a local peculiarity; usually played with a bow, it gave New Orleans bands a smooth, mellow pulse all their own. A white band would likely have a piano and no guitar, but black musicians thought the piano was for "sissies" and "faggots" (Pops Foster again; of all the myriad memoirs of New Orleans, his are the saltiest, and he knows how to dish), and this attitude rubbed off on the Creoles. Obviously, none of 'em had been up to St. Louis to meet Big Tom Turpin.

By 1910, there were dozens of these bands, black, white, and Creole, working the earthier parts of town, stretching their chops on Tin Pan Alley rags ("Hot Time in the Old Town," "Didn't He Ramble"), fossilized blues riffs ("Careless Love," "Alabama Bound," "Make Me a Pallet," our old friend the "Funky Butt" aka the "St. Louis Tickle"), and a goodly number of compositions by the great St. Louis professors ("Maple Leaf Rag" was, as everywhere, a particular favorite). Few out-and-out Coon songs turn up in recollections of what they used to play; whether that's because they'd moved beyond them or because the musicians would rather forget them, I can't say.

The ragtime—dance—bands sure as hell weren't the only game in town. The theaters and restaurants where Topworld went to be seen needed nice, clean music, same as in New York, while the myriad whorehouses of the District—which is what the locals called Storyville—demanded piano men, men who could deliver anything from Puccini to the "Pigfoot Blues." These babies didn't care if the bandsmen thought they were fags; they were pulling in fifty bucks a night. On the street corners, there were spasm bands—a guitar, a mandolin, maybe a kazoo or anything else you could scare up or make from junk (here's where you'd find "Mr. Johnson, Turn Me Loose"). The constant parades called for brass bands, the honky-tonks for blues, usually from nothing more than a cornet or a clarinet with maybe a piano or a guitar to back it up.

But bands like Buddy Bolden's were where the double helix of ragtime and blues got zipped together tightest; where the willful freedom of the Senegambian mode got worked into something musicians could play together, and the tight, regular spaces of ragtime got opened up into uncertainty—into improvisation. One of the bedrock principles of these semi-pro bands was the old battle cry of the working man, "fuck you, Jack, I'm alright"—or, as New Orleans guitarist Danny Barker formulated it, "I'll play what I play and you play what you play." I.e., no fiddle-scratching cute guy calls himself a bandleader can tell me what to play on my clarinet just because he can read it off a page; I'll play my part the way *I* think it should go.

Not that these guys were taking long, speculative solos, improvising as, say, John Coltrane would understand it—for one thing, the rest of the band wouldn't stand for it; anyone who laid off to give a soloist space, put down his horn for more than a minute, wasn't pulling his weight and wouldn't get paid. But there was a lot of highly personal embellishing going on, especially in the blues, which you couldn't find printed on the page anyway. And thus, as much out of plain Underworld orneriness as anything else, jazz—although the name would come later, from outside.

By 1910 there were a score or more Crescent City bands playing this new Senegambian ragtime, hustling and bustling to turn a composer's music into a player's. The roster of their names is as noble and mythologized as the Achaean squadrons in the *Iliad*—the Eagle Band (Bolden's until 1907; after he drank himself into a mental hospital, Frankie Duson's), Jack Carey's Crescent Band, Baby Ridgeley's Tuxedo Band, Jimmy Brown's Superior Band, the Onward Band, Papa Jack Laine's Reliance Band, Tom Brown's band (these last two, white bands, were where Nick LaRocca and his buddies got their chops together, before they started their fateful drive north).

The myth is all we have; none of the first- or second-wave New Orleans bands recorded, back in the pre-ODJB days. The first field recording units made it down there in 1924, but by then it was too late. King Bolden had been locked away for almost a generation, while cornetists—bandleaders—like Chris Kelly and Buddy Petit had been eased out by younger, hipper names. Freddie Keppard, the Creole trumpet king in the teens, did get an offer to make records for Victor as early as 1915—he'd done a vaudeville stint on the Columbia "wheel" (showbiz lingo for "booking circuit") and impressed the right people—but he turned it down. Didn't want everybody copping his stuff, they say. By the time he did record, in the mid-twenties, he was a hopeless drunk and his chops were weak. A couple of Crescent City bands—the legendary King Oliver's among them—recorded in places like Chicago and Los Angeles and New York, but that didn't start until 1922, and they'd all been away from home long enough to change their sound. The only New Orleans band to record before that was the ODJB, although an individual or two snuck in here and there—mostly ofays or Creoles who could pass, like clarinetist Achille Baquet, who recorded at the end of 1918 with Jimmy Durante's band.

But—regardless of what they may tell you—New Orleans wasn't the only place dripping with that jazz-spunk. St. Louis and Memphis were as close to the blues' ground zero as New Orleans, and—as far as anyone can tell, which isn't very—spawned some of the same mutations. Few traces remain. One precious exception is the Columbia personal record (i.e., you pay them money and they press your record) of "Sunset Medley," made in May 1916 by Haenschen's Orchestra. Haenschen's Orchestra was simply W. "Gus" Haenschen on piano and T. T. Schiffer on drums—a couple of German Americans out of St. Louis. The first part of the medley turns out to be "A Bunch of Blues," by H. Alf Kelley (author of the early jazz standard, "Weary Blues") and clarinetist J. Paul Wyer (a star of W. C. Handy's Mississippi band). Chinese boxes: "A Bunch of Blues" is a medley itself, three existing blues cobbled together by two guys who knew the scene well. Chief among them none other than "String Bean Blues"—another precious whiff of the first, unrecorded, wave of blues evangelists. The way Haenschen swaggers his way through the song's descending, chromatic riff—a riff that, as "Cow Cow Blues," was destined to immortality—tells us that he wasn't bullshitting when, fifty-seven years later, he told an interviewer that he used to frequent "some of the so-called dives" where St. Louis's black piano professors practiced their craft. Whatever else they were doing, Haenschen's disc suggests that they were working out how to blue-swerve ragtime on their own without any help from New Orleans.

As for Memphis. In September 1917 somebody finally broke down and hauled old Handy himself out to New York to make some records, fourteen years too late but better than never (if only his Clarksdale Knights of Pythias band had recorded!). Even though he was minus most of his regular men, for whom the idea of black musicians making records was so unlikely as to keep them home in Memphis, and neither of his biggest hits was on the agenda, the ten marvelously swervy sides Columbia issued from these sessions prove that Memphis, too, knew the Senegambian rag. Among them: "A Bunch of Blues" (Col. A-2418), played slower and less urgently than Haenschen and Schiffer's version. Unfortunately, Columbia's recording engineers were unable to do Handy's large ensemble—cornet, trombone, four reeds, three violins, piano, bass, and drums—justice; Victor would've done a better job. Through the fog, though, you can discern a gentle, wistful funk that is far subtler and more emotionally affecting than anything the ODJB was capable of producing.

Even in the places that had to learn their blues from sheet music and vaudeville—basically, the northeast; as Harlem clarinetist Garvin Bushell later recalled, "there wasn't an eastern performer who could really play the blues"—ragtime was changing. In Washington, Baltimore, Philly, and on up the seaboard to New York, the professors were shaking their Joplin up with a stiff shot of Franz Liszt—flash and filigree. On Broadway and in the Big Apple's cabarets, the purveyors of up-to-the-minute dance music were learning to goose the beat along in ways that must've made Scott Joplin weep—drum kits, noisemakers, all kinds of vulgar gimmicks to suggest wild abandon. Meanwhile, Chicago was pulling in carloads of Southern blacks, Appalachian hillbillies, and—until World War I broke out—southern and eastern Europeans, boiling 'em all together and squeezing music out of the resulting mash. Out in the West (and in vaudeville everywhere), Hawaiian music was another craze to stack up next to the ones for dance music and, especially, the blues. With its lush, exotic harmonies and melting melodies on the steel guitar, Hawaiian music had a strong swerve of its own, and in no time rags, raggy pop, and even blues started getting bent, island-style. In fact, the first guitar blues on record was cut by a Hawaiian, Frank Ferera, in 1915. (Then there's the tantalizing 1893 picture of the Kamehameha School for Boys band; its eleven pieces include three guitars, a banjo, a fiddle, and three cornets. Now that's a band I'd like to hear.)

As for the part of Dixie that *doesn't* celebrate Mardi Gras. On April 12, 1911, the fiftieth anniversary of Fort Sumter—closer than World War II is to us now—the South was still powerfully separate from the rest of the country, musically and in just about every other way. Sure, the bigger towns had brass bands and electric lights and citizens with cars and Caruso records just like everyone else. But under that thin crust of homogenized Americanism burbled and sloshed a deep and fetid pool of stubborn, futile, head-in-the-sand *resistance*. Resistance to Yankees, resistance to Topworld, resistance to modernity and everything that stood for it, from integration—especially integration—to industrialization; the bicycle to the saxophone. It was usually violent: lynchings, beatings, brutalization of every kind. Sometimes, it was just petty bitchiness, often ridiculously so: in parts of Mississippi, the postman would cross out "Mr." any time it turned up on an envelope addressed to a black man. You can imagine how general opinion ran regarding the recent Senegambian innovations in ragtime. Down South, they *knew* what black music was supposed to sound like, and it sure as shit wasn't this. Few indeed of the first generation of white jazzmen hailed from Dixie (New Orleans excepted, of course).

In the rest of the country, the minstrel show was a fading institution whose stars were jumping ship for burlesque, vaudeville, Broadway, almost as soon as they were born. Not so in the South; Coonesthesia was still the queen of the musical sciences. In the rest of the country, the only fashionable use for the banjo was to play rhythm chords in a dance orchestra (the very instrument itself was different, having lost that ornery fifth string, the little one that lets you thumb a funky drone to pick against). Not so in the South, where they kept the thumb string and the music that went with it. In the rest of the country, a fiddle was a violin, and you used it to play the lead part—the melody—in a dance arrangement. Not so in the South, where shivarees like the annual Georgia Old-Time Fiddlers Convention (founded in 1913, the year Yankee Topworld started dancing to ragtime) kept the ghost of Dan Emmett from its due repose. You couldn't spit without hitting a string band or backwoods ballad singer of some sort. The more Northern music changed (and Southern black; if there was ever a group that had positively *no* use for nostalgia...), the more Southern white music stayed mulishly the same, all "Old Dan Tucker," "The Picture That's Turned to the Wall," and "Hop Light, Ladies"—Coon songs (and old ones at that), parlor weepers, and pan-Celtic fiddle stretchers.

Of course, the record companies were all in the North, recording being a relentlessly modern industry, and they had no interest whatsoever in getting any of this deliberately old-fangled stuff on record. Besides, right at hand in New York they had their own Coons, and they were far more amenable to modernity.

♪

In the entertainment capital of the new century, a fresh wave of "Coon shouters" was breaking into the professional representation of negritude racket, and their agenda had little to do with the traditional dynamics of Coondom. Sophie Tucker—"Last of the Red

Hot Mamas" and so on and so forth—made her first records in 1910; the next year saw Al Jolson's debut. It was also the year so-called Ragtime King Irving Berlin (ragtime had as many kings as Goethe's Germany had princes) blew ragtime and the Coon song to tiny little bits with his massive hit "Alexander's Ragtime Band," a ragtime song with no rag and a Coon song with no Coon (beyond that "it's the bestest band what am"). All three—Sonia Kalish, Asa Yoelson, and Israel Baline, to give their birth-names—were Russian-born Jews who grew up in the urban slums of New York and Boston; what the hell did they—or their New York–born Coon colleague Isidore Israel "Eddie Cantor" Itzkowitz, for that matter—know or care about America's peculiar institutions? Blackface was just another rung on the ladder to Topworld, and they daubed it on and sloughed it off without nostalgia or backward glance or even much curiosity. Or heat—they had their hot moments, but it wasn't the priority. The net result was a dilution of the already-tenuous relationship between blackface and black America to homeopathic levels. The obligatory exception: in June, 1911 Edison released a new cylinder by Sophie Tucker. "Some of These Days" was by Shelton Brooks, a hitherto unknown black songwiter who had hung around for days trying to pitch it to La Tucker without success, until her black maid finally shamed her into giving him a listen. It was such a hit that it became her signature song and lent its title to her autobiography. Also, in its 1911 version, anyway—there were many to follow—it's one of the most wrenching, emotional, and, yes, bluesy of blackface records, a low-pitched, tortured moan that gets under your skin and won't leave (Ed. 4M-691). She never equalled it, on record anyway. But then again, she didn't have to—all it takes is one record like that for immortality.

At the same time, Topworld was under assault from the black side. The thing that bleached-in-the-sheet Southern Coonophiles like Polk Miller most feared was coming to pass, at least in New York: the "pigeon-tailed coats" and "white shirt fronts" were taking over Georgia minstrelsy. The situation was a lot like that bit in *Blazing Saddles* when, in response to Burton Gilliam's request for "a good ole Nigger work song," Cleavon Little and his track crew launch into "I get no kick from champagne." Starting in the late nineties, a loosely associated group of black musicians, actors, dancers started taking black minstrelsy into new territory—leaving the plantation behind, letting the hero get the girl, etc. Shows like *Clorindy, or the Origin of the Cakewalk* (featuring our old friend Ernest "All Coons Look Alike to Me" Hogan), *The Shoo-Fly Regiment, In Dahomey,* and *Bandanna Land* still had plenty of Coon content, virtual negritude, but under the surface they were honest-to-God black musicals, not just amped-up Coon shows. What's more, they started showing up on Broadway, for all to see. If by the teens this scene had petered out, it had also kicked up two Topworld stars, one in his own right and the other by association, two men who would change the face (or at least the complexion) of American music forever.

Bert Williams was the first black man in America. Emphasis on "man"—he was the first guy for whom the dark (darkish, actually) color of his skin wasn't the only thing most folk needed to know about him (the Frederick Douglasses and W. E. B. DuBoises were too political to find that kind of neutral space). He was an individual; he had personality. And money, which never hurts. What Jack Johnson did for the sweet science, Bert Williams did for entertainment (but without pissing off whitey): before him, a white man could claim that he was the best without worrying if a black man somewhere was better. After him, he'd get the "what about x?" treatment. Back in 1898, when the twenty-four-year-old Williams was just starting his trip to Topworld, he and his partner George W. Walker were the reigning champions of the cakewalk. Word reached them that Cornelius Vanderbilt's great-grandson William K. (II) had been gaining a rep among the four hundred for cakewalking; that he had "appeared in a semi-public exhibition and...posed as an

You better believe it.

expert in that capacity." Williams and Walker challenged him to a showdown to decide, as the public letter they wrote him continued, "which of us shall deserve the title of champion cake-walker of the world." No go. Twenty years later, after Williams's ascension to stardom, Willie Vanderbilt would have had to put up or shut up.

Egbert Austin Williams was born in Nassau, the Bahamas, on November 12, 1874, of thoroughly mixed parentage—African, Spanish, Danish. After that, the facts start to get rubbery. Like his friend W. C. Fields, it seems that Williams never told a story the same way twice; if you were buying it, he was happy to keep on selling. He was the grandson of a Danish diplomat, he had a degree in engineering from Stanford, he studied mime in Paris, etcetera. One fact that is pretty firm is that his family, after ping-ponging around the States, settled in Riverside, California, around 1885 and worked the citrus groves. It was there that Egbert edged his way into showbiz, in the traditional way: church choir—vocal quartet—minstrel show (with a detour in a Hawaiian group, where he passed for Polynesian—thereby inspiring, I suppose, our old friend George "Minstrel to the White House" O'Connor's nasty 1917 musical cowpie, "They May Call You Hawaiian on Broadway, But You're Just a Plain Nigger to Me"). He blacked up for his first big gig, with Martin & Selig's Mastodon Minstrels ("five whites, one Mexican and four colored minstrels; the Mexican drove the four-horse team and played the trombone"— B.W.). He was one end man, and Walker was the other. That was in San Francisco, in 1893. Williams did Jim Crow—slow and country; Walker, Zip Coon—slick and city. Which is pretty much the way their act remained until Walker's tertiary syphilis sidelined him in 1909 (like Hogan and Joplin, it killed him; the price of Underworld stardom). Walker got the girls and Williams got the laughs.

By late 1895 Williams and Walker—"Two Real Coons," as they billed themselves; why should ofays get all the good Coon gigs?— were in Denver; by mid-1896, in Chicago; on September 22, they opened on Broadway—between the last two acts of Victor (*Naughty*

Marietta) Herbert's *The Gold Bug,* which was bombing bigtime.
The desperate producer brought them in to Coon it up in the last
act all the way from West Baden, Indiana (it's near French Lick),
where their march to the sea had petered out. "It was the first time,"
he later recalled, "I had ever seen a musical muke [="mook," "moke,"
as in "Smoky Mokes," q.v.] team stop a show, and they stopped *The
Gold Bug* that night until they eventually gave out physically." *The
Gold Bug* closed anyway, but by then the damage had been done.

Ragtime had come to Broadway. What Williams and Walker
did that night was cakewalk their asses off to Williams's tune, "Oh,
I Don't Know, You're Not So Warm!" (which the pit orchestra hated;
as far as they were concerned, it was a musical "jigsaw puzzle." *Sic
semper*). The song, soon published, came with a special ragtime piano
arrangement—the first time the term "rag" appeared in a piece of sheet
music. Within weeks, the 2RCoons were firmly installed in New
York's—and hence the country's—top vaudeville houses. One fortunate who saw them recalled, "Walker did a neat cakewalk [accord-
ing to one of the dancing Whitman sisters, "he was the greatest
strutter of them all"]...and Bert Williams would follow behind him
doing a slow loose-jointed mooch dance." People dug Walker (including, evidently, a number of white women, among them vaudeville
headliner Eva Tanguay; he was a very good-looking man), but Williams
was the real star.

W. C. Fields's assessment of his friend is pith itself: "the funni-
est man I ever saw and the saddest man I ever knew." Williams's
humor was based on his getting the brown end of the stick, over
and over again. The patient shrug, the slow shake of the head—you
think you got me beat because you're better than me, but, Mister,
you've got nothing to do with it; it's just the way things are. I'm
"the 'Jonah Man' [Williams wrote], the man who, even if it rained
soup, would be found with a fork in his hand and no spoon in sight."
His exquisite timing made it funny as hell, but there's Lucretius's
old *amari aliquid* welling up again.

Everybody loved his act. Blacks, because it was true, and because he robbed the foe of his triumph; whites, because it was true, and because it let 'em off the hook for doing anything about it. Besides, he was laughing right along with them. They came to laugh at him and they ended up laughing with him, at least for a while. Williams was keenly aware of the ironies in all this; Ethel Barrymore (Drew's great-aunt) had a telling anecdote:

> Once when [her brother] Lionel was playing in vaudeville [actually, I quibble, it must have been Maurice, their father], he was standing in the wings to watch Bert Williams' technique, as he did at every performance. One of the stagehands said, "Like him, huh?" Lionel said, "Yes, He's terrific." And the stagehand said, just as Williams came off stage and passed him, "Yeah, he's a good nigger, knows his place." And Williams mumbled, "Yes, a good nigger knows his place. Going there now. Dressing Room One!"

(From time to time he'd play society parties; he'd show up impeccably dressed and start things off by asking the assembled Vanderbilts and whom have you, "Is we all good niggers here?") He was a sensitive, cultivated, proud man who played the Coon so others wouldn't have to.

There's no point in going further into W&W's theatrical career here; they were stars, they were all over the first all-black show to crack Broadway—*In Dahomey*, 1903—they played for Edward VII at Buckingham Palace, and so on. Their triumph came in 1908, with *Bandanna Land*. Even the hardest-assed critics loved it. After Walker fell by the wayside, Williams single-handedly integrated the Ziegfeld Follies and stayed there long enough to become an institution. He made movies (a clip of his famous pantomimed poker game survives). He was an artist; people took him seriously. Like W. C. Fields, he read books—Aristotle, like that. He used words like "desuetude" and "subconscious" and "inconvenient." He was legit. (About that "inconvenient." In the January, 1919, issue of *The American Magazine*, Williams wrote the following: "In truth, I have never been able to discover that there was anything disgraceful in being a colored man. But I have often found it inconvenient—in America." This, his most famous quote, is in fact a sly allusion to one of George Ade's *Fables in Slang*, where a rich, officious old bat goes around "improving" the lives of the poor by telling them things like "it is no Disgrace to be Poor; it is simply Inconvenient, that's all." So when Williams says "inconvenient," he means "a royal pain in the ass." This must be pointed out, because he is frequently taken at his word.)

And, unlike Billy Kersands and Ernest Hogan and all those Georgia minstrel stars who came before him, Bert Williams made records—seventy-eight of them, by my count (excluding various duplicates and rejects), stretching from October, 1901, to a couple of weeks before his death on March 4, 1922. He and Walker started out on Victor, did a cylinder or two for Edison and Zonophone and switched over to Columbia, where Williams stayed from 1906 until the bitter end. Walker dropped out of the proceedings early on: he didn't like the way his voice recorded, and Williams was the one the record companies were interested in anyway (ultimately, he was to appear on only four of Williams's records).

And they sold; Columbia A6141, "Elder Eatmore's Sermon," moved at least half a million units in 1919. Among the masses buying them were a goodly number of black people; blues collectors used to turn them up as far from Broadway as Vicksburg and the Delta. In an if not unprecedented, certainly unfollowed (OK, so that's not a word) failure of greed, the industry at large drew no commercial conclusions from this: black folks weren't a market it knew to recognize or thought to cater to, even as it was starting to churn out Irish, Yiddish, Italian, even Arab and Chinese discs by the carload.

Unfortunately, surviving examples of the twelve titles Williams (and Williams and Walker) recorded for Victor in 1901 are very scarce indeed. Nonetheless, the four I've been able to track down, including two out of the three with Walker, work to validate both Carl Sandburg's boast "I heard Williams and Walker / Before Walker died in the bughouse" and, conversely, the essential accuracy of the Collins-Spencer brand of Ethiopian delineation. Not that I wouldn't like to see the ratio between records made by Collins and Spencer and those by Williams and Walker reversed, but either the white Coons were doing a good job of capturing what the black ones were doing, or vice versa. Then Williams changed the rules of the game.

That didn't happen, on record at least, until 1906, when Williams began recording for Columbia. First out of the gate was Williams's last recording with Walker. "Pretty Desdemone," from the duo's current show, *Abyssinia*, features a chorus with a smooth, powerful kick to its rhythm that owes more to gospel than to ragtime (Col. 3410). The next one Williams belted out of the park. "Nobody" (also from *Abyssinia*; Col. 3423) was one of those songs—like "Born to Be Wild" or "Rapper's Delight"—that define a performer so thoroughly that he just can't get out from under it. Every gig for the rest of your life: play the song, or else. (Williams had to recut it in 1913; presumably the master had worn out from constant re-pressings.) Over a Pryoresque moaning trombone, he lets the words out one or two at a time; they assemble into a lugubrious tale of loserdom and woe with a raggy, smeary kick in the chorus:

I-I-I-I ain't never done nothin' to nobody;
I-I-I-I ain't never got nothin' from nobody, no time:
O-o-o-oh, until I get somethin' from somebody, some time,
I-I-I-I'll never do nothin' for nobody no time.

Going there now—Dressing Room One. Ironically, Arthur Collins was the first to cut Williams's song (Ed. 9084), in 1905—the song that would ultimately put him and most of his kind out of the Coon business.

Williams followed "Nobody" with a string of records—including "Let It Alone" (a third winner from *Abyssinia;* Col. 3504), "All In, Out and Down" (Col. 30039), and "The Mississippi Stoker" (Col. 3575), all from 1906—that played on the same combination of an elastically phrased, rueful verse and a catchy ragtime chorus that put "Nobody" over the top. It's fair to say that these discs blew the canned Coon racket wide open. Sure, Williams played close enough to the trad Coon that Southern distributors wouldn't freak out ("hold on thar, Buford, that's *real* darkey music")—he knew his place—but his records were to your quotidian Coon song as Hitchcock is to Frank Tashlin. And as a result, his act got respect as art in a way that Arthur Collins's or even Polk Miller's never would. What's more, you couldn't imitate him. He had, as his friend Eddie Cantor put it, "a unique way of rendering songs, injecting his talk between rests and catching up with the melodic phrase after he had let it get a head start." He talked a mean song, every now and then getting it up to sing a phrase or two, but always sinking inexorably back to a sly, knowing drawl. There's no way of ever mistaking one of his records for anybody else's.

It's hard to hear Williams's music like Topworld did back when. To us, things like the way the beat stretches on the "I" in the chorus of "Nobody"; the slow tempos; the weariness, stubbornness, dignity: they all spell one thing. The blues. The mode Bert Williams was working in is distinctly Senegambian. The accompaniments may be stiff and unhot (he was always recorded with white musicians of the Broadway variety), the material may tend to the Tin Pan, but there's always that irreducible *wrench* there to bend his records into something that we find familiar but Topworld then found, well.... The subtitle on the sheet music for "Nobody" sums it up best: "Bert William's [sic] Latest Oddity." That oddity, that swerve, would eventually become the cornerstone of American music, and it was Bert Williams who laid it (which is of course not the same as making it).

Williams recorded pretty steadily from the mid-teens until his death, producing numerous gems, but all the heavy lifting was done by the end of 1906 (although 1910's "Play That Barbershop Chord" packs a real wallop on its own, what with its driving rhythm and its swerved, blue harmonies—the "barbershop chord" contains a flatted, or blue, seventh; Col. A-929).

♪

If Bert Williams cried out the advent of the blues, jazz—especially the big-band species—found its John the Baptist in James Reese Europe. What Williams did for show music, the kind you sit down and watch, Jim Europe did for the kind to which you stir your stumps.

Besides being by all accounts a hell of a human being—tall, intelligent, self-assured, a natural leader yet not without a sense of humor—Europe was a perfect embodiment of the cats-in-a-sack relationship between Topworld and Underworld. He was born in 1880 to a freedman pastor and a freeborn schoolteacher, a birth member of the newly coalescing black version of the respectable class—the education-and-quietly-dignified-behavior-will-lead-us-to-acceptance-and-assimilation crew. His death thirty-nine years later was pure Underworld, knifed in a backstage argument. In between, he made the first black band records in America and laid the groundwork for the big band as we know it, half symphony hall and half honky-tonk. And, incidentally, forced ofay America to get used to the sight of black musicians wearing tuxes and ties, not overalls and mule-grade straw hats.

The Europes were a musical family, within which that same high-low dynamic was acted out: ma taught piano, pa fiddled and picked the banjo (much of what follows comes from Reid Badger's excellent and meticulous biography of Europe, *A Life in Ragtime*). Three out of five kids became musicians: Jim's older brother John was a journeyman piano professor (in the Underworld sense of the honorific), his younger sister Mary one of the leading accompanists of black "art" music, and Jim split the difference, composing for banjo orchestras and conducting the funkiest brass band in the Army.

When Jim was nine, the Europes moved from their native Mobile to Washington, D.C., which had the largest black population in the country (around ninety thousand) and was the center of black civilization, at least as black Topworld understood that word. Good schools, learned societies, lots of dicty music. There the Europes lived for a time five doors away from none other than John Philip Sousa (another Topworld-Underworld trimmer), then winding up the Marine Band phase of his career. Jim studied violin and piano—the classiest instruments going—with Enrico Hurlei, Sousa's assistant director. That was all well and good, but when he graduated from high school he found out that D.C. wasn't much of a music town (*plus ça change...*). After a couple of years of proving that to himself, he did what Washington musicians from Edison's pal Len Spencer to Duke Ellington to Van "The Hustle" McCoy and Tina Weymouth have always done: he burned up the Pennsy tracks to New York.

Just to give Europe an extra push, he had a couple examples close to hand of what happens when you bust that move up North: his brother John had been making a bit of a name for himself in Manhattan's Tenderloin, the center of black nightlife before it moved up to Harlem in the teens. If that wasn't enough—and it might not have been; the brothers don't seem to have been particularly close—there was Will Marion Cook.

Will Marion Cook was a *name* in the oughts. If black music's cutting edge—its most thought-out, intellectualized, "developed" expression—was to be found in the musical theatre, then Cook was the guy wielding the razor. He notched up a string of firsts almost as impressive as Bert Williams (many of whose musicals he wrote and directed), he was widely recognized for writing some of the best music of his generation, he mentored talent the likes of Sidney Bechet and Duke Ellington. And yet when he died in 1944 at age seventy-five, he only had two records under his belt, and almost nobody remembered him.

Problem is, Mr. Cook could be a bit of an asshole. He was born in D.C. in 1869, son of two college graduates—rare indeed in the racial climate of the day. He himself attended Oberlin, studied music there. Then he went to Berlin, and studied violin for a spell (sources differ on exactly how long) with Brahms's friend Joseph Joachim. By the time he got back to Washington, in 1889 (the year the Europes hit town), he was feeling pretty damn special, and he didn't care who knew it. In fact, he founded a symphony—a black symphony—with Frederick Douglass's grandson, who was a fine violinist himself. Unfortunately, it went bust. Off to New York to study some more—this time, with Dvořák himself.

But none of that study mattered. There was no way a colored man, even a light-skinned, dashingly mustachioed, and fully conservatoried one like Will Marion Cook, was going to get into the symphonic music racket. Even if, as he angrily told a critic who had called him merely "the world's greatest Negro violinist," he was "the greatest violinist in the world," period (smash violin on said critic's desk and exit fuming—that's the way Duke Ellington heard it, anyway). Doors were closed and noses upturned (it's possible that the famous "Dvořák statement" didn't exactly help open white musicians' hearts). What to do but start writing Coon songs, just like everyone else— "Who Dat Say Chicken in Dis Crowd?" "The Hottes' Coon in Dixie," "Darktown Is Out Tonight." Cook's ma wasn't thrilled: "I've sent you all over the world to study and become a great musician," he claimed she told him, "and you return such a nigger!"

At least he had hits, and plenty of 'em: he wrote whole shows— *Clorindy, or the Origin of the Cakewalk* (1898; the first black Broadway revue, with words by Paul Lawrence Dunbar), *In Dahomey* (1906; with Williams and Walker), *Abyssinia* (1906; ditto—although

Bert Williams and Alex Rogers wrote all the song hits from the show); *Bandanna Land* (1907; again with Williams and Walker—it was poor Walker's last show). He wrote songs. He wrote "serious" music based, à la Dvořák, on the ragtime and spirituals he heard growing up—as James Weldon Johnson put it, "Cook was the first competent composer to take...rag-time and work it out in a musicianly way." On the other hand, he was also the kind of prickly S.O.B. who's firmly convinced of his own greatness, and everyone else's envy of it. Forced to hobnob and collaborate with lesser talents—i.e., the likes of Ernest Hogan, Bert Williams, and James Reese Europe—he dealt, but not gracefully.

If, on paper, Will Marion Cook sounds like a stiff, he sounds a lot better on record. Unfortunately, there was only one (that's not counting the handful of fairly anemic ofay versions of "Who Dat Say Chicken in Dis Crowd," "Darktown Is Out Tonight," and maybe a couple others cut at the turn of the century), and it's pathetically rare. Columbia A-1538 is by the Afro-American Folk Song Singers, a mixed-sex chorus that Cook directed in late 1913 and early 1914. It holds two songs of the three-song suite that Cook published as "Three Negro Songs." I don't know what to say about these sides. They're stunning, sophisticated, titanic. "Swing Along" features (not coincidentally) the same combination of elastic-tempoed recitative and ragtime-powered chorus that Williams was scoring with, but driven home with full gospel power. One minute "Swing Along" is all tumbling vocal leads and tidal wave ensembles, the next it's dignified, deep-toned washes of vocal sound. When, after a long legato section, the ensemble snaps into a reprise of the jaunty opening chorus, it's one of the most exciting moments yet committed to record:

> Swing along, Chillun, swing along de lane,
>   Lif yo' head an' yo' heels mighty high,
> Swing along, Chillun, 'tain't a-goin' to rain,
>   Sun's as red as a rose in de sky.

Come along, Mandy, come along, Sue,
White folks watchin' an' seein' what you do,
White folks jealous when you're walkin' two by two,
So swing along, Chillun, swing along!

That ain't your father's Coon song. The pride, even aggression, in the lyrics is matched by the singers' fierce virtuosity. "Swing Along" lives lives up to its title, and then some. Not until Duke Ellington's Cotton Club band of the late twenties would American music again possess an instrument of such supple grandeur. (That, too, is no coincidence: Ellington was one of Cook's protégés.) The other side, "Rain Song," is no less driving than Led Zeppelin's song of the same name, and a whole lot more moving. O for High Fidelity!

But I digress. As an aspiring D.C. violinist of color, young Jim Europe must have heard nothing but Will Marion Cook. Nor would the buzz have faded when he hit New York in early 1903. Something to aspire to. It took him seven years, but in the end James Reese Europe did it; *he* became the name in black music. He had talent, hustle, and—most important—flexibility. When he found that nobody in New York wanted a violinist, he switched to the mandolin, the hot axe of the day (all those passé banjo clubs were now mandolin clubs). He started writing songs, then revues. By the summer of 1908, when Bert Williams and George Walker got together with nine other sachems of the black musical theatre movement to found the Frogs Club, Europe was one of them and the unclubbable Cook wasn't. When the movement began to tank around 1910—syphilis and (in the case of Bert Williams) Florenz Ziegfeld having carried off the stars, and the movies and dance halls (more on which in a moment) having carried off their audience—it finished off Will Marion Cook as a force in New York music, although he kept in there swinging for another decade or so, to distinctly mixed effect. But hot show music was in eclipse; lucky for James Reese Europe, he also knew how to make people dance.

♪

Now for a brief digression on the state of vernacular dance in Progressive-Era America.

Back in my youth, when the hand of Jimmy Carter was upon the land, a party consisted of a keg of Molson's with a bunch of shaggy dudes holding really big mugs standing around it and a knot of girls wearing painter pants and feather earrings over on the other side of the room. The only thing that brought the sexes together was the need to keep the joints circulating. Nobody danced; who would want to if your choice of groove was the Marshall Tucker Band or the Mahavishnu Orchestra? Besides—more importantly—dancing meant disco, and disco sucked. It was OK for gays and people of color (although the terms in general use were, I'm ashamed to admit, far less polite), but not for manly rebel dudes and the mamas who hung with them. This was the way things had always been—or at least since the late sixties, which is as far as Freakdom's folk-memory went.

Suddenly, in the summer of 1980, "Rock Lobster" and "Take Me to the River" made it out to the burbs, and bimmo! The guys chopped off their hair and discovered shirts with buttons, the girls slipped into something slinkier than the traditional overalls and peasant blouses, and everybody was dancing. Together. What had been degraded was suddenly de rigueur. Before long, the kids were trading in their Outlaws LPs for *James Brown's Greatest Hits* and suchlike. *Mutatis mutandis*, the same exact thing happened in the teens.

Jazz in the larger sense—the craze and ensuing cultural phenom, not just that New Orleans blued-up ragtime—really became inevitable when, a decade or so into the new century, the American middle class said a collective "fuck it!" (okay, perhaps "to heck with it!" is more idiomatic) to their inhibitions and started shake dancing. Sure, respectable people had danced some before that, and not all their dances were sleepy—there were polkas, schottisches, perhaps the occasional one-step, if you were into the strenuous life. But even the quick ones were relatively tame, at least with Topworld hips knocking 'em out—no grind, no twist, no pelvic wobble, no hugging or squeezing; no sex in them. More important, you did it only "rarely, occasionally," as one nostalgic old stiff recalled in the twenties, "with a great sense of the fun of being 'dressed up,' being at a 'party,' having a good time that had been long anticipated." And, when you did do it, it was in private, at your house or your neighbor's, where everybody more or less knew everybody else and the grownups could keep a parietal eye firmly fixed on the youngsters—and each other. Nothing reinforces respectability more than the knowledge that your transgressions are going to reap you a harvest of shit the next day from everyone you know.

Meanwhile, the Preterite were dancing up a storm: the crackers and cowfolk to (more or less Africanized) Celtic fiddle tunes, and the blacks and the more assimilated of the urban working class to ragtime. Dancehalls stretched from coast to coast, low dives—the Animule Hall—pretty much to a one. San Francisco's Barbary Coast supposedly had the wildest: forty-six dancehalls and saloons in three blocks including, as Sophie Tucker nostalgically recalled, "spots such as Purcell's, the hot colored joint [at 520 Pacific], and the Cave, which San Franciscans boasted was the toughest place in the world." All the most salacious steps were cooked up there, or at least served up (most of them seem to have been rooted in the same obscure precincts that had spawned the blues).

Topworld had been watching this with the usual mix of horniness, envy, and lip-pursing that comes out whenever it sees Underworld having fun. But its kids were restless, and—since small-town America was breaking up and moving to the cities—they were getting harder and harder to keep an eye on. The revolution started at the dog-end of the old century, when the cakewalk began pushing its tendrils through the generational cracks in Topworld solidarity like some fragrant, fleshlike jungle creeper. Nor were the old role models helping much to prune them back. As early as 1899, the *Musical Courier* sounded the alarm:

> Society has decreed that ragtime and cake-walking are the thing, and one reads with amazement and disgust of historical and aristocratic names joining in this sex dance, for the cakewalk is nothing but an African *danse du ventre* [= "belly-dance"], a milder edition of African orgies.

You can practically see the sweat-beaded brow behind the prose. At least they got the culprits right: those "historical and aristocratic names." Way back in the tenth century, one Adso of Montier-en-Der—a monk, of course—wrote a most useful little treatise on the Antichrist, where we learn that "first he'll turn the kings and princes

African orgies, British style: two young Brits attempt the cakewalk.

COURTESY OF CHRIS WARE/*THE RAGTIME EPHEMERALIST* MAGAZINE

to him, then, through them, the rest of the people" (*"reges et principes primum ad se convertet, deinde per illos ceteros populos"*). Precisely— remember Willie K. Vanderbilt the Society cakewalk champion? In fact, Teddy Roosevelt himself was reported cakewalking with vim and vigor to "Hot Time in the Old Town" and "Whistling Rufus" at the 1902 White House Christmas party. Perhaps that was just T.R. being T.R.—perhaps (dark looks all around). There has always been a class above Topworld in this country, whether you call it the Society 400, as in Jim Europe's day, or the Jet Set of the sixties, or the whatever-you-call-'em celebrity riffraff of today. In some ways, these fortunate few have more in common with the sans-pisspots of Underworld than with the straitlaced, precarious middle classes of Topworld. They can cut loose without having to worry that some bluestocking will take them for roughnecks—Willie K. could cake- walk until his skinny white buns got numb and he'd still be William K. Vanderbilt II. Inevitably, their Underworld-derived shenanigans trickle down to Topworld (always the last to know). Sometimes the results are pretty innocuous. Sometimes they aren't.

When, around 1910, the jaded wealthlings started poking into a slew of nasty new dances that had begun making their way east from the Barbary Coast and other points west, the old moral order crum- bled. Soon the strapping sons and nubile daughters of the middle class followed. The Texas tommy, the grizzly bear, the bunny hug, the monkey glide, the buzzard lope, the turkey trot, and all the other so-called "animal dances" were quicksteps with a lot of body con- tact and shaking of torsos, tossing of limbs, and—anathema! Moloch!— rotating of hips. Just early versions of the Lindy hop or the jitterbug, according to hoofers who were around long enough to witness both. Whore dances, according to the tutting classes (Dictionary of the Vulgar Tongue: *tommy* = whore). In any case, they were sexy, and wild.

Like the blues, these dances were the creature of the black Underworld, and often held onto a surprising amount of African content—animal imitation, improvised breaks, hip-swinging, etc. (here I'm cribbing from Marshall and Jean Stearns' invaluable *Jazz Dance*). And like the blues, they started their journey to Topworld in black vaudeville, and then crossed over into the white circuits. At the end of 1911, for instance, Al Jolson—then making waves as vaudeville's newest star—brought the black dance team of Johnny Peters and Mary Dewson back to New York with him from Purcell's to do the grizzly bear in his next show; they were supposed to have invented it (Peters is also credited with the turkey trot).

It didn't take long for things to reach the tipping point. Supposedly, the first posh joint to knuckle under and put in a dance floor was Bustanoby's, on 39th Street. That was in 1912, when they got Johnny Peters to demonstrate the dances, after which the patrons, I suppose, would try 'em on for size. I'm not optimistic about the quality of the imitation. (Another Bustanoby's dance model: Rudolph Valentino.) Soon even the Fifth Avenue hotels were following suit, turning themselves into upper crust honky-tonks.

Novelty, novelty, novelty. Steps flying in from everywhere: by 1913, the "early adopters" (as the guys over in marketing call 'em) had moved on to hot Latin steps like the Argentine tango and the Brazilian maxixe. That's when you start hearing rumors of "tango teas" where the "tea" was hooch and the tangoing went on till dawn—you know, raves. Fine for the few, but what about the many? The cakewalk, the Texas tommy, the tango—all the new dances were as tricky as they were strenuous; the average corseted matron or pre-thrombotic commercial traveler of the day must have had a hell of a time with them, no matter how much they might smack of *le bon ton*. "Dance and Grow Thin," the song advised; easier said than done.

Now, you couldn't do the grizzly bear to a schottische or a polka or, God forbid, a march. You needed ragtime. But it's not like just any ragtime would do, either: the delicate lace of the classic piano rag was bound to seem a little anemic to someone busy whirling his partner around by the neck. Unfortunately, it's hard to get a fix on exactly what dance music sounded like before the teens, because little of it got on record, with the important exception of all those cakewalks. What there was of it was generally handled by the banjoists or the military bands—even the so-called Victor Dance Orchestra that cut Ben Harney's "Cakewalk in the Sky" in 1905 (Vic. 4008) is just a gang of Sousa men with a couple of violins tacked on. The typical café orchestra wasn't much in evidence. Old pictures and old-timers' memories can give us an idea of the instrumentation, at least. A New York café dance orchestra around 1910 would have been about seven pieces: if it was white, a violin or two for lead, a mandolin or banjo-mandolin or two to double, a piano for harmony, a guitar for rhythm, a string bass for bottom. There'd be some kind of percussion—certainly a bass drum, and maybe a snare and some percussion things—but the drum kit as we know it was a vaudeville innovation of the teens. You might find a banjo to reinforce the rhythm and a cello for the inner voicings. A white orchestra would have horns—a clarinet, a cornet—instead of a couple of the strings, but outside of New Orleans not a lot of black musicians played them. When Jim Europe was called on to recruit a brass band for the 369th Harlem Infantry during World War I, he had to import half the reeds from Puerto Rico.

But that's getting ahead of the game. It's not until late 1913 that we can get a firm handle on what these dance combos were up to, and we have James Reese Europe largely to thank for that.

When the dance craze hit, Jim Europe was anything but a newbie at getting folks to stir their stumps, be they white or colored. Back in the oughts, one of his gigs (a term that he coined, according to Eubie Blake, a Europe alumnus) had been as codirector of Ernest Hogan's all-singing, all-dancing, all-ragtime-picking Memphis Students. Neither students nor from Memphis—the name was a poke at the Fisk University Jubilee Singers—Hogan's band caused a real commotion on the Topworld-Underworld border when they hit Proctor's Twenty-Third Street Theater with their jumped-up string driven ragging and four-part harmonies. Power pop, in other words. James Weldon Johnson called them "the first modern jazz band ever heard on a New York stage, and probably any other stage"; clearly, he'd never been to the Animule Hall. Still, whatever Hogan's gang was playing, it wasn't the same old ragtime (O that the Memphis Students had recorded!).

The Memphis Students were a string band: a dim 1905 photo has them posing stiffly behind a stack of instruments—a couple of banjos, six or seven mandolins, maybe a banjo-mandolin (alias "bandori," alias "banjorine") or two, a couple of harp-guitars, perhaps a cello and a fiddle. It's hard to make everything out, but there's nary a horn to be seen (they may have added a few later, on tour). This reliance on strings was both "authentically" black (you know, the banjo and all) and practical, what with the relative scarcity of black wind musicians. In any case, when the Students were all snapping out their riffs together the drive must have been titanic.

If talent and experience weren't enough to set Europe up in the dance music business, he also had luck and connections, both mighty useful things in this world. In D.C., his father had been appointed to a clerkship in the postal service by Postmaster General John Wanamaker, a Philadelphian of enormous wealth and social oomph. One day in 1903, Jim happened to bump into Wanamaker's son's private secretary. This led, in the fullness of time, to the whole Wanamaker family using Europe bands whenever they needed music. Now, Society wasn't in the habit of hiring black musicians, but the Wanamakers were progressive and the bands were good, and others in the smart set began to catch the bug. It was a lucrative little sideline; then the dance fever hit.

Suddenly, black musicians were in demand—they had that extra something that made the burghers really shake 'em on down. The problem was, how did you get a hold of them? You couldn't go through the Musicians Union, as you would to get a white band—the union drew the color line. You couldn't just go up to Harlem and wave a roll around. You needed a go-between, someone like James Reese Europe. Exactly like him.

In the spring of 1910, Europe and some of his cronies founded the Clef Club, a combination social club–booking agency–benevolent association for black cabaret musicians (string players almost to a man). With his connections, he'd been making out just fine. But he always thought big. Furthermore, to publicize the club, he organized and conducted a semiannual series of concerts—fantastic affairs that mingled the tenacious traditions of minstrelsy, Will Marion Cook's orchestral ragtime, light classics—Lincke's "Beautiful Spring," if you've ever heard of it (not me)—and what-have-you.

By the fourth one, on May 2, 1912, they were playing Carnegie Hall, their 125-piece orchestra had horns and reeds to supplement the strings, percussion, and pianos (fourteen of them!) that the orchestra had started off with, and they were playing a nice-sized chunk of "serious" music, all by black composers—including, of course, Will Marion Cook. They weren't in overalls or swallowtail coats, they weren't blacked up, and they weren't dishing out Coon songs. Yet the integrated audience (seated together, a novelty) packed the joint, and the critics raved. Big sensation: colored musicians play just as good as real ones, but different; who knew?

This was a turning point in American music: the first viable alternative to European art music that wasn't derivative or cheesy. The Clef Club Symphony Orchestra mixed highbrow and lowdown and made it look natural. The players did unheard-of things: they sang in harmony while they played, they used Underworld instruments like the banjo, they swung. The raw drive and swerve of hot ragtime were incorporated, but not quenched. Just as Will Marion Cook did with the vocal resources of Coondom, James Reese Europe took its instrumental ones—banjos, fiddles, drums, pianos—and

forged them into something powerful, complex and, above all, dignified. While his music wasn't jazz, not precisely, it combined Underworld and Topworld in the same way.

I don't want to say that without the Clef Club Orchestra, you'd
have no Fletcher Henderson, Duke Ellington, Bix Beiderbecke, Artie
Shaw, Charles Mingus, Beatles, Parliament-Funkadelic...—none of
the "there's gotta be more to this music than just grinding" wing of
hot music. But Jim Europe set the cornerstone. At least, that's what
seems to have gone on—nobody thought to get the CCO on record.

That would soon be taken care of, after a fashion. On August 22,
1913, Mrs. Stuyvesant Fish pitched a shivaree at Crossways, her
Newport "summer cottage." Entertainment: the sophisticated, dar-
ing, and yet still respectable (i.e., white and married) dance team of
Vernon and Irene Castle, performing for the first time to the music
of Europe's Society Orchestra. Two chunks of U-235, either one—
although dangerous in the long term—apparently inert; bring 'em
together and bimmo! Alamagordo. The Nuclear Age.

In the fusion between musicians and dancers, the Castles finally
found the beats they'd always been searching for, harder-driving
than any of the polite white bands they'd been using, and swervier
(Vernon—a Brit—was evidently "astonished" at the "instrumental
color" of Europe's band, said color being, I must infer, Senegambian)—yet still polished enough to keep the nice folks in the audience away from the exits. After a couple of years of using Europe,
they were forced for some contractual reason to use Sousa and his
band for an appearance at New York's Hippodrome. Irene Castle:
"He ignored our frantic signals to pick up the tempo and his uniformed arms flailed away with the precise beat of a man conducting a military march, which was exactly what he was doing." Once
you go black, I suppose, you can never go back.

As for Europe. Nine years later, when Louis Armstrong left New
Orleans to make his fortune up north, a bouncer who went by the
name of "Slippers" gave him the kind of advice that comes from

© IRA L. HILL'S STUDIO, N. Y. C.

**Mr. and Mrs. Vernon Castle Dancing
the Fox Trot**

Unlikely revolutionaries.

COURTESY OF ARCHEOPHONE RECORDS

hard experience: "Always keep a white man behind you that'll put his hand on you and say, 'That's my nigger.'" With the Castles to vouch for him, cover his back, Europe was poised to break his music out into the fat pastures of Topworld America, without having to manipulate the minstrel mask or incarnate the Coon.

The dividends came fast. Right after the Fish affair, the Castles hired Europe as their personal musician: wherever they went, he and his gang went too. Furthermore, they took the extraordinary step of stipulating this in all their contracts. They were the most popular act in America. If you wanted 'em, you had to swallow the fifteen or twenty tuxedo-clad black men that went with 'em. (Polk Miller—the "Old Virginia Plantation Negro"—died in October; my theory: this is what done him in.) That fall, the Castles opened a nightclub (the cover: a cool hundred dollars) and a dancing school, encouraged in the latter by a bunch of society matrons who wanted "a place where their children could go to learn the dance without being exposed to the discredited elements." Europe supplied the musicians for both.

That was only the beginning of Europe's infiltration of Topworld: on the penultimate day of 1913, Europe led fifteen of his A-echelon syncopators into Victor's New York studio (probably the same one that the ODJB would use) and produced the first records made in America by a black band: two rags, a tango, and a maxixe. They cut the rags first, and, with a quick one-two combination, did to recorded ragtime what Jack Johnson had done to Jim Jeffries. "Down Home Rag" and "Too Much Mustard" (released back-to-back on Vic. 35359) are to Vess Ossman what Led Zeppelin's "Communications Breakdown" is to Chuck Berry—the basic premise of the music might be more or less the same, but the execution is all force and crackling, almost contemptuous speed (Hogan had taught him well).

The minute Europe's Society Syncopators kick off "Down Home Rag" (a Wilbur Sweatman number that had been recorded the year before by the Victor Military Band), it's clear what musical territory we're in. The herky-jerky fiddle riffs, topspun in the wildest Celtic style; the manic banjication; the rat-a-tat drumming; all the various and sundry whoops, hollers, and guffaws from the band—we're back in ol' Dan Emmettland. There have, however, been some improvements made, and it's not just the matter of the addition of a trumpet and a clarinet to add punch to the lead lines. The rustic high spirits (whether real or assumed) have been replaced by a deliberate, crushing precision. The Society Syncopators were the first masters of the modern power riff: as they blaze along at something like 244 beats per minute, there's not one guy spitting out the fiddle part, but three; not one banjo-mandolin, but five. There are even two pianos. Where the Victor Military Band, just the year before, cantered through their version with style and not without brio (Vic. 17340B), Europe's men fly through theirs with propeller screaming and machine guns blazing. Suddenly the violence with which the ODJB executed "Dixieland Jass Band One-Step" doesn't seem so anomalous.

Occasionally, when studying the course of history, one gets an unpleasant feeling that somewhere a gear has slipped, a cylinder has misfired, a switch has closed too soon or late—that something has kinked up the orderly procession of events. One such locus occurs on Victor 35359. It has to do, in part, with the ugly, hacking rhythm of the banjo-mandolins. But mostly it's Buddy Gilmore. Gilmore, another ex-Memphis Student, was one of the pioneers of a new instrument, the drum kit. (The technology to combine all the traditional kinds of band percussion in the hands of one individual had only been around for twenty years or so, and its true potential for mayhem was just then being realized.) The thing is, Gilmore's work went on record in December, 1913—a full eight months before Europe (the continent, not the man) and the rest of the "civilized" world would experience the full horror of the relentless tap-tap-tapping of the machine gun, a sound destined to resonate throughout the twentieth century. And yet, proof perhaps that a hidden hand guides the course of events, here's that very tap-tap, embodied in Gilmore's

GILMORE
Mascot of Society   Not wonderful but good

"ROYAL CHAMPION DRUMMER OF THE WORLD,
FORMERLY WITH MR. AND MRS. VERNON CASTLE,"
as the back of Gilmore's card informs us.

COURTESY OF SHERWIN DUNNER

drumming in all its pitiless, mechanical fury. Curious. This disc alone must have taken ten years off Scott "It is never right to play 'rag-time' fast" Joplin's life.

There was another, tamer session in February (four songs), and an abortive one in October (two songs, none released), and then silence until 1919, which we'll get to in a moment. I don't know why Victor was so tight with the bag; Victor 35359, at least, seems to have been a hit (if the frequency with which copies still turn up is any guide), and they kept "Castle House Rag" (from the February session) in print for five years. But that's all there was; perhaps Southern distributors complained, perhaps Europe held out for a white man's wage, perhaps he was just too busy with his other commitments to pick up chump change recording; this far down the road, we'll never know.

The year 1914 was a busy year for Europe: besides recording (what there was of it), backing up the Castles in all their local activities and pulling in innumerable society gigs on the side, he found time to put together a replacement for the treacherous Clef Club (who had kicked him out), the Tempo Club. And to promote it with the obligatory big concert at Carnegie Hall. And he found time for the Castle Whirlwind Tour: thirty cities in twenty-eight days. As if the sight of Irene, slim, sexy, and utterly, completely un-Victorian wasn't signal enough to the assembled Midwestern burghers that a new world was dawning, there were Europe and his men, all tuxedo-clad and without visible trace of Coon. Many couldn't stomach it: "A lot of darky musicians sit in the regular music makers' places, and if it was a traveling medicine show I could sense it out, but what those society people are putting down good coin to see it for is what gets me"—thus the *Minneapolis Journal*'s humor columnist. But not everyone was quite so shitheaded.

And he found time to "invent" the foxtrot. The old cakewalk and especially the new "animal dances" were all well and good, but better to watch than execute unless you were comfortable enough with who you were to work up a serious sweat and inflict disarray on your *habillement*. To really get the householders dancing, some clever bugger had to come up with a new step, genus lite—slower and simpler, yet still savoring of the dance forbidden. Actually, it took three clever buggers: the Castles supplied the gymnastics, Jim Europe the beats. That was in 1914, and the step was the foxtrot (originally fox trot), destined to dominate the American dance floor until the end of social dancing.

At some point during the Whirlwind Tour, Europe and the Castles were hanging out, Europe—as usual—at the piano. He started picking out the familiar riffs of Handy's "Memphis Blues"—he was the first bandleader to play it—and wondered aloud if they could work something up to go with it; maybe throw it in for contrast with all the uptempo flag-wavers. Vernon was skeptical, "the world of today demanding staccato music," but they gave it a try. Big, big hit with the audiences. So now the blues goes Topworld, works its peculiar wiggle right into the foundations of middle-class movement. In the hands of couples less dicty than the impeccably Topworld Castles, the foxtrot would always be prone to carnality—the only thing hotter than fast sex is slow sex. The foxtrot always had that potential.

Would that we had a record of Europe's Society Orchestra digging into the "Memphis Blues." Along with Ben Harney doing "Mr. Johnson, Turn Me Loose," Ernest Hogan and his Memphis Students doing "All Coons Look Alike to Me," Scott Joplin (at the height of his powers) doing the "Maple Leaf Rag," and Buddy Bolden's Eagle Band doing "Make Me a Pallet on the Floor," it's one of the greatest records that never got made. Would it have been the first undisputed jazz record? Drive—and how!—and swerve; ragtime and the blues, brought together by black musicians in the lens of the Venn diagram where Topworld and Underworld interpenetrate each other: yeah. It would have.

Might-have-beens are sweet. Just how sweet is demonstrated by Dan Kildare, the Clef Club man who, right around the time Europe was cutting "Down Home Rag" and "Too Much Mustard," deposed him from the club's presidency and took his place. In early 1915, a few months after making a few Society Syncopator-lite type dance records as leader of Joan Sawyer's Persian Garden Orchestra (Sawyer was trying to cut into the Castles' action; among her dance partners was the young Rudolph Valentino), Kildare took a bunch of Clef Club musicians over to London to play at the swank and rather decadent Ciro's Club.

Sometime around August 1916 his band began recording for the British branch of Columbia Records—as "Ciro's Club Coon Orchestra." At a mere six pieces, his band was a more intimate and infinitely more relaxed version of the Society Syncopators: a banjo, a banjo-mandolin, Kildare's brother Walter on cello, Kildare on piano, plus string bass and drums. It took them a while to get around to it, but after a longish string of pleasantly funky, albeit not blatantly hot, pop records—there are exceptions—they finally did a W. C. Handy blues—not "Memphis Blues," but the other one. The "St. Louis Blues" (Col. [E] 699).

If Ciro's Club's was no back-country juke joint and its Coon Orchestra no casual assemblage of horny-handed sons of labor fresh from their agrarian toil, this is nonetheless the first blues to be recorded by a black string band, and it's surprisingly funky. True, it does preserve some of the delicate precision of the 1906 Ossman-Dudley Trio, but the way Kildare's men dig into the beat wouldn't be out of place on a record by, say, the Memphis Jug Band or the Mississippi Sheiks or one of the other blues-based string bands of the late twenties.

Kildare's weren't the only Clef Club musicians in England at the time, or even the first ones to record. Murray's Club, on Beak Street in raffish Soho, had their own aggregation, who recorded four sides in February 1916 as the Versatile Four. They did two fast numbers and two slower ones, which don't concern us. The obligatory "Down Home Rag" (HMV 654) and, especially, "Circus Day in Dixie" (HMV 645) demonstrate that the incandescence the Society Syncopators achieved was no one-time thing. Machine gun drums, shellburst cymbals, flashing banjo-mandolins, shouted vocals— all the hallmarks of the old Jim Europe style are here. "Circus Day in Dixie," with its minstrel themes transformed by pure musical testosterone, is one of the hottest records I've ever heard. Ironically, Murray's Club was the site of one of the first meetings that led to the development of the tank—the machine gun's antidote.

♪

Although Jim Europe cracked Topworld, lodged himself in it, he never got to exploit his success. In 1915, the war swallowed up Vernon, who was to survive over a hundred combat missions with the RAF only to cop it in a training accident. The Castles were Europe's ticket to Main Street; without them, he was stuck in New York, a blackbird in a gilded cage. He still had plenty of Society work, but nowhere to go with it. In September 1916 he joined the 15th Infantry Regiment (Colored) of the New York National Guard—the Harlem regiment. War was coming, and in it a substantial slice of black America (Topworld-oriented optimists, mostly) saw an opportunity to prove its patriotism, its mettle, its manhood. After the war, there'd surely be a new deal. (No.)

At any rate, although Jim Europe joined up to fight, not play music—he was training to be a machine gunner (again, that hidden hand)—inevitably, the regiment's C.O. recruited him to build the regimental band. Europe had little interest in brass bands (strings, he thought, were more "characteristic" of black music) but he knuckled down and did his duty. When war came in April, he threw himself full-time into the new band, recruiting top musicians from all over the country, including no less than Bill "Bojangles" Robinson as drum major (not to mention those reed players he went to Puerto Rico to get). By the time the 15th Harlem was ready to ship

out for France, in November, it had the best band in the Army—
and the only one that swung. Europe made sure to whip a goodly
number of Harlem favorites—rags, blues—in with the obligatory
marches. And by the time these guys recorded, two years and hundreds of concerts all over France later (not that they spent their
whole time over there syncopating: Lieutenant James Reese Europe
was the first black American officer to lead troops in combat), they
were absurdly tight, yet still light on their feet. But they didn't
sound anything at all like the Society Orchestra. The 369th Infantry
("Hellfighters") Band (the Army had renamed the old 15th Harlem
in 1918) had been infected with the new jazz, and the mix of songs
they cut in their four 1919 sessions proves it: out of twenty-four
sides, four are blues—W. C. Handy, mostly—and another eight are
straight jazz numbers, including the ODJB's own "Clarinet Mar-
malade."

The Hellfighters records are tight, driving, hot. They're also
anachronistic—the cutting edge of hot music was with the folks who
were exploring the parameters of freedom that the Senegambian
mode allows, not with folks who were training military bands to
play pickled jazz riffs in unison. The distance between these records
and the small-band jazz records that were trickling out into the
marketplace isn't quite as stark as, say, the difference between James
Brown and his Famous Flames doing "I Feel Good" and the Kansas
State University marching band doing it, but it's not that far off. I
don't want to be too harsh about the Hellfighters. There are some,
even many, truly exciting moments—the bit in "Indianola" when
the chorus kicks in, Frank DeBroit's flutter-tongued cornet cadenza
on "Darktown Strutters' Ball" (both on Pathé 22081), the all too
brief swinging trombone break at the very end of "Memphis Blues"
(quite possibly by Ward "Dope" Andrews, whom we shall encounter
again; Pathé 22085)—and the standards of arranging and musician-
ship throughout are impeccable. The Hellfighters represent the
apotheosis of military band ragtime. But military band ragtime, indeed

military band *anything,* was music of the past. Still, they must've been something to see.

Two days after the Hellfighters' fourth session, James Reese Europe was dead—the Underworld, on the knife-edge of which he'd been walking his whole musical life, caught up with him at last. On May 9, 1919, while he was backstage at Boston's Mechanics Hall for intermission, Europe reprimanded Herbert Wright, one of his drummers, for a bit of unprofessionalism on stage. Wright took it as a dis and shanked him. It was just a little cut, but they couldn't stop the bleeding. Europe was the first black man in New York City history to receive a public funeral.

Jim Europe's sudden death devastated the strivers' wing of black music. By almost single-handedly making ofay America accept "a kind of symphony music," as he put it, "that, no matter what else you may think, is different and distinctive, and that lends itself to the playing of the peculiar compositions of our race," he took up the talking stick for black musicians coast to coast. He was the man, soul brother number one (Bert Williams, the only guy who could challenge Europe's title, had too fine and ironical an eye to set himself up as anything but Bert Williams).

But while Europe had been busy fooling around with socialites and machine guns, and guys like Fred Van Eps had been adding trap drums and saxophones to their acts and learning how to make people dance (his Van Eps—Banta Dance Orchestra even did their own version of "Down Home Rag," in 1916), guys like Freddie Keppard and Nick LaRocca and Larry Shields had been draining north from New Orleans to Chicago and kinda layin' 'em dead with their peculiar bluesy wiggle. I don't know what Jim Europe thought about the ODJB; I doubt he heard the band live—like all downtown nightspots, Reisenweber's drew the color line—but he must have heard the records. I suspect they bothered him. In 1918, he discussed jazz with a reporter for the New York *World.* Although he came out for the swerve—it was natural and good for black musicians to put a spin on each note—he also revealed a kind of timidity in the face of it: "I have to call a daily rehearsal of my band to prevent the musicians from adding to their music more than I wish them to." He was a dance musician, at heart, addicted to the collective effort of the groove, and the "hey-lookit-me" individualism inherent in a musician taking off into the wild blue yonder must have troubled him deep down. Even his wildest records were all about keeping the uncheckable in check, if only just.

Looking down the road, I can't convince myself that had Europe lived he would have embraced free spirits like Louis Armstrong or Sidney Bechet—in fact, he auditioned Bechet on his 1919 homecoming tour with the 369th; he was impressed, but...pass. It's a glum thought that Herbert Wright just possibly allowed a hundred flowers to bloom: that without that one towering, heroic figure, the Boss, to prune and shape and expedite the flowering of Senegambian-mode dance music, the blossoms were perhaps slower to bloom and more delicate, but also richer in color, in fragrance, in variety.

In any case, by 1919, jazz had won; ragtime was disarming itself, beating its spiky staccato riffs into something flatter and smoother. It seems like all it took was one listen to "Livery Stable Blues" and everybody who liked to play things hot, from the exalted James Reese Europe to the tent-show queen to the brilliantined small-town bad boy, knew just what he or she had to do. The ODJB—or their records, to be precise—were like that grain of whatever it was you dropped into the beaker of clear solution in eighth-grade science class to make all that white stuff start precipitating out.

Two Crazes:
Jazz, 1917–1921; The Blues, 1920–1924

After one year from the ratification of this article the manu-
facture, sale or transportation of intoxicating liquors within,
the importation thereof into, or the exportation thereof from
the United States and all territory subject to the jurisdiction
thereof for beverage purposes is hereby prohibited.

—THE EIGHTEENTH AMENDMENT

It was a one-two punch. First the ODJB and its disciples jabbed
hard for Topworld's breadbasket, already considerably softened up
by the punches it had been taking from the likes of Williams,
Europe, and the handful of New Orleans bands who had filtered
into vaudeville and Yankeeland cabarets. Then, in 1920, Mamie
Smith and the blues singers floated in a lovely roundhouse to the
heart and goodnight, sweet prince. Topworld fell. So hard, in fact,
that its music—the stuff to which it was OK to listen, which didn't
brand you as weird or betray unsuitable class origins—stayed warm
for almost thirty years, until the Patti Page era set in.

Even when they were still at Reisenweber's, the ODJB blew a
lot of minds and called forth a lot of censorious yelping. About a week
after they opened, *Variety* sent someone down to take a gander: "This
'jaz' thing, five pieces (the Reisenweber's bunch being white) sounds
like a trio of musicians trying to draw business to a side show. There
is a piccolo screech and a drum for prominence. It's what would be
called 'stewed music,' for you have to be feeling that way to like it."

So much for jazz. "Piccolo" indeed—obviously, the guy didn't
even bother to stroll by the bandstand: the ODJB had no piccolo,
saxophone (another reviewer), slide whistle, Maxim gun, or coal-
scuttle. Cornet, clarinet, trombone, piano, drums; that's all. (It probably didn't help that the boys went around saying things like "none

of us know music"—not true—and, after the postwar influenza epidemic killed Ragas in early 1919, "I don't know how many pianists we tried until we found one who couldn't read music"—also not true; J. Russel Robinson, Ragas's replacement, was an accomplished pop composer. But punks will be punks, and you take their inflammatory pronouncements seriously at your own peril.) More importantly, the article closed by noting "the 400 Club is placing a cover charge against all chairs not ordering food." In other words, the boys were making pots of money. A cool thousand a night, in fact.

Which fact did not go unnoticed by their fellow musicians: within weeks, jazz bands started springing up in places where there had been none before. Example: in December 1916 *Variety* ran a little squib about Earl Fuller, a novelty drummer who led the house band at the extremely posh Rector's restaurant/dance club, about half a mile from Reisenweber's at 48th and Broadway. Nary a hint of jazz. Six months later, we find Earl Fuller's Famous Jazz Band—himself on piano now, a cornet, a drummer, and a couple of ex-klezmers on clarinet and trombone—cutting discs for Columbia (including a swervy version of Pryor's "A Coon Band Contest," the only cakewalk recorded by a first-wave jazz band). They were a big hit, although Fuller's men were to the ODJB as the ersatz rock 'n' roll bands in fifties movies were to Elvis: guys who made little attempt to really understand a music they felt was beneath them and hence played it for laughs, exaggerating its comic potential and ignoring its subtleties. In other words, doing to the ODJB what the ODJB was doing, if less deliberately, to the music of black New Orleans.

Still, in 1917 Fuller's band was better than nothing. Garvin Bushell, then a fifteen-year-old black kid living in Springfield, Ohio (nobody's idea of blues country), recalled that Fuller's "Li'l Liza Jane" (Vic. 18394, b/w "Coon Band Contest") came with the brand-new Victrola his family bought for Christmas that year. "I played this record over and over. Noticing the lift the clarinet [played by former klezmer and future star Ted Lewis] gave to the last chorus,

I decided to forget about Bach, Beethoven, and the others I had been studying on the piano for the past four years. The seed of jazz had definitely been sown."

Fuller's gang wasn't alone, or even the first: on May 10, a California reedman named Rudy Wiedoft managed somehow to wrangle a session out of the stiffnecks at Edison for his Frisco "Jass" Band, a weirdly jerky blend of Fred Van Eps–style tack-it-down banjication and Pryoresque trombone smears. But even before them, another new-style act had edged its way onto record. What's more, it was black.

Wilbur C. Sweatman (nobody can find out what the "C" stood for) was a trouper. He'd been in vaudeville (and circuses, and minstrel shows—he even did a stint with Mahara's Minstrels, under W. C. Handy) since he was a kid back in the nineties, playing clarinet. Three of 'em, actually, all at the same time. Show music. But he also led bands, and wrote songs—including, of course, "Down Home Rag." He was also supposed to have done "Maple Leaf Rag" for an Edison subsidiary way back in 1903–04, but no trace of the cylinder has ever been found. In any case, he'd managed to sneak in front of the recording at the end of 1916 to cut his own, not-unfunky, version of "Down Home Rag" with a white studio trio (not counting Polk Miller's or Bert Williams's vocal efforts, the first interracial session in hot music). While this disc ain't exactly jazz, it ain't exactly ragtime, either (Emerson 7161). Then, in April—about a month after Victor released "Livery Stable Blues"—Sweatman, with an "and His Jass Band" tacked onto his name, did six numbers for Pathé, among them Handy's "Joe Turner Blues" and a certain "Boogie Rag." Sure, the Jass Band was made up entirely of saxophones, with Sweatman's clarinet noodling a gentle lead—no cornet!—but it still kinda swung, with a subdued funk alien to the ODJB's more strenuous conception of the music.

Yet, taken all together, surprisingly little of the new music was making it on record. As 1917 wore into 1918, the catalyst worked its transformation in young musicians coast to coast, whether inspiring them to slavish imitation (tales abound of guys slowing down ODJB records to learn them note for note) or just lending them a beat here and a lick there or even the bare idea that it was OK to play the song how *you* thought it should go, the printed arrangement be damned. (For some, of course, jazz was just a flag of convenience, a handle to attach to what they'd been doing all along.) But the record companies, the only chroniclers we've got for what people were actually playing, kept it all at arm's length.

There were exceptions: in August 1917, Eubie Blake, more or less running Europe's Tempo Club while Himself was smiting the Kaiser hip and thigh, cut a ragtimey version of Earl Fuller's "Jazzin' Around" with another pianist and a drummer who may be Buddy Gilmore. This was also for Pathé (maybe the fact that headquarters for this label was in Paris had something to do with its willingness to go black). The next month, W. C. Handy got his turn, as noted above. But the exceptions were few.

This is especially surprising, since a war was on and cabarets were heavily restricted—dancing leading to sex, sex leading to syphilis, and syphilis leading to the Kaiser kicking our ass. (In New Orleans, they closed down the District; if all those funky professors wanted to maintain their diamond-tooth lifestyle, they'd have to hit the rails to do so.) In practical terms, this translated into a boom in record sales; Victor, for example, moved about 15 million units in 1916; in 1919, with folks still winding down from the recent unpleasantness in Europe, the figure was 31 million. If you couldn't go out, you'd have to bring the cabaret into your parlor. A natural opportunity for the new wiggle to grow like kudzu, especially since the European acts Topworld had been drawn to were lying doggo. But, as far as I can tell, that's not what happened. Victor, Columbia, Edison, Brunswick, and the others by and large let jazz pass until 1919 or 1920, at least two full years. And since the familiar system whereby independents fill niches not catered to by majors wasn't yet in place, the smaller labels—content to chip and shave the majors' markets, follow and imitate—did likewise. Sure, they made sure they had a tame jazz band on the roster, to fill that niche, but they made no effort to expand the market or track down local talent around the country.

I don't know what the suits were thinking. Of course, a fad is a fad: they had no way of knowing what this stuff would become. Far as they saw it, it was just Underworld music, not to be distinguished from the vulgarities of the nigger blues and the dumbshit sounds of the hillbilly rubes. Besides, the stuff was polarizing: if parts of Topworld were attracted by it, other parts were totally and quite vocally repelled. And they were, by and large, the parts with the money. The parts who lived next door to the suits, who stood beside them at the saloon or sat behind them at the Temperance League. Why make waves?

Here, from the editorial page of the New Orleans *Times-Picayune*, of all places, is a perfect expression of what jazz—and, by extension, blues and everything else where drive met swerve—was up against. It's worth quoting this in full; what richness the eight decades since this was first uncorked have added to our recorded music, they have subtracted from our prose.

Why is the jass music and, therefore, the jass band? As well ask why is the dime novel or the grease-dripping doughnut. All are manifestations of a low streak in man's tastes that has not yet come out in civilization's wash. Indeed, one might go further, and say that jass music is the indecent story syncopated and counter-pointed. Like the improper anecdote, also, in its youth it was listened to blushingly behind closed doors and drawn curtains, but, like all vice, it grew bolder until it dared decent surroundings, and there was tolerated because of its oddity.

We usually think of people as either musical or nonmusical, as if there were a simple line separating the two great classes.

The fact is, however, that there are many mansions in the house of the muses. There is first the great assembly hall of melody—where most of us take our seats at some time in our lives—but a lesser number pass on to inner sanctuaries of harmony, where the melodic sequence, the "tune" as it most frequently is called, has infinitely less interest than the blending of notes into chords so that the combining wave-lengths will give new aesthetic sensations. This inner court of harmony is where nearly all the truly great music is enjoyed.

In the house there is, however, another apartment, properly speaking, a kind of servants' hall of rhythm. It is there we hear the hum of the Indian dance, the throb of the Oriental tambourines and kettledrums, the clatter of the clogs, the click of Slavic heels, the thumpty-thump of the negro banjo, and, in fact, the native dances of the world. Although commonly associated with melody, and less often with harmony also, rhythm is not necessarily music, and he who loves to keep time to the pulse of the orchestral performance by patting his foot upon the theater floor is not necessarily a music lover. The ultra-modernists in composition go so far as to pronounce taboo upon rhythm, and even omit the perpendicular lines on their bars of written music, so that the risk of a monotonous pulsation is done away with.

Prominently in the basement hall of rhythm is found ragtime, and of those most devoted to the cult of displaced accent there has developed a brotherhood of those who, devoid of harmonic and even melodic instinct, love to fairly wallow in noise. On certain natures, sound loud and meaningless has an exciting, almost an intoxicating effect, like crude colors and strong perfumes, the sight of flesh or the sadic [sic] pleasure in blood. To such as these the jass music is a delight, and a dance to the unstable bray of the sackbut gives a sensual delight more intense and quite different from the langour of a Viennese waltz or the refined sentiment and respectful emotion of an eighteenth-century minuet.

In the matter of jass, New Orleans is particularly interested, since it has been widely suggested that this particular form of musical vice had its birth in this city—that it came, in fact, from doubtful surroundings in our slums. We do not recognize the honor of parenthood, but with such a story in circulation, it behooves us to be the last to accept the atrocity in polite society, and where it has crept in we should make a point of civic honor to suppress it. Its musical value is nil, and its possibilities of harm are great.

They ran that on June 20, 1918, just five days before their homies in the ODJB cut their epochal "Tiger Rag" (in New York, of course). "If there arise among you a prophet," Deuteronomy warns, "that prophet shall be put to death."

So. Your choices: total stiff or vulgar, flesh-ogling sadist fit only for the servants' hall—in other words, your typical razor-toting Coon (just who do you think supplied the servants in New Orleans?). There were, as always, plenty of folks who didn't give a shit what the likes of the *Times-Picayune* thought (a few high-class music critics among them), and they bought records. But, as always, there were more who did, and so did they. And, being on firm moral ground, they were the ones more likely to cause trouble.

♪

If the ODJB and their spawn were punk, what the record companies needed was new wave: a safe, disciplined, poppy new sound with just enough of the "unstable bray of the sackbut"—the shock of the new—to give it a little static-electric spark. The answer came along in the nick of time, in the unlikely form of a rather sickly, self-taught thirty-three-year-old pianist/drummer from San Francisco.

Along with everybody else, Art Hickman had put together a dance band back in 1913—his being for, of all things, the evening recreation of the Pacific Coast League's San Francisco Seals (the team where DiMaggio was to get his start twenty years later) while they were in training camp somewhere in the wilds of Sonoma.

Scoop Gleeson, sports guy for the San Francisco *Bulletin,* thought having the band up there was a pretty good angle: the Seals, he wrote on March 6, "have trained on ragtime and 'jazz' and Manager Del Howard says there's no stopping them." In fact, "the players are just brimming over with that old 'Texas Tommy' stuff and there is a bit of the 'jazz' in everything they do." And what *is* this 'jazz' stuff? "Why, it's a little of that 'old life,' the 'gin-i-ker,' the 'pep,' otherwise known as the enthusiasalum." Scoop lived up to his moniker here: this was, as far as anyone knows, the first time that particular four-letter word made it into print.

That doesn't mean Hickman's little combo—trumpet, trombone, piano, two banjos, himself on drums—could have gotten over at the Animule Hall. Enthusiasalum is one thing, the blues is another. Hickman, later on, claimed that he had learned his shit straight from the source, back when he was a Western Union boy: "I used to greet with joy the chance to deliver a message to some hop joint, or honky-tonky in the Barbary Coast. There was music. Negroes playing it. Eye shades, sleeves up, cigars in mouth. Gin and liquor and smoke and filth. But music! There is where all jazz originated." Maybe so, but he quit that job when he was sixteen (circa 1902) and, judging from those of his eighty-six records I've heard—only a few of them have ever been reissued, and few collectors are interested in them—that was the last time he listened to a black musician. He did record four blues of the Handy variety, but whether he had ever actually heard a blues singer is another story.

From the sound of his band, not bloody likely. No matter; in 1919, the San Francisco *Chronicle* crowned him "King of Jazz" (a title soon to be usurped by Paul Whiteman; see below). Hickman didn't care for that; it gave folks the wrong idea: "They expected me to stand before them with a shrieking clarionet and perhaps a plug hat askew on my head shaking like a negro with the ague"— the plug hat and clarinet being trademarks, by the way, of Ted Lewis, Earl Fuller's erstwhile clarinetist, who had by then gone solo to killing effect. There was, of course, no danger of taking Hickman for a Negro of any sort whatsoever.

Probably connected to that fact is another: Hickman made himself and his boys a massive pile of pelf. His gig at the uber-swank Rose Room in the St. Francis Hotel was the most popular thing in San Francisco and the whole West Coast. They paid him enough that he saw no need to accept any of the offers to come to New York that kept rolling in. Victor had tried to get him to record in 1917, but that fell through. Finally, two years later, Columbia managed to pry him away from the Rose Room by sending a private Pullman car to bring him and his boys to New York. Between recording and the gig they held at the Biltmore Hotel for the two weeks they were in town, the band pulled in over forty thousand dollars.

Those two years of stubbornness were crucial: the band that finally recorded was enriched by three new members, Clyde Doerr and Bert Ralton on saxes and one Ferdinand Rudolf von Grofé handling the arrangements. Ferd Grofé had played violin in the Los Angeles Symphony Orchestra and piano in a selection of Barbary Coast dives. Topworld and Underworld. With Hickman, he bent his classical skills to arranging improvised ragtime with a dance beat. Different arrangements for each chorus, saxophones and brass in contrapuntal sections, improvised leads over ensemble choruses— all Grofé innovations.

On record, the Art Hickman Orchestra was a smooth, clean, disciplined aggregation with a strong rhythm section—two (barely audible) banjos, string bass (ditto), piano, and drums—and a lead that was carried not by the cornet, not by the clarinet, but bounced back and forth between Doerr and Ralton's saxophones. This is entirely unremarkable now, but in the teens the sax was where the synthesizer was in the early seventies, a novelty instrument just beginning to be used seriously. It's clear that they're working from the same basic premises as Europe's Society Syncopators, but lightly. The band's tone is bright, clean—no dirty slurs, growls, or bends— and optimistic, and so is the beat: where Europe's records facilitate the bacchanalic turkey trot, Hickman's are strictly for a foxtrot world. The 4/4 is steady, not too fast, not too slow, and not too loud. And not hot—not overtly, anyway, although you can still find that enthusiasalum, that something new, in it, if you know how to listen for it.

Most of the band's material was either polite stuff with titles like "Good Bye, Pretty Butterflies" and "Rainbow of My Dreams" or minor-key, but still polite, exotica such as "On the Streets of Cairo," "Song of the Orient," and "Rose of Mandalay." It takes a while to notice it, but there's actually a surprising amount of improvisation going on in all this. While the sweet, pleasant ensembles tick-tock away, there go Doerr and Ralston quietly spinning out smooth, fluid leads that owe little to the Senegambian mode. No blue tonalities, no roughness, moaning, or buzzing, no sickening lurches or wild blasts of sound. The swerve here—and there is definitely swerving going on—is melodic and harmonic, not rhythmic and tonal.

Not even the temptation of playing an actual blues could call those effects forth from the band—the two blues medleys they cut are about as free from dirt as an issue of *Highlights for Children.* Even Handy's great "Beale Street Blues" couldn't shake 'em loose. (Columbia issued both medleys back to back, as if to get them out of the way; Col. A-2813). Still, when the rhythm wakes up a bit— e.g., in the A-part of "Cairo" (Col. A-2858)—the band at least manages to get a bit flustered.

Their sole masterpiece was destined to become one of the all-time dance band classics, recorded by the likes of Duke Ellington, Fletcher Henderson, and Benny Goodman. "Rose Room (In Sunny Roseland)" is Hickman's own composition; he recorded it on September 20, 1919. It begins blandly enough but then unfolds into a sweet, sappish chorus that sticks in your head, all swelling strings and saxophones burbling away—improvising freely—underneath, over a gently rocking 4/4 rhythm. There's a sophisticated, rolling piano solo in the middle courtesy of Frank Ellis, an incisive bridge, some more swell and burble, and out (Col. A-2858). Pop heaven. Compare this to the New York–based Joseph C. Smith Orchestra's lightly jazzed version from the year before, and the true genius, if that's the word I want, of Hickman's organization becomes clear. The Smith disc isn't laughable, to be sure, but the rhythm's clunky and the only improvisation comes from Harry Raderman, the rather lugubrious trombonist (Vic. 18473). The Hickman one is, well, creamy and lightly effervescent, like a well-made Ramos gin fizz (San Francisco always was a great cocktail town).

Columbia was so excited by the results of their two-week mega-session they issued the first four records in an album—the first. It sold phenomenally well. For a year or so, Hickman was riding high. But he didn't like New York, or the road, and he was a stubborn S.O.B. After one more stint in New York, working for Flo Ziegfeld as "the highest paid orchestra leader in America," he took his act home pretty much for good and ran out his days playing dance music in California. He died in 1930. Fame has blown off countless musicians, but few indeed have blown her off. For whatever reason (hardly anything has been written about him; who knows?) that's what Art Hickman did.

But the Earth (as the proverb goes) is to the strong, and the fruits thereof. Hickman's abdication of the new wave throne left the field open to Victor's counterpunch, which came in the deceptively non-threatening form of an Oliver Hardy–lookalike from Denver. Paul Whiteman's Orchestra was strictly in the Hickman mode—he had absorbed the gospel straight from the source, having put together a band for San Francisco's Fairmont Hotel to compete with Hickman's at the St. Francis. What's more, by the time he recorded in

1920, he had managed to put none other than Ferd Grofé in the piano chair. But where Hickman was strictly self-taught, a honky-tonk musician at heart, Whiteman was a trained violinist of the symphony variety, willing and able to push his music to levels of dicty pretension far beyond Hickman's grasp. And he liked publicity. Loved it.

It didn't take long for Paul Whiteman to hijack this new "symphonic jazz," as he called it—to stamp his jowly mug on it and drive it into all the nooks and crannies of the Topworld market where plain old jazz jazz was just too rough, large, vital to penetrate. By 1922, he was a rich, rich man. Like James Reese Europe, he had a bunch of bands playing around under his name, but his got paid a hell of a lot better. In 1924, he staged his own triumph, the famous Aeolian Hall concert, whose climax was a new piece commissioned specially for his band: George Gershwin's "Rhapsody in Blue." It was the first show he lost money on; he didn't do it again. The King of Jazz maintained his popularity through the early 1930s, going through some interesting changes in the process (including very publicly dieting off a hundred pounds of his trademarked blubber). At one point or another, he managed to hire just about every white musician of the hot variety from Bix Beiderbecke to Bing Crosby and file them away in one of his capacious sections, there to trot out the occasional warm chorus and then sink back into the background of plush. The number of jazz standards that began their lives as Whiteman hits would fill a fake book.

But, no surprise here, Whiteman has few fans these days, especially in the jazz establishment—he's stiff, exploitative, phony, confused, dull, pretentious, and very, very white. Not Jazz. (As for Hickman, he's just been flat out ignored.) The problem is, these guys and their fellow-travelers—there were many—seemed to throw their lots in with the enemy; to agree with the *Times-Picayune* and all the other haters of jazz. It doesn't help that they went around spouting off to the effect that "jazz is merely noise, a product of the honky-tonks, and has no place in a refined atmosphere" (A.H.,

1920). In 1924, one of them even went so far as to sponsor a national contest to find a new name for the music, one more respectable than that awful "jazz." He got over 700,000 responses, every last one of 'em lamer than McCloskey's mule. A few of the finalists: "Fron-Fron," "Melody-Rhythmic," "Rhythmic-Reverie," "Rhapso-doon," "Rigsody," "Peppo," "Ufon," "Exilera" (GlaxoSmithKline take note), "Merry Hop," "Hades Harmonies," "Syncodavis" (a brazen attempt to influence the jury: the contest was run by Meyer Davis), "Jog-Hop," "Dancial," "Paradisa," "Swazee," "Syncosway," "Glide-ola," "En Cadence," "Syncomelo," "Mah Song," "Gee Miss" (watch it!), "Melojings" (?!?), "Beato Music," "Joy Music" (multiple entries). And the winner: "Synco-Pep," contributed by Alvin Bert, "manager of the Keystonians Orchestra of Pittsburgh, PA."

Unfortunately, too many critics have taken this kind of malarkey at face value and written its peddlers off without noticing the truly subversive nature of their music and achievement. Sure, Synco-Pep was polite in a way that good, hot jazz never is, but its politeness nevertheless fronted for a smooth drive and a carefully disguised swerve that could and sometimes did break out into raw excitement. Art Hickman and Ferd Grofé succeeded in building a framework that could contain extreme heat without itself being overtly hot, sort of like the magnetic fields that contain a fusion reaction. Ragtime couldn't do that; one player blasting away would throw everything out of whack—kind of like if Chank Nolen dropped the staccato guitar chords in the middle of "Papa's Got a Brand New Bag" for a long, interpretive solo. (Would it be interesting? Sure. But whither the groove?) Nor would Jim Europe stand for those kinds of willful shen-anigans; improvisation had to be kept squished under his thumb. But with this stuff—as long as the players kept the dirt out of their tone, kept Senegambia carefully veiled—they could stand right up and back out a fat one and none be the wiser. This was Topworld's cleverest gambit for dealing with the raw sounds of Underworld: scrub them up and set them on display against a cushion of nice.

In fact, Hickman and Whiteman—names out of Trollope—were every bit as revolutionary as the ODJB (more so, in a way: they invented their music while the ODJB more or less absorbed theirs). Although their bands, especially Whiteman's, read notes off a page, they always left a margin blank, a space for deviation. Through all the precise, sedate patterns you can catch glimpses of something wild, and you know it'll eventually break out. A little more push on the beat, a little more wrench in the lead, and the elephant—placid, dull, lumbering—stampedes and rips up everything before it. Neither Whiteman nor Hickman ever let their own bands get away like that (although a bunch of Whiteman's boys used to get together regularly to blow off steam on record as the Virginians, perhaps not the hottest of hot bands but not ice cubes, either). The idea of a synthesis between Synco-Pep and the free-form Senegambian-mode blue ragtime of the ODJB and their followers was both natural and attractive, and when you start wading through the records left by the myriad tuxedo-draped saxophone and music stand outfits who trod their path over the next three decades, you find it realized time and again.

It really kicked into gear after 1924, but that's another book. Nonetheless, at the very dawn of the twenties, the voice of things to come was not entirely unheard. You can hear it in Louis Panico's laughing cornet effects and hot (well, reasonably hot) breaks on the Isham Jones Orchestra's 1921 smash, "Wabash Blues" (Br. 5065). You can hear it that same year in "Baby Girl" by Fletcher Henderson's Dance Orchestra (not yet the superbly hot jazz orchestra they were to become), when the clunky verse opens into a swervy chorus where everybody's suddenly springing apart (Bl. Sw. 2100). You can hear it in the soaring clarinet lines with which ofay Atlanta bandleader Charles Fulcher decorates "The Eskimo Song," an odd little slab of rhythm he recorded for Okeh in June, 1923 (Ok. 4889). You can hear it in the beautifully funky "Mean, Mean Mama" Vic Meyers and His Orchestra—a pretty standard white dance outfit out of Seattle—turned in two months later, complete with wah-wah cornet chorus and hot trombone breaks by Jim Taft (Br. 2501).

In 1920, though, when Hickman and Whiteman were all the rage, this was still to come. The *Times-Picayune,* surveying the state of American pop at the beginning of the year, must have felt pretty damn smug. Jazz, "the indecent story syncopated and counter-pointed," while not eradicated root and branch, seemed nonetheless to be cleaning up its act or withering away. The ODJB had just scored their biggest hit ever with "Margie" (Vic. 18717), a rather syrupy confection with a prominent sax (they had to hire somebody) and not a lot of noise. Nor had the few black acts who had managed to bend the color bar succeeded in removing it for their fellows. Even minstrelsy was in rapid decline. The denizens of the servants' hall of rhythm seemed to be keeping to themselves again and not bothering respectable folk.

A year later, catastrophe. The servants were in open revolt, hot music was everywhere—worse, hot *black* music. Even Paul Whiteman was burning up the charts with "Wang Wang Blues"—pure jazz, and funky, too (Vic. 18694-B). Two things happened in 1920 to keep Synco-Pep from taking over everything: Prohibition and the blues.

Prohibition had been conceived by Topworld as a supreme act of self-sacrifice to clean up Underworld. In the mid-teens, the prolific newspaper humorist Don Marquis, creator of the immortal Archy and Mehitabel, ran a particularly wicked series of columns in which a Society girl favors us with her thoughts on the issues of the day (they were collected in 1916 as *Hermione and Her Little Circle of Serious Thinkers*). In a column entitled "Taking Up the Liquor Problem," Hermione neatly (if viciously) summarizes Topworld thought on the matter:

The Working Classes would be so much better off without liquor. And we who are the leaders in thought should set them an example. So a number of us have decided to set our faces very sternly against drinking in public. Of course, a cocktail or two and an occasional stinger, is something no one can well avoid taking, if one is dining out or having supper after the theater with one's own particular crowd. But all the members of my own particular little group have entered into a solemn agreement not to take even so much as a cocktail or a glass of wine if any of the working classes happen to be about where they can see us and become corrupted by our example.

Even if you banned saloons and liquor stores, you'd still be able to get a drink at the Club, right? If not, well, with privilege comes responsibility, and that would be a sacrifice you'd just have to make. And besides, you of course can take the stuff or leave it alone, not like those unfortunate, undisciplined Working Classes. Thus the Noble Experiment.

Unfortunately, once the Volstead Act—the teeth in the Eighteenth Amendment—went into force on January 16, 1920, things didn't work out like that. First off, leaving it alone was harder than it seemed. The carefully stocked cellars started running dry faster than anyone would have thought, and there was no replenishing them. And sure, the workingman's saloons were shut down, but along with them went the hotel bars where the well-upholstered congregated and then, one by one, their fancy restaurants and dicty cabarets. Rector's and Reisenweber's folded within months—without the markup on drinks, they couldn't make a profit. The same thing happened everywhere. A whole culture closed—only to reopen in Underworld precincts.

If there's one thing that the long and sordid history of legislated morality proves, it's that to make something that a majority perceives as harmless and fun illegal is not the same thing as to make it go away. If anything, quite the opposite. I can remember, back in the mid-seventies, MIT students doing hits on massive, home-engineered

Bert Williams contemplates the end of an era, 1920.

COURTESY OF ARCHEOPHONE RECORDS

bongs in the aisle of Amtrak's Boston–New York express. Like the dope years—1965–79—the dry years were a gross national wallow of Thelemitic cast. Do what thou wilt was the whole of the law: everyone from bank president to iceman was united in a nationwide fraternity of vice. Often they'd be drawn to the same salt lick, Topworld and Underworld rubbing elbows at the neighborhood speakeasy, buying their hooch from the same hoodlum, sleeping it off in the same drunk tank. And for the first time women could join the men in their elbow bending: saloons had kept them out, but speaks couldn't afford to be that choosy. All in all, it was a fine mess. By the end of the twenties, Henry Ford, a notorious Dry, was supporting repeal—so that people would cut down on their drinking.

The closing of the cabarets didn't mean the end of live music. People still wanted to step out, and new clubs popped up to accommodate them. Some of these nightclubs occupied the old spaces; Rector's, for instance, reopened as the Café de Paris. Only now, to get by, a club owner had to be willing to supply hooch, deal with hoodlums, bribe cops, protect his turf—basically, be a gangster. Solid citizens like Louis Sherry and Jacques Bustanoby were out; in were punks like the "horse-faced racketeer" Larry Fay (forty-six arrests) and Owney "the Killer" Madden (nine years in Sing Sing: premeditated murder). Topworld pretensions met Underworld realities. The booze was generally counterfeit, the dancers vulgar, and the music loud. Jazz fit right in. Like acid rock in the sixties, it became a banner. "I like jazz" = "I drink"—and dance, swear, fight, fuck without benefit of a license, live—whatever, as long as it ain't Victorian. The jazzheads' creed was no more consistent or coherent than that of their grandkids forty years later, and it raised the same kind of hackles. A 1922 Ladies' Home Journal piece on jazz dancing trots out all the standard phrases: "unwholesome excitement," "boy-and-girl couples," "dangerous disturbance," "blatant disregard of even the elementary rules of civilization," "statistics of illegitimacy," and so forth.

So 1920 did not see the end of hot-combination jazz, despite the best efforts of the Synco-Peppers—and their efforts were pretty impressive: Whiteman's quintessential foxtrot "Whispering" (Vic. 18690) from August went double platinum, only to be eclipsed by prolific mediocrity Ben Selvin's Hickmanesque "Dardanella," which went an astounding *quintuple* platinum (Vic. 18633). Even worse, in the dog days of August, the real sound of Harlem made it on disc. Black musicians playing black music for black people—that had never happened before. From then on, everything was going to be different.

♪

The second stage of Underworld's musical insurrection ignited slowly and smoldered quietly for a few months before bursting into open flame. The spark came from a skinny young Harlem pianist and song plugger. Perry Bradford was twenty-six, a sixteen-year veteran of Georgia minstrelsy out of Montgomery, Alabama, via Atlanta and Chicago. He was no Baby Seals or String Beans, but all those years touring the South in black vaudeville ensured one thing: he knew the blues. He used to catch shit for it, too, from an unexpected quarter: his fellow black musicians. James Reese Europe had been dead less than a year, and in New York his shadow was still tall—black musicians had to show class, not wallow in downhomity (to coin a word).

Regardless, Bradford stuck to his guns. He was the lucky possessor of the one thing that is a predictor of success in this world far more than any other: not intelligence, although he was no dummy; not education, luckily for him, as he had none; not loving parents, a nurturing home life, or faith in God; but iron-headed persistence in the teeth of repeated rejection. The nickname his fellow musicians hung on him was "Mule."

Although he was pretty much a nobody, with only a couple of published songs and piano rolls under his belt, Bradford nonetheless spent the long, hot summer of 1919 (black America thought, after the war, it deserved a new deal; white America disagreed, violently) bugging the various New York record companies for a session. He had this singer, you see, who was tearing up the boards in a show called *Maid of Harlem* uptown at the Lincoln Theater—her hot number was a little thing called "Harlem Blues," by guess who— and he just thought she should make records. So what if no black woman had ever done that before; so what if he kept hearing that black singers' diction was all wrong, that their timbre wouldn't record, that there was no market, that black folk were too poor to buy records or phonographs or too ignorant to operate them. So what.

Finally, the president of the struggling new Okeh label, one Otto Heineman, gave in—even though his recording director, Fred Hager, supposedly advised against it on account of a boycott threat from, as Bradford recalled, "various Southern and Northern pressure groups" for any label that broke the color bar (Bert Williams didn't count; he was, well, something else). Bradford could bring his singer into their studios (at 25 West 45th Street; I give the address because the building still stands, unblemished by plaque or other historical remembrance) and they'd give it a try. The date: Valentine's Day, 1920. (I should mention another fruit of Bradford's persistence: a month before the Okeh session, he managed to get his singer an audition at Victor. Pass.)

The girl, Mamie Smith, was a beauty in an age when beauty had not yet been wholly conquered by the new flapper ideal as staked out by the slim, boyish, and radiant Irene Castle. Mamie was built to a more generous scale. Doe-eyed, lush-hipped, milk-chocolate-complexioned, encrusted with diamonds and wrapped in sequins and furs and such—she dropped three thousand dollars on an ostrich-feather cape to wear for one show—she was something to look at. Strong men wept, blind men saw, etc.

She could sing, too. Mamie Smith was not, however, a "blues singer." Ma Rainey and Bessie Smith were blues singers—everything

OKeh Records
BLUES! BLUES!

MAMIE   SMITH

AND HER JAZZ HOUNDS

4228 10 in. $1.00	MEM'RIES OF YOU, MAMMY -	Mamie Smith and Her Jazz Hounds
	IF YOU DON'T WANT ME BLUES -	Mamie Smith and Her Jazz Hounds
4194 10 in. $1.00	THE ROAD IS ROCKY - -	Mamie Smith and Her Jazz Hounds
	FARE THEE HONEY BLUES -	Mamie Smith and Her Jazz Hounds
4169 10 in. $1.00	CRAZY BLUES - - - -	Mamie Smith and Her Jazz Hounds
	IT'S RIGHT HERE FOR YOU -	Mamie Smith and Her Jazz Hounds
4113 10 in. $1.00	THAT THING CALLED LOVE - - - -	Mamie Smith
	YOU CAN'T KEEP A GOOD MAN DOWN - - -	Mamie Smith

The luscious Ms. Smith.

they sang was the blues or got bent into it. Not Mamie; she was equally comfortable with raggy pop and Synco-Pep. That doesn't mean she *couldn't* sing the blues, as pecksniffian purists have used this flexibility to maintain. (By like logic, because Louis Armstrong could play "Body and Soul" he couldn't play the blues; hogwash— he was ten times the bluesman a guy like Peetie Wheetstraw— 160 sides issued, each more uninspired than the last—ever was.) Somewhere along the way—like Bradford, she'd been in vaudeville since she was a kid—this Cincinnati girl had mastered the Sene-gambian mode. But on her first record, released as Okeh 4113, no blues.

"That Thing Called Love" and "You Can't Keep a Good Man Down" were Bradford compositions, both raggy/slightly jazzy pop things; nothing new. Hager wanted to play it safe (no surprise here: he'd been producing records since the turn of the century). Against a tame accompaniment from the (white) Rega Orchestra—Okeh's house band—Mamie puts them over convincingly. Yet there's nothing here that hadn't been done before by Sophie Tucker or especially the great Marion Harris, a Kentucky-born Vernon Castle discovery who'd been shaking up the field of Coon shouting (black audiences bought her records, thinking she was one of the race—then and now the highest praise for a white musician). Still, Mamie sings beautifully, with gentle ripples of Senegambia throughout, and the songs aren't bad.

Okeh, still hesitant, sat on the record until July and then let it slip out without any publicity. The black press picked up on it nonetheless (nudged, no doubt, by Mule) and it started selling, especially in Harlem. Okeh's next move would have been good business if it hadn't been so clueless: getting things precisely backward, they tried to get Sophie Tucker to cut Bradford's "Harlem Blues." It must have been the songs that moved the first disc, not that colored girl; how much better if they had someone really famous (and, of course, whitish) for the follow-up.

Luckily for everyone but her, Sophie couldn't shake free of her contracts. Heineman gave in again: Bradford could cut the song with Mamie Smith, but he had to get that "Harlem" out of the title (the "Southern and Northern pressure groups" again?). August tenth would be the date.

Had Okeh stuck with the Rega Orchestra, it's safe to say that "Crazy Blues," the new title, would've been no more than a footnote in American music. But Bradford had talked them into using a black band (organized by guess who) to put a little rhythm into the proceedings. As Samuel B. Charters and Leonard Kunstadt tell the story in *Jazz: A History of the New York Scene,* "Nervous" Hager "took Perry aside [before the session] and explained to him that it was very important to have a sweet, singing accompaniment for Mamie's voice. A little rhythm was all right, but keep it light. Perry nodded, went into the studio, and just winked at the musicians. When the recording light flashed on, they backed off a little from the . . . recording horns and gave it everything they had."

Right off the bat, the lurching tones of Dope Andrews's trombone—formerly heard with Europe's Hellfighters—announce the revolution. The Jazz Hounds, as they were christened, were anything but sweet: loud, tough, funky (and not over-concerned with such niceties as intonation), they were, in short, a full-on, driving, swerving jazz band. Never before had one accompanied a singer on record (well . . . the Hellfighters had cut a couple of vocals, but nothing near as gutbucket as this). The song was in the Handy mold, a twelve-bar blues with a couple of ingrafted pop sections and plenty of room in the vocal line for Mamie to work the Senegambian bends and everyone else to slur, bark, twist. The only record before this that sounds anything like it is "Livery Stable Blues"—but now, there are words that you can sing along to, words that can stab you right through the pericardium.

From the first verse—

> I can't sleep at night,
> I can't eat a bite,
> 'Cause the man I love,
> He don't treat me right.

—to the last—

> I'm gonna do like a Chinaman,
> Go and get some hop;
> Get myself a gun
> And shoot myself a cop.
> I ain't had nothing but bad news—
> Now I got the crazy blues.

—"Crazy Blues" is the most riveting recording of American music the record industry had yet produced. It's the first record to present American music as a fully realized art, capable of moving emotions as well as hormones, hearts as well as feet. Like European opera, it integrates the full range of human musical expression, instrumental and vocal, rhythmic, melodic, and harmonic. Like opera, it has love, death, beauty, and pain. And yet it's *not* opera. There's no score.

Unlike the ODJB, who jiggered up their parts in advance and then played 'em pretty much the same way every time (as garage bands have always done), the Jazz Hounds didn't have that option. They were a pickup band, and they had to make things up as they went along. Which they did, weaving elegantly around each other, coming together occasionally to punch out a big riff and then sliding, skirling, churning away from each other until the next time. Improvising—and not like Hickman's band, where a couple of guys are discreetly winging it while everybody else is coloring within the lines. Not only is "Crazy Blues" the first real blues record, it's the first real jazz record, too.

"Crazy Blues" finally came out in November, backed by another Bradford pop thing (Ok. 4169). Okeh gave the record their usual buildup—none—until, at the end of the month, one of their bean-counters noticed that somehow they had sold 75,000 copies of the thing in Harlem alone. At first, they thought it was a bookkeeping error—no way the colored folk would be buying that many records. It wasn't.

While not earth-shattering, 75,000 was pretty sweet: the minors had been having a hard time chipping into the majors' sales. Victor, Columbia, and Edison had unbreakable contracts with the top performers, so even if you had a hit song they'd rush out a version by someone better and skim off the cream. Here was a pool of performers the majors hadn't locked up, a market they hadn't tapped.

Between 1916 and 1919, half a million black men, women, and children escaped the South; during the twenties, a million more followed. World War I—the bright side: Northern factory jobs for black Americans. With European immigration choked off, suddenly they were in demand for more than just chopping cotton. Jobs meant money, and money meant customers. It took "Crazy Blues"—which eventually sold a pleasant quarter million or so copies—for record companies to see that, but once they did, foofaraw about "pressure groups" and suchlike was conveniently forgotten and so was the color bar. Besides, some of them *needed* the black folks' money: after radio took off in 1921, Topworld wasn't buying records like it used to; although Edison and Victor were pulling through just fine, others weren't. The mighty Columbia was even forced to declare bankruptcy.

So it wasn't pure altruism that prompted Okeh to start a special "race" series in 1921, the same year the first black-owned label, Black Swan, appeared (Dictionary of the Vulgar Tongue: *race record* = a record made by a (usually) black, (usually) Underworld performer, pitched at a black audience; black Synco-Pep and instrumental jazz, to which Topworld ofays liked to dance, was usually excluded). Paramount followed in 1922, Columbia in '23, Edison (briefly) in '25.

Vocalion waited until 1926 and Victor until '29, but they had both been issuing (a few) blues records since 1923.

A few labels—the ultra-cool Gennett—were bold enough to fold all their black Underworld music into the general run of their other discs. (It wasn't always such a good idea to mix the races, even symbolically, as Columbia learned when they issued a disc by the top-selling Allen Brothers, a hillbilly act, in their race series: the boys filed a quarter-million-dollar lawsuit and switched to Victor. Nice.) In any case, from now on both sides of the dialogue in American music would be heard.

Birth of a New Art: Enrico Caruso, a Whole Bunch of Other Guys, and Louis Armstrong

By mid-1921, the record companies knew three basic ways to make it hot for their customers. There were the blues singers, usually women: after Mamie hit, the industry, with its usual attention to nuance, hauled every black woman in New York with vaudeville experience (and hence some Topworld gloss) in front of the recording horn and paid her to belt out a couple of the sumbitches, whether she had a clue or no. Most often, the companies kept their expenses down by backing their finds up with nothing more elaborate than a piano, and not a particularly swinging one at that. There was swerve, but precious little drive.

Then there were the Synco-Pep bands, long on drive but pretty swerveless. And finally, Uncle Nick LaRocca's children, the "Originals"—the Original Memphis Five, the Original Louisiana Five, the Original Georgia Five, even the Original Indiana Five (although what Indiana has to do with Dixie I don't see—in any case, Tom Morton, their guiding light, was really Tommy Monaco, an Italian kid from Brooklyn). There were myriad others—all made up of five or six guys, still almost always white, almost always Yankees (or at least Northerners), playing a politely swervy, Senegambian-inflected (lightly, lightly) ragtime over blues changes or simple pop progressions. Nineteen twenty-one saw more than a dozen new ones get on disc, including Ladd's Black Aces, with the young Jimmy Durante on piano (I must confess to a particular fondness for their "Shake It and Break It," Gen. 4762). As the Original Memphis Five, but with Frank Signorelli taking over from the Schnozzola, they'd go on to make more jazz records than any other band in the twenties. At their best—especially when they had a good blues singer fronting them—these combos had drive and swerve both; at their worst, they still had a nervous, herky-jerky momentum.

It's pointless to cite individual records: each band had its good ones, and they all blur together into an endless stream of jangly and often quite skillful riffing (one exception is the very fine series of records Frank Guarente's Georgians turned out in 1922 and '23, which display an unusually relaxed, even funky energy; but Guarente was from New Orleans and had, supposedly, traded cornet lessons with King Oliver). All in all, there's a lot of kinetic energy being splashed around, but less of the thermal kind than one might expect. On record, anyway, the music of the Fives lacks what the hot vocal music—the blues—of the day has: emotion; drama.

Let's get back to concepts for a moment, to drive and swerve. Each of these values carries within it a statement about the function of music, a statement that, broadly, defines a genre of music. There's dance music—drive music—and what we can call "show music." Music that compels us to move, and music that, by in some way making us wonder what's coming next, compels us to listen, to observe. Dramatic music. In dance music—be it James Reese Europe or James Brown; Michael Coleman, Joey Dee and the Starliters, or the Chemical Brothers—what counts is the collective product, the groove. The musicians can express themselves within that groove, as long as they don't bust it up (Michael Coleman's fiddling is a master class in the subtleties of this art). Show music, on the other hand, is all about the individual—be it the razz-a-matazz instrumental soloist, the vocal diva, the star conductor, or even the large-browed composer.

Like drive and swerve, dance and show aren't mutually exclusive. Some sorts of music heavily favor one or the other: the "modern"—that is, nineteenth-century—symphonic and operatic repertoire is almost exclusively show music (even though much of its original, conceptual swerve has been fossilized through constant repetition), while techno, particularly in its earliest incarnations, is pure dance music. Other sorts partake much more evenly of both—West African music, for example, has a long tradition of fusing dance with drama, participation with spectacle. As we've seen, in America, this fusion had unraveled far enough to generate separate dance and show traditions, culminating in ragtime and the blues, respectively. If Mamie Smith and her Jazz Hounds heralded their final reintegration, it would take a few more years for instrumental music to hear that call. Not even the Jazz Hounds themselves could pull it off unaided, judging from the two instrumentals they cut in January 1921 (the first to be recorded by black musicians)—although Dope Andrews with his active trombone struggles manfully to break out of the box, and almost succeeds.

The Jazz Fives made dance music. There's nothing wrong with that; it's a legitimate end in and of itself. (Well-executed dance music can of course be as rewarding to listen to as any show music—provided the listener harbors a musicianly appreciation for instrumental interplay and other such subtleties of the musical craft.) But every species of dance music contains within it the seeds of a show music, and these seeds rarely go uncultivated. Some musicians, curious, ambitious types, get tired of playing more or less the same thing over and over again. Before long, they get to fiddling with it, and next thing you know they're saying, "Hey, lookit me! Look what I can do!" Thus Jimi Hendrix, in the 1960s, and thus Louis Armstrong, whom I'll get to shortly. Or maybe one of 'em starts throwing in a little vocal whatnot, just to give the groove some variety (true dance music won't tolerate lyrical content much heavier than simple exhortations to move your movables, jocular balderdash, or sheer nonsense—cf. "Fly, Robin, Fly," by the Silver Convention, a song which mystified me to no end back when it hit in 1975). Bit by bit, he (or she, of course) gets to taking that nonsense more seriously, and next thing you know disco, one of the most faceless of dance musics, is giving birth to rap, one of the showiest of show musics. Whatever the exact mechanism, this showification (to coin a truly atrocious word) happens time and again. The sarabande and the minuet begin their lives as lowlife dances and end up as parts of Topworld symphonies; the Afro-Celtic dance music of the rural South becomes the stage music of the urban North.

It doesn't hurt that there are often pronounced class and economic advantages to going show. Dance music, with its emphasis on the *corpus humanum* in motion—the reciprocal oscillation of the limbs, the heaving of the excited breast, the distillation of sweat from the heated brow—is always an uncomfortable resident of Topworld, and rarely if ever a native one. But it's not only that. A dance musician has to repress his ego, subordinate it to a common goal. A show musician, on the other hand, has to nurture it, cultivate it, display it. A dance musician is a craftsman, a show musician an artist. Topworld respects artists, even the louche, unrefined kind, the kind that still emit a bracing whiff of the streets. Perhaps especially that kind—case in point: Bert Williams, who began as a cakewalker, a show dancer, and, sidling crabwise farther and farther away from the world of dance as he went, ended his life's journey some twenty-five years later as the most popular and (arguably) respected black man in America.

In 1921, American dance music had been nurturing the seeds of show music for two decades. Every once in a while these seeds would send forth a sprout—be it a little bud like Arthur Pryor's time-suspending smears or Fred Van Eps's hyperactive prestidigitation, or a full-blown shoot like Scott Joplin's ill-fated venture into opera, *Treemonisha*, or the explorations in theatrical ragtime of Will Marion Cook and his circle. In the teens, the sprouts start coming in thick: they're there in the over-the-top trap drummers and the other ragtime instrumental virtuosi who are circulating in vaudeville (the bottom rung of the ladder to Topworld—as O. Henry noted in 1911, tongue only partly in cheek, "Vaudeville has risen to such a respectable plane in the last few years"). They're there in the ODJB's eargrabbing squeals and squawks and, especially, in the multimedia spectacle that was Mamie Smith. By 1921, they were gathering themselves to bloom.

There was, however, one basic structural problem that the musically ambitious jazzbo had to address. If the Senegambian mode was proving to be a wonderfully flexible and exciting tool, the twelve- (or fourteen-, or sixteen-) bar blues song upon which it rode into Topworld consciousness was not. The resulting music had small-scale drama to burn—every note, every space was susceptible to manipulation; was a potential source of suspense. Yet it lacked, well, architecture. It was repetitive, even monotonous; its choppy phrases worked against continuity and flow and, with their cadences falling predictably at the end of every couple of bars, were incapable of ambushing the listener with something truly new. Not even the intervention of the Tin Pan Alley songwriters could change that. A song such as Irving Berlin and Harry Akst's 1921 "Home Again Blues"—about as close as Izzy ever got to the real thing—curbs the slangy unpredictability of the music's Senegambian phrasing without significantly enlarging its range. The solution wasn't to be found in shuffling chords around or adding pop-derived bridges. It had to come from the performers—in the Senegambian mode, they're the real composers. The story of hot music in America in the early Prohibition years is first and foremost the story of how a ragtag assortment of Underworld dance musicians transformed themselves from sidemen into stars and, in the process, made jazz into an art.

They weren't traveling entirely blind on this journey. They had examples. In 1921, the ability to read music was widespread, and folks used it. Opera and symphonic music were much more widely and deeply understood (and much stronger signifiers of Topworld culture) than they are today. Even a pimp and whorehouse professor like String Beans's friend (and fellow vaudeville blues evangelist) Jelly Roll Morton could play, as one black newspaper noted in 1914, "classics and rags with equal ease." Of course, Mr. Jelly Lord, as he styled himself, wasn't necessarily dealing from the top of the deck when it came to the dicty part of his program—the same paper went on to note, "his one hand stunt, left hand alone, playing a classic selection, is a good one." Show music. No matter; the point is, many of the folks who gravitated toward the new music were old-timers in the unpatrolled borderland between high art and low. When looking for an answer to a musical problem, they were as likely to look up as down.

Looking up, the first thing they would've seen was Enrico Caruso, if only because he was so large. In the first two decades of the twentieth century, no musician was more visible or had more to offer, on almost all levels—not ignoring the commercial one. An affable, even goofy kid from the slums of Naples with, to lift a line from the *Paradiso,* "una voce modesta / forse qual fu dall'angelo a Maria"— "A voice so fine it could have been the Angel speaking to Mary"— Caruso was Topworld by acclaim, Underworld by nature. He was a fun guy, not one of those high-hat stiffs. He drew caricatures, most often of himself. He *liked* America, rather than just tolerating it.

His trajectory across the American firmament began in 1904, when he signed a contract with Victor Records to make ten sides for four thousand dollars (plus forty cents royalties per disc sold). And for another two thousand a year, he agreed not to record for anyone else for five years. For Victor, the fourteen grand was a pittance. Caruso's voice, with its rich midrange, was uniquely suited to the acoustic recording process. Those ten discs, and the many subsequent ones he did for them, were the cornerstone of their new Red Seal imprint. Victor's pop records went for seventy-five cents to a dollar. They priced their ten-inch Red Seal records *beginning* at two bucks apiece; Caruso's twelve-inchers ran at three dollars, his duets at four— except the ones he did with Australian diva Nellie Melba, which were five dollars—and the quartet from *Rigoletto*, with Caruso and some other luminaries, went for six. The sextet from *Lucia*: seven. That's for a single-sided 78, four-and-a-half minutes of music, max (in twelve-inch; three-and-a-half in ten). That's balls. Dinner for four at Delmonico's, the swankest restaurant in New York, wouldn't set you back more than a fin.

You can predict what happened next. Topworld went nuts—here was pressed, stackable class; the price tag proved it. You could buy it and spread it around the house whenever you wanted. Your neighbors would know you had it. Sales zoomed, especially when Victor introduced the super-deluxe Victrola to play the things on: all the ugly mechanical stuff cleverly contained and hidden in a mahogany cabinet. Two hundred dollars; must-have. With Caruso leading the charge, opera brought music to the classes and relegated Edison and his phonograph to supplying Coon songs and parlor weepers to the Southern market at thirty-five cents apiece. (In 1910, Edison's propaganda organ, the *Edison Phonograph Monthly,* characterized his public with supreme condescension as the "good old 'ragtime-coon songs-Sousa-Herbert-monologues-sentimental ballads' crowd.") Enrico transcended Opera; he was the first pop star of the recording age. Topworld and Underworld (at least, the more urbanized parts of it) could agree on this one. And he could sing.

Caruso even recorded a goodly number of poplike things, but they're just not hot (unlike his Red Seal stablemate Alma Gluck, whose 1911 "Old Folks at Home" was the first million-selling record, he refrained from minstrelsy). Take his number-one selling 1918 version of "Over There" (Vic. 87294), sung in English and French. This proves conclusively that he ain't got rhythm: he bulls ahead at a good clip all right—it's rousing—but he shoves a steamship through the syncopation. What's left wouldn't fit into a shot glass. There's just no snap to it, no funk. With Caruso, you've got to forget about drive (although check out "*La danza (Tarantella napolitana)*" from 1912; Vic. 6031); look for the swerve. And swerve means arias. Start with that "*Vesti la giubba*"; everyone else did.

Victor 6001, recorded March 17, 1907, is an overwhelming record. There's a reason the icon of Enrico Caruso that still resides in popular memory is wearing a clown suit and banging on a drum. "*Recitar! mentre preso dal delirio; Vesti la giubba* (Act I)," to give it its full title, starts off sensibly enough. Caruso's thick, muscular voice calmly lays out the basic situation over some organ-like chords from the simple orchestra:

> *Recitar! mentre preso dal delirio*
> *Non lo so piu quel che dico e quel che faccio—*

> To perform! while, lost in delirium,
> I don't know what I'm saying or doing—

Suddenly, stop-time; he shouts a word or two: "*forzati!*"—force yourself!—and this *laugh* comes out. Skittering, arrhythmic, maniacal. The next phrase, "*Tu sei pagliaccio*," "You're a clown," is bitten off with a startling vehemence. Then the restrained, bitter verse: dress yourself, people are paying you to make them laugh, etc. All very dramatic. But then the tension increases, the melody marches up the scale, and Caruso just lets it loose. His voice swells, throbs wordlessly, twists into a phrase—"*Ridi, pagliaccio...*"—and now all language is lost, dissolved into pure agonized sound; the voice reaches apogee, hovers, falls, barely under control; words form again—"*...ridi del duol.*" A couple more words, and the orchestra quietly carries the body out. But that moment, the eighteen seconds between 1:37 and 1:55, is one of the hottest things ever recorded. It's pure swerve:

you expect a climax, but he wrenches it into something beyond expectation through sheer animal force. It's a moment too vulgar, too orgasmic to be called classical.

One could go on; Caruso made about 250 records. At his best—"Testa adorata" from Leoncavallo's La Bohème (alias "La Vie Bohème II") is another K.O. (Vic. 6012)—Caruso makes all melody swerve: it's new, it's a discovery, carved out by force and effort; even though he's following notes on a page, he's not. Every syllable is slightly tweaked, spun. Every note is *alive*. And it wasn't all blast and thunder: when the suit was hearts, he was a teddy bear. His 1907 duet with Melba on Puccini's "O soave fanciulla," from the "real" La Bohème (Vic. 95200) is ravishingly lovely—and still hot. He had a dramatic gift like Sinatra's and his voice was an instrument like Billie Holiday's. Or rather, vice versa to both.

It would be dumb to suggest that the Jazz Fives and other hot dance bands of the early twenties all set out to deliberately imitate Caruso records and their ilk, and we strive not to be dumb. However, the era in which ragtime had come to maturity—say, 1870 to 1895—was one essentially untouched by the phonograph. If you wanted to learn to rag, you had to do it from somebody else, or from sheet music. Jazz, on the other hand, grew up with the phonograph. Between 1895 and 1920, the quarter-century in which jazz came together, recorded music went from being an amusing novelty to a staple of home entertainment, one that had reached all levels of society save the the bindlestiff hobo and the deserted mother of ten who takes in washing. In 1919 alone, the phonograph industry churned out 2,225,000 of the devices. At the same time, Underworld-derived hot music made up only a tiny portion of the available software for these machines; you wouldn't—couldn't—*just* listen to ragtime or dance music. And going by the sales statistics, what there are of them, it's clear that in among the displaced accents and Tin-Pannery there'd be a fair number of Caruso's arias and John McCormack's Celtic *bel canto*; violin solos by Fritz Kreisler and—and let's let Louis

Armstrong flesh out the picture. When, around 1918, he was able
to buy his first Victrola, he bought a stack of ODJB records, to be
sure—"they were the first to record the music I played," as he later
explained. But that wasn't all. "I had Caruso records, and [pop tenor]
Henry Burr, Galli-Curci, Tetrazzini—they were all my favorites.
Then there was the Irish tenor, McCormack—beautiful phrasing."
Q.E.D.

Sometimes the result of European art music's gravitational pull
on the musical vernacular is pretentious dreck—there's a long tradition of crappy classical-inflected pop, from the stiffly enunciated
ballads and flashy-fingered ragtime runs at Liszt of the teens on
through Rick Wakeman and Emerson, Lake, and Palmer in the seventies (just because they were Brits doesn't let 'em off the hook).
Sometimes it's cheap theft; "Avalon," the Al Jolson–Vincent Rose
perennial, was a quick lift from Puccini's "*E lucevan le stelle*"; in
1921, Puccini sued and recovered a bundle. Sometimes it's genius.

I'll get to the genius in a moment. There's no point in mounting a
detailed assault on the period between the beginning of 1921, when
the blues craze started shifting into high gear, and the end of 1924,
when the final elements of what we recognize as modern music fell
into place. So many of the Great Names in American popular music
stepped forward during those three years that the story is, if not
immediately familiar, then at least uncoverable with minimal effort.
Recording debuts—now for the first time a reasonably accurate indicator of when Underworld musicians began their escalade of Topworld's walls—tell the tale. February 1921: Fletcher Henderson;
March 1921: Ethel Waters; August 1921: James P. Johnson; May 1922:
Coleman Hawkins (with Mamie Smith); October 1922: Fats Waller;
February 1923: Bessie Smith; April 1923: Louis Armstrong (with
King Oliver's Creole Jazz Band); June 1923: Jelly Roll Morton; July

1923: Sidney Bechet; October 1923: Earl Hines (accompanying singer Lois Deppe); December 1923: Ma Rainey; February 1924: Bix Beiderbecke; November 1924: Duke Ellington. And that's just the A-list.

The B-list is wide and deep. Some examples: the blues brought forth the smooth and sexy Memphian Alberta Hunter and Birmingham's raw and funky Lucille Bogan; from New Orleans there came Lizzie "The Creole Songbird" Miles and banjo-toting Papa Charlie Jackson (he swung it like a guitar, in anything but a rustic style); the Southeast produced Ida Cox, the "Uncrowned Queen of the Blues," and "The World's Greatest Moaner," Clara Smith, while Virginia ponied up the Norfolk Jazz (and/or Jubilee) Quartet to yank the music of the Unique and Standard and Dinwiddie and all the other Colored Quartet(te)s out of the age of minstrelsy. Synco-Pep, which was being rapidly reinfected with jazz, saw the debut of the Coon-Sanders Nighthawks, the California Ramblers, and the fine orchestras led by Isham Jones and Jean Goldkette (all white, and all objects of cult worship to this day); there were black Synco-Peppers, too—besides Fletcher Henderson's outfit, there was Erskine Tate's Vendome Orchestra and Doc Cook's Dreamland Orchestra (both from Chicago, and both employing Creole cornet king Freddie Keppard) and a couple of others; they generally played things a bit swervier than their white counterparts, but then again, they were expected to. Out-and-out jazz was being committed by the likes of Kid Ory, Clarence Williams, the New Orleans Rhythm Kings, Phil Napoleon (aka Filippo Napoli), Red Nichols, Bubber Miley, Bennie Moten's Orchestra, Johnny Dodds, Muggsy Spanier—all names to be reckoned with in the Annals of Hot. The C-list was wider and deeper still; between 1921 and 1924, some four-hundred-odd blues- and jazz-oriented acts recorded, and that's not counting the Synco-Pep acts, who flourished like grass of the earth.

Most of these artists—particularly the jazz and Synco-Pep ones—were still building up to their best work. The Senegambian mode of music isn't easy to master, and there was an awful lot of what we perceive these days as awkward stiffness in the music. But the bands were learning nonetheless—even the pure dance musicians were getting looser, more conversational, bluesier. To compare a relatively unambitious (but competent) ofay dance outfit such as George Olsen and His Music, which first recorded in 1924, to Art Hickman's band of five years earlier is to understand the permeating nature of funk.

While the ensembles were busy getting loose, though, the soloists were doing something more, and they're the ones with whom I shall end this book. Every previous form of American music had been essentially egalitarian: each man had his part, and he stuck to it, and they were all equally important. This held as true for the Virginia Minstrels and Europe's Society Syncopators as it did for, say, Sousa's Band. This democracy wasn't perfect—there were of course soloists, as the careers of Vess Ossman and Arthur Pryor attest—but the difference between soloist and accompanist was one of degree, not of kind. The soloists were more precise, faster, purer of tone—things that theoretically can be mastered through application and diligence, like grammar.

At first, the spread of jazz didn't seem to put this egalitarian state in peril. True, the parts were no longer fixed as they had been, but where every man is responsible for making up his own, every man is still an equal. Then Art Hickman put his saxophonists to improvising (leaving aside the open question of where he got the idea to do that), and only them, and everything changed. Suddenly there are two kinds of musicians: those whose job it is to create, and those who just, well, re-create, play what's put in front of 'em. That can have its own joys and rewards (just ask any good bass player), yet as the proverb says, *"alterius non sit qui suus esse potest"*—"he would not belong to another, who can be his own."

Hickman and his school didn't make a big thing out of this, and it took bands a while to see the writing on the wall. But as the twenties wore on and jazz began to exert more and more influence on Top-world music, all those polite, clean dance bands found themselves in a bind. People wanted a little hot, dirty razz-a-matazz along with their Synco-Pep. Not a lot of it, mind you, but just enough to give the music an illicit tinge. Problem was, Senegambian improvisation wasn't as easy as it looked—it wasn't just a matter of blowing funny noises and hamming it up. That may have worked for Earl Fuller's crew in 1917, but four or five years down the road it wouldn't cut it. The kind of bent-note, on-the-fly swerving that was coming into vogue took chops well outside the grasp of the average band musician—and not only chops; it took a different attitude. In 1922, on one of his first jobs, the teenaged Eddie Condon had his boss tell him, "There is no use trying to convert the older musicians to jazz" (shades of Arthur Pryor). You wanted a "hot man"—a ringer to come in and do the dirty work, and it didn't even matter if he couldn't read music. You could hire plenty of guys who could do that. "Since you can't read music you have nothing to unlearn," as Condon's boss put it.

At first, the older guys regarded the hot men with condescension; if they couldn't read music, how were they musicians? They couldn't even get into the union; you had to read for that. When, in November 1924, the crack, modern Jean Goldkette Orchestra set up to record for a Victor field unit then in their hometown of Detroit, they were prepared to show off their new hot man, a dreamy-eyed young fellow with an odd name. Bix Beiderbecke. They ran through their first number, a piece of pop fluff called "I Didn't Know." Bix took the whole second chorus. When they finished, Victor's producer—a man by the name of Eddie King, who, ten years earlier, had been trap drummer in the Fred Van Eps Trio—took one listen and called the band manager over.

"Who the hell's that kid on the cornet?"
"That's Bix Beiderbecke.... He's the last word these days, hottest thing around. Big hit on the campuses."
King scowled and snapped his suspenders. "Yeah? Well, let

the college kids have 'im, then. That's not the kind of jazz we want here."

So the story goes, anyway (it's worth noting that Victor sat on that take until 1960).

Bix's experience is an extreme example, but the hot men often had a pretty hard time of it, not least from the other guys in the band. When Eddie King delivered his judgment, I'd be very much surprised if there weren't secret smiles from some of the section men. Even Louis Armstrong himself, when he left his mentor King Oliver's Creole Jazz Band and Chicago forever behind for the big time as Fletcher Henderson's hot man in New York, came in for a hazing. You can't blame the guys, though. Increasingly, the hot men were the stars, and were getting treated as such. Everyone else was there to back them up.

Borders are porous and talent is difficult to contain. Before long, this principle of subjugation began casting its influence over the libertarian precincts of jazz: the small combos. The kind of everybody-in-the-pool more-is-moreism that the Original Fives peddled was exciting, but it presupposed a good deal of self-censorship on the part of the better players. After a certain point, it's a zero-sum game: the more music you play on your cornet, the less the guy sitting next to you gets to play on his clarinet. He might take exception to that. And besides, where everyone is playing something different, the only way significant amounts of drive will be generated is if everyone keeps a close eye on the beat and doesn't stray too far from it. Phrases have to be short and punchy, solo breaks brief and propulsive.

In the early twenties many of the best jazz cornetists/trumpeters and, to a lesser degree, clarinetists, trombonists, and saxophone-wranglers, black and white alike, were also working as hot men, either knocking out choruses over Synco-Pep bands or spinning out mournful obbligati behind blues singers (usually with nobody to step on their lines but a pianist). Cases in point: Phil Napoleon, guiding light of the Original Memphis Five, who spent much of the early twenties flitting back and forth between them and various New York Synco-Pep aggregations (the Ambassadors, Sam Lanin's Orchestra, etc.); James Wesley "Bubber" Miley, who went from Mamie Smith's Jazz Hounds to the lead trumpet chair in Duke Ellington's Washingtonians, while still finding time for plenty of blues work. Naturally, these guys got used to a lot more instrumental space that the tight, overheated structure of small-band jazz could afford. When they went home to their jazz bands, they started rearranging the furniture to suit.

One of the first surviving fruits of this came in December 1921, when Johnny Dunn, star of W. C. Handy's band and the Jazz Hounds, set himself up as bandleader and cut two sides for Columbia with a seven-piece band (Col. A-3541). While there's still a lot of swerving around from the supporting cast—particularly Herb Flemming on trombone—there's no mistaking who's in charge: Dunn's cornet is front and center, right in front of the recording horn. Unfortunately—and here's where we get back to Caruso—there's a depressing lack of drama to the sides. "Bugle Blues" is probably the best of the two, and it's not that good—a sequence of rather stiff blues choruses, each one pretty much like the one before. There's no "*ridi, pagliaccio*" moment, no climax, and the supporting characters keep throwing in interjections at the most inopportune times.

Let's skip ahead two and a half years and thirteen issued sides. In April 1924, Dunn was back in the studio, recording his "Dunn's Cornet Blues" (Col. 124-D). He's learned a thing or two about the art of being a cornet star, and it's not just that he's cut the supporting cast back to a chord-chunking banjo and a piano, tinkling away discreetly in the background. Here he's stretching his notes out until you can hear the ache in them, there he's squeezing 'em together until they yelp. There's a story being told. A somewhat disjointed one, perhaps—Dunn hasn't yet figured out how to stitch the discrete segments that make up his aria together into a seamless whole—but a story nonetheless.

Now, the lazier sort of jazz orthodoxy holds that Louis Armstrong pretty much single-handedly invented the jazz solo in 1925, when he made his first records under his own name. This is of course utter bullshit. He may have perfected it—only a fool would deny that. But there were plenty of guys like Johnny Dunn moving the ball forward. Some of them—not Dunn—were doubtless more or less under Armstrong's influence, although before early 1925, they'd have had to see him live (i.e., in Chicago or around the Midwest) to catch that influence: not until late 1924, when he left Chicago for New York, did he record any significant solos.

In 1922, after a bunch of biographical stuff that it would be pointless to repeat involving extreme poverty and Colored Waifs' Homes, military bands, whores' bars and riverboats, the twenty-one-year-old Louis Armstrong found himself in Chicago, playing second cornet in his idol Joe "King" Oliver's Creole Jazz Band. Oliver was thirty-seven years old and had been one of the last Crescent City cornet kings—old enough to remember Bolden, young enough to still have his chops together (his favorite weapon: the mute, of which he had mastered all the known kinds and then some, using them to distort, bend, swerve, and vocalize the sound of his horn). He'd been in Chicago since 1918, leading his own band since 1920. By 1922, after a hardening stint on the West Coast, his was the premier black band in town; its gig at Lincoln Gardens (459 E. 31st Street) was the one any wannabe hot boy had to catch. The young Bix Beiderbecke and Paul Mares—cornetist for the New Orleans Rhythm Kings, the best white band to come out of the Crescent City (they started recording in 1922)—were fixtures, along with a murderer's row of budding jazz talent, black and white. The Lincoln Gardens even put on a midnight show one night a week, for ofays only (the rest of the week it was strictly black); the crowd was all musicians, including a whole lot of Synco-Peppers. The university of jazz was open for business (when the young Bud Freeman, later a tenor sax stylist of some repute, would show up the bouncer would crack, "Well, it looks like the little white boys is out here to get your music lessons").

Nobody knows why he sent down to New Orleans for Armstrong—a weird move, since Crescent City ragtime bands never had more than one cornet. Maybe his gums were bothering him, a problem that would eventually end his career as a cornetist (the fact that one of his favorite pig-outs was a bowl of sugar poured into a hollowed-out loaf of bread couldn't have helped there). Maybe he was just tired—the cornet's a workout. Maybe he wanted to be able to concentrate on conducting the band; maybe he missed the brass (i.e., marching) band he used to run back home, with Manuel Perez seconding him on cornet. Maybe he just needed the extra noise— the Lincoln Gardens wasn't small, and odds are the crowd didn't sit around drinking in the band in respectful silence. Nobody really knows; Joe Oliver died broke and sick and far from home in 1938, and he didn't leave any memoirs. Whatever the reason, the King caught his homeboy midleap—Louis Armstrong was in the middle of making a mental adjustment like the one Charlie Parker made twenty years later and Jimi Hendrix twenty years after that: of taking a complicated music and putting another kink in its tail—and gave him a place to work things out.

That place wasn't, however, on record. The King and his gang— Johnny Dodds and his brother Baby on clarinet and drum, Honoré Dutrey on trombone, the great Bill Johnson on bass and banjo, and Miss Lil Hardin of Memphis, Tennessee, on piano (a chair often filled by women in the early days of jazz; they had actually paid attention to those music lessons)—weren't interested in the new principles of subjugation. He ran a tight, old-fashioned shop, every tub on its own bottom. Armstrong's job was to back up the King in the ensembles and take the occasional break—not solo; there were no long, improvised solos in jazz the way King Oliver's band conceived of it—with him, or occasionally in his place. His breaks were spectacular enough to get him noticed, to be sure, but they weren't what the band was all about. It was a dance band, and they played a dense, powerful funk that was impossible to imitate, a strange but seamless weave of sunny, Caribbean lilt, topspun Celtic stomp (see particularly "Canal Street Blues," Gen. 5133), deep blues, and bent Synco-Pep. I won't discuss or recommend any individual records of theirs; that would be like choosing between your children. The band cut thirty-seven sides between April and December 1923 (not including the six that were, alas, never released); there's not a bad one in the bunch. They represent the swan song of the pure egalitarian ideal in American jazz—at least, until the free jazz movement briefly resuscitated it in the 1960s.

In any case, that leaves a hell of a lot of guys that had nothing to do with Satchmo. Some of them were geniuses in their own right. In 1923, the recording horn also turned its face toward another son of the Crescent City, Mr. Jelly Lord, Jelly Roll Morton (it was only some fifteen-odd years after his vaudeville debut). In June, through the aegis of black A&R man J. Mayo "Ink" Williams, he cut two sides for Paramount Records in Chicago (Pm. 12050) with a gang of ex–W. C. Handy men on trombone, clarinet, alto sax, and drums, and one of New Orleans' finest—Natty Dominique? Tommy Ladnier? Freddie Keppard? (the experts differ)—on cornet. They're pretty nice, but the next month Morton really showed his stuff when he went out to Richmond, Indiana, and taught the world how to play jazz piano.

The twenty-odd solos he recorded there for Gennett Records between July 1923 and June 1924 are nothing but pleasure, a relaxed, rippling stream of funk. But they're more than just rhythm. Consider "New Orleans (Blues) Joys," as it was titled, from his first session (Gen. 5486; specifically, I'm considering the second take). After two choruses of impeccably played blues, full of drive and microscale swerve, he proceeds to demonstrate just how jazz is different from ragtime and the blues. The third chorus starts off conventionally enough, but then...you know what happens when you drag a stick against a flowing stream? That moiré pattern that you get between the current of the stream and the wake of the stick? When Jelly Roll starts laying improvised, right-hand runs against his steady, rocking left, that's pretty much the effect he creates. The rhythm—the stream—flows unabated, but not unquestioned—he pushes it almost to the edge of breaking. Everything else in the performance leads up to this moment. That's drama.

Some of the ball-carriers, it must be admitted, were pretty damn unlikely. Consider the Mound City Blue Blowers: three young guys from St. Louis (aka "the Mound City"), wielding, in order of decreasing likelihood, a banjo, a kazoo, and a tissue-paper-covered comb (you blow on it, if you've never tried). In New Orleans, they called this sort of ragtag aggregation a "spasm band." I don't know what they called it in St. Louis. They were common enough, anyway, although few of them got on record, and those that did tended to be pretty rustic affairs. Not these guys, no matter what jazz purists might think (the instrumentation is so...*declassé*). Their first record, from February 1924, was Spencer Williams's "Arkansaw Blues" backed with "Blue Blues" (Br. 2581). It sold over a million copies— and not without reason (pause while jazz purists grumble and scoff). "Arkansaw Blues" was perhaps the first truly hot instrumental hit in seven years, since "Livery Stable Blues." Over Jack Bland's taut banjo chording, Red McKenzie (the comb) and Dick Slevin (the kazoo) give out with the horn imitations—first, the unison riffing, then the swervy, fluent solos. I don't want to make too much of it, but the fluidity and self-assuredness on display here are demonstrative of the way the soloist's art was beginning to come together.

Others—the bulk of them—were the sort of skilled journeymen who do most of what actually gets done in this world. Thomas Morris, Lovie Austin, Jimmy O'Bryant, Paul Howard, Doc Behrendson, Frank Guarente, on and on—the list is long. But to offer a mere roster of names would be pointless. A master of the art of the Senegambian cornet (as he knew it, anyway) like St. Louis's Charley Creath, whose December 1924 "Market Street Blues" (Ok. 8201) is a benchmark of elegant blues playing, deserves more than a mere notation that he existed, but usually he's lucky to get even that. Like Johnny Dunn, these folks weren't the Carusos of hot music, but they weren't mere spear-carriers, either—not yet, anyway: once the Armstrong revolution got going in full gear, many of 'em would be unable to make the conceptual leap, to spin out the instrumental arias that people came to expect.

Take the rather sad case of Creole trombone slider Edward "Kid" Ory. In the teens, he'd led one of the Crescent City's most popular bands, with first Freddie Keppard on cornet and then Joe Oliver— "he was rough as pig-iron," Ory recalled; "you know how rough that is—I tamed him down." In 1919, he moved out to California, where New Orleans-style jazz was doing good business (Morton was out there, too). Sometime in June 1922 (although it may have been earlier), in the unlikely location of Culver City, California, his band froze two instrumentals and four blues accompaniments on disc.

Spikes' Seven Pods of Pepper—the Spikes brothers owned the label—were from New Orleans, and they were black—or at least Creole. Some have used those two facts to label their sides the first jazz records. While that may be total bullshit, they were still the first Creole band to record, to tell the Creole side of the New Orleans jazz story. Not only did one of their songs—"Ory's Creole Trombone" (Nordskog 3009)—go on to become a Dixieland standard, in Papa Mutt Carey on cornet, Ed "Montudi" Garland on string bass, and, of course, Kid Ory on trombone (they were also known as Ory's Sunshine Orchestra), they had some topflight talent. "Ory's Creole Trombone," with its sliding breaks throughout, is a pretty fine demonstration of the old Crescent City style of jazz; if it had come out on Victor in 1917, it would've been a sensation. But Sunshine records (somehow affiliated with Nordskog records) was tiny and, worse, jazz had moved on. Next thing you know, it's November 12, 1925, and he's recording with Louis Armstrong—as a sideman. Louis Armstrong, the kid who used to hang around his band trying to get cornet pointers from King Oliver. (Ory didn't lead a band again until the trad-jazz revival of the 1940s. He spent most of the 1930s farming chickens.)

In November 1925, Louis Armstrong was a star. Not yet a pop star, perhaps, but anyone with a serious interest in hot music knew him, respected him, even worshipped him. In November 1924, he wasn't. A month or so before, at the prodding of his band mate and new wife, Lil Hardin, Armstrong had finally left the Oliver band, already in disarray, and accepted an offer to join Fletcher Henderson's lightly jazzy Synco-Pep outfit in New York. This was an opportunity too good to pass up. He'd be playing with one of New York's most popular bands, one that had a nice Topworld gloss to it. What's more, New York was the capital of the recording industry, and hot men were in demand. Armstrong hit the ground running: he cut two songs with Henderson on October 7, four more on the thirteenth, three more on the sixteenth as part of a Henderson unit backing up the legendary tent-show queen Ma Rainey; at some point in October, the same unit also did four songs behind black blues vaudevillians Coot Grant and "Kid" Wesley Wilson. On the seventeenth, Armstrong joined homeboys Clarence Williams and Sidney Bechet (both big men on the New York music scene) and a couple other guys to knock out two accompaniments to blues singer Virginia Liston, plus an instrumental. He was back in the studio on the thirtieth with the full Henderson band for two more sides. November, December, and January offered more of the same.

Out of all this hustle and bustle, I'll select but a single song—the last song in this book but one. On December 22, a little combo got together at Gennett Records' New York satellite studio, at 9–11 E. 37th Street (the building's still there). Vocalists Clarence Todd and Eva Taylor (some say it was Alberta Hunter, but Taylor claims it), plus the Red Onion Jazz Babies—Louis Armstrong, Charlie Irvis on trombone, Sidney Bechet on clarinet and soprano sax, Buddy Christian on banjo, and, sitting in for Clarence Williams, Lil (Hardin) Armstrong, who had finally quit King Oliver herself. They cut three songs. The last one (Gen. 5627) was a zippy, rather old-fashioned little ditty by Clarence Williams (or "by" him), Henry Troy, and veteran black songwriter Chris Smith (he had written for Bert Williams back in the oughts and hit it big in 1913 with "Ballin' the Jack"). "Cake Walking Babies (From Home)" is, I suppose, at root not much more than a catchy little ditty about a dance fifteen years out of date.

The performance, though—that's the thing. Christian and Miss Lil lay down a titanium-edged, supercharged 2/2 beat, over which the three horns just plain tear. Bechet's flying soprano sax (like a clarinet, except of course louder) is performing aerobatics in the foreground, with Armstrong's muted cornet under it handling the melody—"handling," as in "touching, examining, subtly refashioning"— and Irvis's trombone riffing up the midrange. They pause for the vocal chorus, which Taylor lines out with Todd echoing:

Here they come (oh here we come), those struttin' syncopators,
Goin' some (oh goin' some)—look at those demonstrators,
Talk of [the] town, Green and Brown,
Pickin' 'em up and layin' 'em down.
Prancin' fools, that's what I'd like to call 'em,
They're in a class all alone.
The only way for them to lose is to cheat 'em;
You may tie 'em but you'll never beat 'em.
Strut's their stuff,
They don't do nothin' different:
Cakewalkin' Babies from home!

The words may hearken back to minstrel days, what with the high-stepping black syncopators. But they're belted out with a fierce, exultant pride—"the only way for them to lose is to cheat 'em"—that's pure rock 'n' roll.

After the vocals, steeplechase: Bechet and Armstrong go tearing after each other, spinning out music like Spider-Man does webs. The breaks they take—leaping, tumbling, time-defying torrents of notes—would've been inconceivable even two years earlier. Drive and swerve, dance and show, high and low—this was music that encompassed all dichotomies. Lil Armstrong's mom had called the blues "wuthless immoral music, played by wuthless, immoral loafers expressin' their vulgar minds with vulgar music." No longer.

Judging by this record alone, it's clear that instrumental jazz had found its Caruso—the only problem is figuring out which one of them, Armstrong or Bechet, it was going to be. In many ways, Bechet would've been the careful investor's choice. A twenty-seven-year-old "Creole of Color" from New Orleans with peripatetic habits, Bechet grew up in a musical family and had played with most of the Crescent City greats before he was out of his teens. Not only that: in 1919, he joined Will Marion Cook's Southern Syncopated Orchestra as, essentially, hot man on the clarinet (no, alas, they did not record), where he attracted a good deal of attention, especially in Europe, where they toured in 1919 and 1920. After being deported from England (don't ask), Bechet ping-ponged around the New York music scene, doing surprisingly little recording. What little he did, however, revealed him as the only man alive who could cut Louis Armstrong—as he arguably does on "Cake Walking Babies."

But that's not the whole story. Two weeks later, the same bunch, but with Williams back on piano and no Todd, did the song again, this time for Okeh (Ok. 40321). The rhythm's benefited from a tune-up: it's just as powerful, but smoother. Eva Taylor (this time there's no question) belts for all she's worth. Bechet does his thing pretty much the same way he did it the first time. Why mess with perfection? But here's why it was Louis Armstrong who became the Jazz Caruso, and not Bechet: in those two weeks, he rethought everything he played. His final break on the first version was a fluent, funky bit of juggling in rhythm. Now, it's something else entirely—a dizzying demonstration of the art of temporal manipulation. Notes fly ahead of the beat and suddenly pull up short; soar up and spiral down. It's pure swerve. Lucretius would've loved it.

Emmett's Children, or Hillbilly Music

Just as this new thing arrived, this sophisticated, fully realized American art music, able to challenge European music in its complexity without being subservient to it, the same forces that allowed it to develop and flourish were simultaneously unleashing something else: something very old, very shaggy, and very, very rough.

Now, if black acts of any kind were scarce on record from 1890 to 1920, and Underworld ones scarcer, the only folks scarcer than them were their cracker neighbors. The hillbilly, the hayseed, the rube (Thomas Edison's word) was just as minstrelized, as mimicked, as the Coon. Difference is, he didn't mind so much. The canny Yankees at Edison, pretty much the only label that showed any interest in the rural population, seemed to satisfy them by rustling up maybe a fiddle (usually studio crackerjack Charles D'Almaine), maybe a banjo (Vess Ossman or Fred Van Eps, of course), maybe even a piano—what the hell—and having the usual suspects—Collins, Spencer &c.—crack spavined hillbilly jokes over it. Hee-Haw.

On June 29, 1922, a thirty-five-year-old fiddler from central Texas dressed in rodeo cowboy drag and an honest-to-God Confederate veteran in full uniform, fiddles tucked under their arms, marched into Victor's New York offices and demanded to make records. And they did (OK, they may have had an itty bitty in through Victor's lawyer, but nonetheless). Over the next two days, Eck Robertson (the cowboy) and Henry Gilliland (the Reb) made the first commercial country records—the first, anyway, that captured the real pop music of the rural (i.e., Underworld) white South. Their fiddle tunes sold OK, as did the fiddle-and-vocal ones Atlanta fixture "Fiddlin'" John Carson cut the next year. For a couple years, there was just a trickle of rural artists, white or black, making it over the dam. In 1924, though, after thirty years of holding Underworld at arm's length with nostrils pinched, the recording industry caved; the dam broke. Hillbilly music was in full swing. (It's the familiar story: "That's not a market...that's not a market...hey, that's a market! Let's saturate it.") And just what was this hillbilly music?

Let's turn things over to Uncle Dave Macon, from Readyville, Tennesse, who's taking a quick swig of something white and oily out of an old fruit jar. He puts the jar down, picks up his five-string banjo (none of those new-fangled, jazzy four-string tenor or plectrum models for him), and spits. "Hallo, folks, you know I been a-pickin' and tryin' to pick a banjo for forty years or more. I used to just play the imitations, but now I'm a-gonna give you a little of the *var*-iations of Casey Jones." And so he does, emitting a healthy blast of ornery, cross-stitched banjication that owes nothing to Vess Ossman (Uncle Dave was born in 1870, only two years after Plunk), a lot to "that's the way we always done it 'round these parts"—and not a little to frets, steel strings, and other industrial-age innovations. After forty-five seconds or so, he pulls up the reins. "Genchlemen [At least, that's what I *think* he says]. Now, folks, I'm gonna give you a little of Ol' Dan Tucker, containing more heterogeneous constapolicy, double flavor, and unknown quality than usual." And it's "Old Dan Tucker." Like he means it (Vo. 5061o*).

The ghost of Daniel Decatur Emmett walks. And like all ghosts, its face is white—Uncle Dave wasn't billed as an "Ethiopian delineator," a "Coon shouter," or a minstrel of any kind. He could tickle the banjo (or, in his case, spank it), mangle the King's English, and sing Coon songs until the hams got smoked, and all he'd be doing is playing, as they were billed at the time, "old, familiar tunes." Country music. American music.

Records

Traditionally, a book like this will have appended to it a list of the various CDs and LPs that contain the records discussed, or at least however many of them have been reissued. But labels that specialize in the kind of music we've been dealing with tend to be small—sometimes exceedingly so—and ephemeral, and print runs conservative; in other words, good luck actually finding that CD (let alone LP). Fortunately, we live in the Age of Google: a little determined surfing and you should be able to turn up just about everything I've touched on and determine its availability. Which, by the way, is ever increasing: not only are more and more folks burning their 78 and cylinder collections onto CD and marketing the results online, but there's also an astonishing number of early recordings available on MP3, never to be lost or out of print again.

Accordingly, I've dispensed with the discography as unnecessary, and will confine myself to recommending one Web site and a few record labels. You can find biographies and streaming audio for just about anyone who's anyone in early jazz at www.redhotjazz.com. Well worth a visit. As for the labels: not all reissues are created equal. The best ones will give you informative notes and clean, carefully remastered copies of interesting records. Some labels specialize in that: for early recording, the name of the game is Archeophone (www.archeophone.com), who do everything in an exemplary way (and I'm not just saying that because they're doing the companion CD to this book). Among the other good ones are the Web-only labels Phonozoic.com, which has a particularly useful Coon song anthology, Tinfoil.com, which specializes in stuff that was recorded on cylinders, and Besmark.com, whose catalog is all recorded off a Victrola, so you can kinda hear the music as it would've sounded then. When it comes to early jazz, there's much more to choose from: Jazz Oracle and Sensation from Canada, Frog from England, and Timeless and Retrieval from Holland all produce meticulously researched volumes with impeccable sound (which is no surprise, since they all rely upon John R. T. Davies, the best in the biz, to do their transfers). For American vernacular music—blues and hillbilly records—Yazoo Records and County Records are the gold standard, while Document Records has everything—*everything*—but with generally lousy sound.

Books

Rather than list every last scrap of paper I've consulted in the years I've been working on this book, I'll focus on the books with the best combination of information and readability, the ones I find myself going back to again and again, the ones that I'd want to read even if I weren't being paid for it. Before I get to them, however, there are three indispensable works which I must mention, for I couldn't have written this book without them. They are *Blues and Gospel Records, 1890–1943*, by Robert Dixon, John Godrich, and Howard Rye (4th ed; Oxford, 1997); and two by Brian Rust: *Jazz Records, 1897–1942* (4th ed: 2 vols; Arlington House, 1978; there's a new, expanded edition that has just come out as I write this, featuring more ragtime, but it's not yet fully indexed) and *The American Dance Band Discography, 1917–1942* (2 vols; Arlington House, 1975). These are discographies—dry, unadorned lists of who recorded what, when; if you rely only on other people's histories for this crucial info, without an independent and reasonably precise knowledge of what was actually recorded, you're driving without a map, trusting in directions given by laconic rustics whose bias and ignorance you can't calibrate. Unfortunately, these books, despite their wonderful utility, are no help with the related issues, such as who wrote a particular song and when, and who popularized it—who had the hit. For those, some recourse may be had to Nat Shapiro's far-from-comprehensive *Popular Music: An Annotated Index of American Popular Songs* (6 vols; Archon, 1964–70), which is (naturally) out of print, and occasionally to Dave Jasen's *Tin Pan Alley* (Omnibus, 1990), although the decision to exclude song titles from the index ensures that this will be a last resort.

So much for the books you consult. As for the ones you actually read: for American pop in general, from the Revolution to *Frampton*

Comes Alive, be it hot, warm, cool, or Frost King, Charles Hamm's *Yesterdays: Popular Song in America* (Norton, 1979) is a good, if somewhat stiff, overview (with lots of parlor songs). For the history of the recording industry, Andre Millard's *America on Record: A History of Recorded Sound* (Cambridge, 1995) is comprehensive and up-to-date, although Roland Gelatt's *The Fabulous Phonograph, 1877–1977* (2nd ed: Collier, 1997) is a better read. Russell and David Sanjek's *Pennies from Heaven: The American Popular Music Business in the Twentieth Century* (Da Capo, 1996) is the standard history of the biz in general.

Among the hundreds of books I consulted (or half-remembered) for the general context of hot music in America, a few really stick out. Joel Chandler Harris's *Uncle Remus: His Songs and Sayings* (1880) is essential for understanding the illusions of the Old South, and how easily they were undermined from within. Leon Litwack's *Trouble in Mind: Black Southerners in the Age of Jim Crow* is so fierce and unsettling that those who wish to maintain those illusions should avoid it at all costs—and then be forced to read it at knifepoint. By contrast, there are few more entertaining books than Herbert Asbury's oft-reprinted 1928 *The Gangs of New York,* and few more compelling portraits of white, urban Underworld; in fact, one of the chief strengths of Luc Santé's popular *Low Life* (Vintage, 1991), which covers much of the same territory, is that it's unafraid to invite Asbury to come in and sit a spell. Randy Roberts's *Papa Jack: Jack Johnson and the Era of White Hopes* (MacMillan, 1983) capably tells the story of Jim Crow America's greatest hobgoblin. For the big picture, the meaning and form of the universe in which hot music plays a key symbolic role, there's Lucretius. No translation really satisfies; you could try the one by Rolfe Humphries (*The Way Things Are;* Indiana, 1968), but it's entirely worth learning Latin to read him in the original:

Te sequor, Romanae gentis decus, inque tuis nunc ficta pedum pono pressis uestigia signis.

Part I

Minstrelsy has been getting a good deal of attention lately from the thought gang. Eric Lott's 1993 *Love and Theft: Blackface Minstrelsy and the American Working Class* (Oxford) was even burning up the academic charts for a while. It's a fine book, as long as you don't have to read it—unless, of course, you find yourself at home with verbiage like "libidinal body," "social antinomy," "Herderan notion of the folk," and "Lyotard." For me, it's one of those books that subtracts reading from life's pleasures and adds it to its burdens. Far more readable is Dale Cockrell's excellent *Demons of Disorder: Early Blackface Minstrels and their World* (Cambridge, 1997), but it ends in 1843 and I may hence deem it—in that most useful of academic phrases—"beyond the scope of this study." *Inside the Minstrel Mask* (Wesleyan, 1996), Annemarie Bean *et al.*'s scattershot anthology of modern and nineteenth-century writing on the topic, has a couple of good pieces on instrumentation and such, but its nineteenth-century bits are poorly chosen and the modern ones tend to wallow in jargon. Hypnotized by the racial politics of minstrelsy and the cleverness of their own insights into it, none of these books talk much about the music—a fault shared by Robert Toll's *Blacking Up: The Minstrel Show in Nineteenth-Century America* (Oxford, 1974), which is more or less the standard history of the institution. Not that Toll's is a bad book—you can read it, and it's got a lot of information, although he lacks a compelling angle on the whole thing and tends to be frustratingly vague about what precisely they were doing on those stages.

For my money, the best book on minstrel music and its performance is still musicologist Hans Nathan's *Dan Emmett and the Rise of Early Negro Minstrelsy* (U of Oklahoma, 1962)—he's a little old-fashioned in his racial attitudes, although not evilly so, but he has the fascination with facts that used to be the mark of the scholar.

Minutiae abound. And he includes scads of songs. Nick Tosches
has an excellent, if brief, bit on the phenomenon in *Country: The
Twisted Roots of Rock & Roll* (Da Capo, 1996), and his style is as
hot as the stuff he's writing about. He returns to the topic in *Where
Dead Voices Gather* (Little, Brown, 2001), his wild pitch biography
of last-days white Coon Emmett Miller, which has much to cogi-
tate and much to puzzle through.

After Nathan, there are few good books about individual figures
from the age of minstrelsy; the best I know—and it's a fine book
indeed, at once judicious and snappy—is Ken Emerson's *Doo Dah:
Stephen Foster and the Rise of American Popular Culture* (Simon &
Schuster, 1997).

There's even less that's palatable about brass bands. H. W.
Schwartz's *Bands of America* (Doubleday, 1957; rpt. Da Capo, 1975)
is indispensable, if you can find it: vividly, fluently written and full
of captivating detail: one of the best books ever written on American music, it's out of print and likely to remain so. After that, the pick-
ings are slim. Margaret and Robert Hazen's *The Music Men: An
Illustrated History of Bands in America, 1800–1920* (Smithsonian,
1987) is more illustrated than history: burdened by the modern
academic disdain for history that tells a story, it offers lots of scattered detail but no grand framework on which to hang it. Still, it
has a plethora of pictures, and covers some interesting angles not in
Schwartz.

Part II

Ragtime has more to offer the discerning reader. Begin with Rudi
Blesh and Harriet Janis's 1950 masterpiece *They All Played Ragtime* (reprinted variously). This is the book that brought ragtime
back from the grave, that made Scott Joplin an American Bach.

Enough of the old ragtimers were still around when they began researching this that Blesh and Janis could get much of their information first hand, but—unlike many—they knew how to properly weigh old men's tales and temper them with more reliable sources. It's a bright, passionate book; everyone should read it. Edward Berlin's *Ragtime: A Musical and Cultural History* (California, 1980) will appeal to the more sober-sided reader, salted as it is with footnotes and precisely noted musical examples; but it is intelligent, readable, and pleasantly brief, and opens new ground on the importance of the Coon song (neglected by Blesh and Janis). Paul Oliver's *Songsters and Saints: Vocal Traditions on Race Records* (Cambridge, 1984) is essential on what black Underworld was making of and out of the Coon song. Once you've digested these, you can fill in some of the inevitable gaps from Terry Waldo's *This is Ragtime* (Da Capo, 1976), David Jasen and Trebor Tichenor's *Rags and Ragtime: A Musical History* (Seabury, 1982), and Ian Whitcomb's *Irving Berlin & Ragtime America* (Limelight, 1988)—Whitcomb seems to have found one of Louella Parsons's old style sheets and gone to great lengths to follow it in this weird but fun book. Tim Gracyk's *Popular American Recording Pioneers: 1895–1925* (Haworth, 2002) is a unique compendium of workmanlike biographical essays on the hot and not-so-hot alike. *Jazz: A History of the New York Scene* (Doubleday, 1962), by Samuel Charters and Leonard Kunstadt, has some useful stuff on how early ragtime was playing out away from the Midwest. Little that's truly compelling has been written on individual ragtimers; about the best of the crop is Edward Berlin's impressively researched and meticulous *King of Ragtime: Scott Joplin and His Era* (Oxford, 1994). Finally, mention must be made of Mr. Chris Ware's *Ragtime Ephemeralist,* an irregular review which presents a unique farrago of unidentified old photographs, tantalizing biographical snippets, random snatches of sheet music, and accurate and insightful articles on all things ragtime.

Part III

Once we come to the hot music of the twentieth century, we're graced with a dazzling chorus of the authentic voices of its protagonists, a great many of whom, assuming they were provident enough to survive until at least the 1930s, were debriefed by jazz scholars (a profession that would have had entirely different connotations in their youth). The two standard works are *Jazzmen*, edited in 1939 by Frederick Ramsey, Jr., and Charles Edward Smith, a collection of historical essays drawing heavily on the musicians' experience, and Nat Shapiro and Nat Hentoff's 1955 *Hear Me Talkin' to Ya: The Story of Jazz As Told by the Men Who Made It*, which just lets the guys talk (and is thus much more fun to read). Quite a few of these folks, stars and spear-carriers, told their stories at book length. Four of these—W. C. Handy's 1941 *Father of the Blues*, Eddie Condon's 1947 *We Called It Music: A Generation of Jazz*, Alan Lomax's 1950 *Mister Jelly Roll: The Fortunes of Jelly Roll Morton, New Orleans Creole and "Inventor of Jazz,"* and Louis Armstrong's 1954 *Satchmo: My Life in New Orleans*—are among the jewels of American biographical literature, whether you care an iota about jazz or the blues or not. Would that Bert Williams and James Reese Europe had lived to add their own voices to that chorus; there's still no satisfactory biography of Williams, but at least Europe's story has been brilliantly told by Reid Badger in *A Life in Ragtime* (Oxford: 1995).

A few particularly useful books on general background: no book better dispels the myth of Jolly New Orleans than William Ivy Hair's *Carnival of Fury: Robert Charles and the New Orleans Race Riot of 1900* (Louisiana State: 1976). Thomas Riis's *Just Before Jazz: Black Musical Theater in New York, 1890 to 1915* (Smithsonian: 1994) efficiently recuperates an almost lost history. *Jazz: A History of the New York Scene* (see Part II) is packed with interesting information, as is William Howland Kenney's more academic *Chicago Jazz: A Cul-*

tural History, 1904–1930 (Oxford: 1993). Gunther Schuller's *Early Jazz: Its Roots and Musical Development* (Oxford: 1968) is still the best of its kind, although its focus is far too narrow. Finally, I must mention Lynn Abbott and Doug Seroff's groundbreaking article, whose title alone demonstrates its utility: " 'They cert'ly sound good to me': Sheet Music, Southern Vaudeville, and the Commercial Ascendancy of the Blues" (*American Music*, Winter: 1996).

Index